William Nelson Pendleton

A Witness for the Bible

William Nelson Pendleton
A Witness for the Bible
ISBN/EAN: 9783337096953
Printed in Europe, USA, Canada, Australia, Japan
Cover: Foto ©Lupo / pixelio.de

More available books at **www.hansebooks.com**

SCIENCE

A

WITNESS FOR THE BIBLE.

BY

REV. W. N. PENDLETON, D.D.

PHILADELPHIA:
J. B. LIPPINCOTT & CO.
1860.

TO

THE CHURCHES,

AND TO

THE SCIENTIFIC PUBLIC

IN GENERAL;

AND IN PARTICULAR TO HIS

GRATEFULLY REMEMBERED ALMA MATER,

THE MOST DISTINCTIVELY SCIENTIFIC EDUCATIONAL INSTITUTION OF THE COUNTRY,

THE U. S. MILITARY ACADEMY AT WEST POINT,

AND TO

THE MANY ACCOMPLISHED ALUMNI THEREOF,

HIS ESTEEMED FELLOW GRADUATES,

This Volume

IS RESPECTFULLY AND KINDLY INSCRIBED

BY THEIR FRIEND,

THE AUTHOR.

PREFACE.

THE topics discussed in the following pages may be regarded either separately or in their mutual relations. With this twofold view, accordingly, the discussions are conducted. Each is intended to be complete in itself, and yet to constitute an appropriate part of a larger whole.

Trusting that he may, in the series, have done something toward promoting right convictions on great questions, with regard to which science is sometimes represented as at issue with Holy Scripture, the author commits it to His blessing, "without whom nothing is strong, nothing is holy."

LEXINGTON, VIRGINIA, June 1, 1860.

CONTENTS.

DISCUSSION I.
SCIENCE AND REVELATION.. PAGE 9

DISCUSSION II.
THE HUMAN FAMILY.. 62

DISCUSSION III.
THE CHRONOLOGY OF CREATION.. 145

DISCUSSION IV.
THE AGE OF MANKIND.. 199

DISCUSSION V.
THE MONUMENTS OF LOST RACES....................................... 287

(vii)

ERRATA.

"these," should be *those*, page 13, line 6 from top.
"imperfect," should be *impatient*, page 147, line 11 from top.
"sepultures," should be *sculptures*, page 322, line 5 from bottom.
"varieties," should be *verities*, page 341, line 4 from top.

SCIENCE A WITNESS FOR THE BIBLE.

DISCUSSION I.

SCIENCE AND REVELATION.

ONE of the greatest questions of our age is undoubtedly that respecting the actual relations between Natural and Revealed Truth, between Science and Scripture.

Toward conveying, at the outset, a just impression of the bearings of this great question, and of its controlling importance at the present time, we shall need no apology for quoting from the lamented Hugh Miller the following instructive testimony:—

"Before the churches can be prepared competently to deal with the infidelity of an age so largely engaged as the present in physical pursuits, they must greatly extend their educational walks into the field of physical science. The mighty change which has taken place during the present century in the direction in which the minds of the first order are operating, though indicated on the face of the country in characters which cannot be mistaken, seems to have too much escaped the notice of our theologians. Speculative theology and metaphysics are cognate branches of the same science: and when, as in the last and the preceding ages, the higher philosophy of the world was metaphysical, the churches took ready cognizance of the fact, and, in due accordance with the requirements of the time, the battle of the evidences was fought on metaphysical ground. But, judging from the preparations made in their colleges and halls, they do not now seem sufficiently aware—though the low thunder of every railway, and the snort of every steam-engine, and the whistle of the wind amid the wires of every electric telegraph, serve to publish the fact—that it is in the departments of physics, not of metaphysics, that the greater minds of the age are engaged,—that the Lockes, Humes, Kants, Berkeleys, Dugald Stewarts, and Thomas Brownes, for the most part belong to the past; and that the philosophers of the present time, tall enough to be seen all the world over, are the Humboldts, the Aragos, the Agassizes, the Liebigs, the Owens, the Herschels, the Bucklands, and the Brewsters. In that educational course through which candidates for the ministry pass, in preparation for their office, I find every group of great minds which has in turn influenced and directed the mind of Europe for the last three centuries, represented more or less adequately, save the last. It is an epitome of all kinds of learning, with the exception of the kind most imperatively required, because most in accordance with the genius of the time. The restorers of classic literature—the Buchanans and Erasmuses—we see represented in our universities by the Greek and what are termed the humanity courses; the Galileos, Boyles, and Newtons, by the mathematical and natural philosophy courses; and the Lockes, Kants, Humes, and Berkeleys, by the metaphysical course. But the Cuviers and Huttons, the Cavendishes and Watts, with their successors the practical philosophers of the present age—men whose achievements in physical science we find marked on the surface of the country in characters which might be read from the moon—are *not* adequately represented;—it would be perhaps more correct to say, that they are not represented at all; and the clergy as a class suffer themselves to linger far in the rear of an intelligent and accomplished laity, a full age behind the requirements of the time. Let them not shut their eyes to the danger which is obviously coming. The battle of the Evidences will have as certainly to be fought on the field of physical science as it was contested in the last age in that of metaphysics. And on this new arena the combatants will have to employ new weapons, which it will be the privilege of the challenger to choose. The old, opposed to these, would prove but of little avail. In an age of muskets and artillery, the bows and arrows of an obsolete school of warfare would be found greatly less than sufficient in the field of battle, for purposes either of assault or defense."

That this statement is in the main just cannot be doubted, and it certainly indicates a misapprehension, as perilous as it is prevalent, in regard to the relation which subsists between the lessons of revelation and the teachings of science. We would do somewhat toward arresting this evil and averting the dangers that follow in its train. And to this end we here present to notice certain great facts and principles going to show what is really and justly the relative position of scientific achievement and of scriptural teaching.

Just one hundred years have elapsed since a celebrated philosopher of North Britain gave to the world an account of certain remarkable researches, by which he had liberated from a solid form in limestone, magnesia, and other substances, a peculiar gas, entirely different from atmospheric air. This discovery, altogether due to a steady application by Dr. Black, of the Baconian doctrine of experiment and observation, may be regarded as the real starting-point of modern chemistry. Nay, by the questions which it forthwith suggested, and the impulse it gave to the sagacious mind of its detector, this fact became the immediate precursor of another scientific triumph of unrivaled value, by the same great man,—the discovery, that, when water passes into steam, a vast amount of heat becomes absorbed, and is rendered imperceptible or latent, but that it is made again prodigiously effective for warming purposes, when the steam is recondensed into water.

This law at once revealed the secret of many a grand phenomenon of nature, and placed in human hands the control of some of her mightiest powers. Here was seen the sceptre of the storm-king, and the subtle energy whereby are sent forth hail and snow. Here were disclosed the processes of congelation and vaporization, and the parentage of rain and dew. And here mankind learned how to make the vapor of water the most useful of servants, to convey genial warmth through the largest dwellings, to supply healthful baths at all seasons, to minister culinary appliances for congregated crowds, and to furnish the arm to color or to cleanse, and the breath to dry, all articles of human apparel. And more than all, in this same discovery was found the key, which Watt was at the very time seeking, to these improvements in the steam-engine, which have made it, this half century, the mightiest agent in man's material progress.

This instance may serve to illustrate the diffusive influence and beneficent power of true science. How the accurate ascertainment of even one great natural law opens to the human mind a world of associated truths, and places man in a condition to secure, for his well-being, that dominion over the whole lower creation, to which, the sacred book tells us, he was at his birth ordained!

And it is in this way that science has become so controlling an element in modern civilization. It is undoubtedly one of the two prime agencies by which civilized man is distinguished in these latter ages. It is the grand material element of human progress.

We say science is one of two chief influences by which the leading races of mankind are this day actuated. The other is, of course, that moral element of culture which has been given us in Revelation. It reaches far deeper than the material in its bearings on the great interests of human life. Farther back lies its power, and incalculably more essential is it to the right development and final regeneration of our race.

Witness one instance of its benign operation, exactly

coincident in time with Dr. Black's scientific discoveries. The very year, now a fraction over a century past, which witnessed the promulgation of the earlier of these achievements, saw captured, by a French privateer, a sick, bereaved, lonely Christian man, who was crossing the British Channel, partly to recruit, in the genial air of Lisbon, energies which had become enfeebled in his afflicted English home.

The prisoner, in common with many others, was confined to a loathsome dungeon, and for months subjected to treatment the most inhuman. And the experience there gained ultimately directed the earnest devotion and undying sympathies of an obscure servant of Christ, into that course of heroic practical charity which has changed the whole character of prison discipline in Christendom, and which will impart to the name of John Howard the charm of sweet music in the ear of a grateful world, so long as our earth bears upon its bosom a receptacle for the lawless or an asylum for the unfortunate.

This extract from his recorded meditations may show the spirit in which he wrought. "O my soul! in the amiable light of redeeming love, keep close to Him whose presence makes the happiness of every place... Remember thou art a candidate for eternity ... Lift up thine eyes to the Rock of Ages, and then look down on the glory of this world. A little while, and thy journey will be ended; be thou faithful unto death!"

And the work, in this spirit accomplished by the world-renowned philanthropist, was, in the language of another, this: "He saw that in the many-chambered dwelling, framed for them by their Father, men could not live together and in peace. The roof and spires of that dwelling seem to rest in sunshine; in the higher apartments is the voice of mirth and gladness; lower down, the darkness of sorrow begins to thicken; and beneath all, there have ever been lightless dungeons, from which, through the whole course of human history, have arisen the broken groans of agony or the low wailings of despair. By a stern and awful necessity, these dungeons were never empty; men were compelled to chain down their brethren in the darkness, lest, like maniacs, they should plunge their knives into the hearts that pitied them, or, like fiends, bring on all the destruction of Sodom. Never out of the ears of humanity could pass the doleful voice of lamentation, crying, like the conscience of the race, 'Fallen! fallen! fallen!' Meanwhile, they who had thus flung their fellow-men in fetters out of their sight, looked down upon them with the fierce glare of indignation, as if their chief duty was to load the whip and whet the axe. Or they turned from the anguish, whose existence they would forget, and deafened the walls through which sounds of woe might ascend, and urged on the dance, and the laugh, and the song, or listened to the chantings of solemn organs, or the trembling of bridal music, unsaddened by any cloud that floated up from below. Yet calamity was waxing greater and greater there, writing its pale emblems on too many faces; famine, pestilence, torture, and all injustice might enter unseen; and groans of agony were going up to heaven, though unheard by man on earth. Into these dungeons of the world Howard penetrated, and compelled men to hear the voice of agony beneath their feet. The result was a response of pity throughout society, and a resolve among civilized men that henceforward the lighted lamp of justice should be committed to the kindly hand of love."

This is but one illustration of that benign energy which Christianity exerts upon mankind, a single specimen of efficacy in that great moral element of our civilization which the Scriptures furnish, and which, reaching to lower depths in human necessity than does any scientific disclosure, and bearing upon interests more intimate and precious, limits not its benefits, as science ever must, to this transitory life, but points onward to that endless existence, where purity is unimpaired and knowledge unimpeded by the hindrances of earth.

Now between these two grand elements of human wellbeing, the material and the moral, so far from there being essentially any antagonism, there is a most important relation of mutual service, which, as already indicated, is, to this day, strangely misunderstood, not only on the infidel side, but on the part of Christian people otherwise well informed.

Emanating, as they do, from the all-wise Author of nature and reason on the one hand, and of revealed disclosure on the other, it is of course impossible, not only that they should really conflict the one with the other, but that they should not sustain and enforce each other. The works of God explained by a genuine science, and his word expounded by a just interpretation, not only cannot be at issue, but each, when rightly understood, must both harmonize with the other, and exhibit it to human view in a light more glorious and worthier its divine origin.

And yet, plain as is this principle, there is more than the depreciative neglect of which the Cromarty philosopher gives warning. The attempt indeed is not seldom made to array, as if in deadly opposition, these two mightiest agents of man's welfare. Ever since the fatal Inquisition, actuated by a timid and illiberal distrust, the direct opposite of that noble freedom with which the Bible challenges inquiry, dared to arm itself with the fierce energy of bigoted delusion, and to torture old Galileo into a repudiation of his senses, has something of a like spirit been exhibited by not a few, who should have learned a better lesson, from that calm, tolerant tone of conscious strength, which breathes in every page of the inspired book they profess to honor. And injustice so flagrant on the one side could not but provoke more than retaliation on the other, until the errors of certain of its advocates have, in no small measure, subjected religion itself to the sneering reproach of being the jealous, unworthy enemy of thorough human culture.

If feebleness on the side of right, and harm to the great interests of religion, result from the mere quiescence which Hugh Miller justly deprecates, how much more serious the mischief to be expected from this actual antagonism, founded, as it demonstrably is, in a double mistake! He therefore who can, in any important measure, contribute toward counteracting the evil, will be so far subserving the best interests of mankind.

It is this conviction which induces us to submit the views we are about to present concerning the actual relations between the disclosures of the Bible and the progress of scientific inquiry. Of the correctness of these views we have not the slightest doubt, nor of their tendency to remove prejudices which now hinder alike the material and the moral elevation of our species. We would contribute our mite toward the harmonious development of that wisdom which makes man triumphant over nature, and of that which fits him for heaven. So long as the leaders in Christian thought remain indifferent to the advances of physical research, and the body of Christian people retain the idea that scientific investigation tends on the whole to skepticism, and so long as the ungodly scientific mind both has the field mainly to itself and can avail itself of the pretext of persecution to brand religion as the foe of science, so long must disparagement and defiance exist between these mighty powers. And so long must detriment accrue to those interests of our race which belong only to this world, on the one hand, and on the other to those which pertain to a future and eternal existence.

That there is, in truth, an entire harmony between the moral and the material agencies that have been mentioned, between the triumphs of Science and the teachings of Scripture, nay more, that they are so thoroughly intertwined and blended in their relations to the human mind, as to prove their common origin in the Source of all wisdom, it will be our first endeavor to show. Perfectly clear is it to our view, that discoveries in the wondrous plan of nature, made by rightly-directed inquiry, have aided the human faculties to a better understanding of the documents of inspiration, and a firmer grasp of the precious verities they disclose. Nor is it less evident to us, that influences proceeding from Revelation have opened the way to those right methods of investigation which constitute the basis, and have resulted in the miracles of modern Science.

Indeed it must, we think, be to all obvious, on reflection, that, addressed as are Natural and Revealed truth, to the same creatures, and to faculties in them altogether inseparable, reciprocal relations of action and reaction cannot but exist in the mental processes by which they are respectively realized. Hence may it be conceived how Revelation, though embracing in its plan no direct instruction for mankind, in regard to things naturally cognizable, has, nevertheless, through its influence upon the cognitive faculties, incalculably promoted that amazing scientific progress which we witness in Christendom, and nowhere else. And hence may be understood the service which scientific discovery is rendering the interpretation and the evidences of the sacred records.

These views we now proceed to expand and illustrate. We shall endeavor to establish the position that mankind are largely indebted to influences derived from the Scriptures for that intellectual revolution in modern Christendom which has emancipated the mind, as it was never liberated before, and which has placed the keys of nature even in the hands of children. And then it will be our aim to point out, as only second to this, a debt on the other side, to the all-wise Author of nature, for the scientific methods to which he has adapted the faculties of creatures made in his own image. To exhibit the reciprocal influence which Science exerts in correcting inadequate apprehensions of things revealed; and in placing divine truth in a fortress so strong that enemies, however inveterate, must forever assail it in vain, and so lofty that the celestial light thence emanating shall at length reach every eye that will behold.

We maintain, then, in the first place, that, for that simple and humble process of inquiry into facts, and that systematic ascertainment and application of natural laws, which constitute what we mean by Science in its every department, man owes, incalculably more than the mere scientific reason supposes, to influences connected with Christianity. And in support of the position, we appeal to the nature of things, and to the evidence of history.

That the scientific method of seeking truth is of comparatively recent introduction among men, and was, in fact, never dreamed of, save in modern Christendom, is a circumstance as significant in the premises as it is in itself undeniable. It is generally known to have been inaugurated less than two and a half centuries ago, as the new organ of investigation and discovery, announced by Lord Bacon, in his celebrated "Novum Organum," and substantially contained in the first aphorism of that immortal work. "*Man, as the minister and interpreter of nature, does, and understands, as much as his observations on the order of nature, either with respect to things or the mind, permit him, and neither knows nor is capable of more."*

Now, that this principle, obvious as it appears when once established, and the systematic applications of it, which constitute the various branches of modern science, should have been so long undetected, by human intelligence, is, of itself, a phenomenon sufficiently remarkable to suggest, that there must have been in the nature of man, or of the world, or of both, some cause or causes seriously interfering with his thus applying his powers to the problems of the universe. And a slight attention to certain indisputable facts in the general aspect of the material world, and in man's own character, suffices, if we mistake not, to reveal such causes with convincing certainty.

There is, for instance, in the vast array of material things, a complexity so intricate as thoroughly to baffle the conjectures of an uninstructed mind. Particulars so infinitely various, and combined in ways apparently so confused, disorderly, and fortuitous, present, to the uninitiated, a scene which cannot but perplex thought, and make inquiry seem hopeless. Nor is it difficult to conceive how potent the influence of this seemingly inextricable confusion in the world must have been toward preventing those systematic observations of associated facts, which might have conducted the mind to a knowledge of certain general laws, and thence, by a wider induction, to generalizations still more extensive, and so on, to an approximate understanding at last, of the grand and beautiful order existing under such seeming chaos. The idea of such ascertainable system in a universe so infinitely various and complex, might well appear, we can readily understand, about as reasonable or natural, as to expect to find an orderly arrangement in the leaves scattered by autumn winds, or to trace a definite meaning in the mazy dance of insects on the summer air or on the tremulous bosom of a rippling lake.

It is true that, amid this vast assemblage of seemingly disarranged elements, certain obvious instances of order, calculated more or less deeply to impress the mind, present themselves to notice. But it is soon found that they are, for the most part, such as rather increase than diminish the perplexity occasioned by nature on the whole. The recurrence of day and night, and of the seasons; the lunar phases, and other periodical changes in the heavens; and the great diurnal heavings of the ocean, are of this character. Their very grandeur, however, and the immensities which they involve, are well calculated, it is plain, not to relieve, but the more to embarrass the mind, when an uninstructed man turns from them to contemplate the things more immediately about him. The intricacy or disorder here, seems so out of keeping with the fixedness of system there, that it is scarcely possible for thought, under the circumstances supposed, of actual ignorance once existing, to associate them together as elements of one great plan, pervaded by order in every part.

Where he discerns order, uninformed man finds himself

impotent; and where his energies can act, complexity and confusion baffle his understanding.

Allow, then, all that can by any be claimed for human reason, (and for it, under right guidance, much should indeed be allowed; wonderful is it when thus conditioned,) and it is still clear, that, apart from all other impediments, these very circumstances in the constitution of nature, and in man's relation to the world around him, must interpose hindrances of the most formidable character, in the way of his attaining a method of investigation which may unlock for him the secrets of the universe. If, therefore, no other adverse influences operated in this direction; if there were no impediment in the original approaches to the paths of science, besides the complications of the material world, and the limited power of direct penetration which the human mind is known to possess, it might be safely alleged, that many ages must pass (who shall say how many?) before the casual notices of successive generations could, if indeed they ever could, furnish a clue whereby the remotest approximation might be gained toward the entrance of the mighty labyrinth of nature.

But these are very far from being the only or the most formidable difficulties by which access to a true philosophy of investigation, on the part of mankind, must, it would appear, have been prevented. There are in man himself, in the processes of his own constitution, and the elements of his character, hindrances in the way to an effectual plan of inquiry, which would seem to render its attainment well-nigh hopeless. They consist not so much in the feebleness, as in the complexity and disordered condition of his faculties. He is notoriously a being of fitful, wayward, and impatient will, and of turbulent passions, as well as of conscience, affection, and vague, but occasionally lofty, aspiration. And such is the want of harmony among these elements, that his breast is for the most part a scene of wild confusion; nay, of actual warfare, between the moral sense and the selfish purpose, the dictates of reason and the promptings of appetite, the groveling lust and the aspiration after unknown good. But in this warfare, alas! as the history of the race has everywhere shown, the forces of downward tendency, where man is left to himself, really enslave and hold in bondage those that might otherwise elevate him to knowledge and power.

Such, then, is the condition of the individual mind, and considered by itself, without now bringing into view those accumulated barriers, which are, as we shall presently show, crowded in the way of truth, by the aggregation of such minds in society, it is obviously most unpropitious for successfully undertaking a search into the hidden things of creation. Energies thus discordant are manifestly unadapted to that calm, patient, protracted, ever-vigilant course of systematic observation, which alone could conduct previously uninformed man to a point whence, amid hitherto unresolved confusion, he might behold even one of those inner bands that connect the wheels of nature's vast machinery.

And there is another characteristic of human intelligence, somewhat different, which incalculably increases the difficulty, namely, that an understanding so limited must aid itself by general notions. It is the necessity of rational faculty such as man's, that it must generalize. Under the pressure of particulars endlessly accumulated, it sinks overburdened and exhausted. And hence, will it ever seek relief in contrivances, however arbitrary or delusive, for arrangement and combination, as the arm avails itself of lever and pulley, to lift masses beyond its unassisted strength.

Now this generalizing tendency, associated as it is with impatience, and other disturbing influences in the mind, not only prevents a true, but leads directly to a false philosophy of investigation. And a false philosophy once inaugurated by genius, especially if adapted to the very conditions of mind and of nature out of which it arose, as almost of necessity it must be, is little likely to be rectified merely by advancing time. Rather would it be fastened, most probably, on human thought for indefinite ages.

How such delusive system would arise is obvious. Since generalizations must be had, and there is neither inducement in the appearances of nature, nor patience in restless human beings, to seek for them by assiduous observations on actual phenomena, they are assumed in certain abstract conceptions of the mind. And then, arbitrary as are such assumptions, and wide of the truth as they may be, they become the very engines with which the mind, deluded by their imposing show of potency, works, age after age, upon the great problems of nature, very much as a band of the ancients might be conceived, battering with huge catapult the fortress of Gibraltar, and with about the same result, of impotence, failure, and despair.

Of such assumed generalizations, of the readiness with which the mind of the race becomes enslaved by them, and yet of their impotency toward opening the treasures of nature, the celebrated system of Aristotle, which in this connection we may appropriately designate physical logic, and which gave law to mind in the civilized world for two thousand years, is a perpetual monument. And the agreement of that system with what our analysis has indicated as the natural course of philosophy which man, as he is, unaided, would evolve, in such a world as this, strikingly confirms the truth of that analysis.

This is the way in which that greatest genius, perhaps, of antiquity, solves the question respecting the immutability and incorruptibility of the heavens:

"Mutation is either generation or corruption. Generation and corruption only happen between contraries. The motion of contraries is contrary. The celestial motions are circular. Circular motions have no contraries. Because there can be but three simple motions—to a centre, from a centre, round a centre; and of three things only one can be contrary to one; but motion to a centre is manifestly contrary to motion from a centre; therefore motion round a centre, that is, circular motion, remains without a contrary. Therefore celestial motions have no contraries; therefore among celestial things there are no contraries; therefore the heavens are eternal, immutable, and incorruptible."

In this specimen of a method, the inevitable rise of which we have just traced, we see indeed exercised certain great capacities of thought, but we see also a vain conceit and proud self-confidence, which must only and forever delude ignorant creatures in a world whose complexity, like the adamantine walls of some grand temple, effectually hides from view its inner wonders. Into that temple there is only one entrance, and over its portals is inscribed, in characters never to be effaced, the simple ordinance: "Before honor is humility." "Access to the kingdom of man, which is founded on the sciences," says Bacon, with characteristic felicity, "resembles that to the kingdom of heaven, where no admission is conceded except to children."

But if the tendencies of the individual mind, amid intricacies so perplexing, thus exclude man from the temple of truth, how greatly do those tendencies, as they operate among masses, multiply hindrances in the way to that inner entrance. Here arise interests which sway him, complications which encompass, and necessities which control. Here have birth endless influences which stimulate passion and add inveteracy to prejudice. Here irregular desire and impatient will, ambition and rivalry, antagonism and malignity, while unchecked by influences which earthly wisdom never furnished, seethe, as dire elements of mischief, in the mighty caldron of aggregated humanity. Hence usurpation and tyranny, disquietude and contention, restlessness and revolution, and the death-struggles of tribes and nations, in perpetual round through all the centuries.

Surely, under such conditions, human intelligence, otherwise, as we have seen, sufficiently disturbed, is about as likely by its own glimmering to discover the way to wisdom's treasure-house, as the poor mariner in frailest wicker-boat, by a feeble rushlight, safely to track the dark, tempestuous ocean, lashed to fury by all the winds of night.

Such, then, are the causes, deep seated in the nature of things, in the structure of the world, and in man himself, which so inveterately prevent the ascertainment of that simple process, whereby modern science received being, and was sent forth conquering and to conquer. They include those "*idols* of the *tribe*, of the *den*, of the *market*, and of the *theatre*," of which Bacon delineated the mischiefs: the passions and prejudices common to all men, which he calls the "idols of the tribe;" the special evils incident to particular minds, which he characterizes as the "idols of the den;" the distortions of reason occasioned by disorders in society, which he designates the "idols of the market;" and the power derived by false principles from deceptive show before the multitude, which he denominates the "idols of the theatre."

Now, if this be a representation of the case, even approximately correct, it must be admitted that any great influence coming in to control these tendencies, to awaken juster thoughts, to suggest principles of order not before apprehended, to allay the strife in man's breast, and to quiet the turmoil of society, to loosen the iron bands of unlawful authority, and to whisper in the ear of reason hints of a true method of inquiry, could not but tend to open the way to the dwelling-place of truth, and assist the mind in gaining access thereto. But whence could such influence come? That brilliant speculative philosophy nurtured beneath the shadow of the Athenian Pallas, peerless acknowledged among achievements of unaided intellect, proclaimed, as we have found, with voice that may ring through all the ages: "It is not in me." And he that will listen, hears ever echoed back this voice, from the banks of the Euphrates, the Nile, and the Tiber. It comes also to his ear from the frosty wilds where were cradled Alaric, Attila, and Clovis, and from the sunny clime that cherished the arch-imposter of the Koran. But what neither Babylon, Egypt, Attica, Italy, Scythia, nor Arabia could furnish, has gone forth from the hills of Palestine, to illuminate the world and speak order into the chaos of human opinion, to hush the tempest roar of passion and bid away invincible prejudice, to exemplify right processes of testing truth, and, in throwing open for man the kingdom of heaven, to unbar to him also the kingdom of nature.

This, we say, the Bible was adapted to do, ever tended to accomplish, and ultimately did achieve. Its very first sentence, received as from the Creator of heaven and earth, could not fail to carry with it ideas of a plan that must awaken inquiry. And then its whole series of providence, and prophecy, and law, could not fail, in the end,

3*

fully to confirm such ideas. But if such suggestions concerning the universe, indirectly given by its Maker, when revealing himself for purposes moral and spiritual, were calculated so to arouse the mind and present it with inducements to seek for order in the Divine works, with what inestimable efficacy to the same end are not those wondrous doctrines invested, accompanied as they are by vital energies, which, in disclosing the great features of God's moral government, both humble and elevate the human spirit! Those admirable precepts, also, examples and promises, which furnish alike the rule and the incentive to all excellent action, can their ultimate influence be computed, toward promoting effective intellectual exertion, by harmonizing human breasts and securing peace in an agitated world?

But, besides all these ways, in which the Bible, though designed for other ends, was calculated to dispel a false and develop a true philosophy of nature, there is in it one other marked characteristic, more immediately operative to this end, perhaps, than all the rest. The simple inductive method of determining truth, is appealed to in all its teachings. Significant facts agreeing in their indications, are adduced as the standard of a right judgment. "The works that I do, they bear witness of me," was the memorable dictum of unerring lips. And this lesson, as mighty as it is simple, pervading too, as it does, the whole Bible, could not go abroad in the world, especially in conjunction with all else that the inspired word discloses, without in the end overthrowing the "idols of the tribe," "den," "market," and "theatre," emancipating the mind from the chains of delusion and the dungeon of ignorance, and putting in its hand the key of an humble but truthful philosophy, wherewith to unlock the great palace of nature, and give free access to its richly-furnished halls, where the sciences wait as handmaids to dispense to mankind refreshment and comfort.

And now, in verification of the argument thus derived from the nature of man, of the world, and of the Holy Scriptures, we appeal to the great facts embodied in the history of our race. And as an appropriate connecting link between the *a priori* proofs already given and the evidence from facts presently to be offered, we adduce the judgment, indirectly rendered, by one who is certainly not prejudiced in favor of our view, and who will be recognized as no less reliable for his intelligence than for his fairness in the cause. In his statement, it will be seen that we have not over-estimated the tendency of such disclosures and influences as those contained in the Bible to guide aright the human faculties in their relation to nature. Humboldt, in his sketch of the intellectual phenomena of the world, thus describes the state of the Hebrew and Christian mind, as contradistinguished from that exhibited among other portions of the human family:

"It is characteristic of the poetry of the Hebrews, that, as a reflex of monotheism, it always embraces the universe in its unity, comprising both terrestrial life and the luminous realms of space. The Hebrew poet does not depict nature as a self-dependent object, glorious in its individual beauty, but always as in relation and subjection to a higher spiritual power. Nature is to him a work of creation and order, the living expression of the omnipresence of the Divinity in the visible world. Hence the lyrical poetry of the Hebrews, from the very nature of its subject, is grand and solemn; and when it treats of the earthly condition of mankind, is full of sad and pensive longing. Their epic or historical narrations are marked by a graceful simplicity, almost more unadorned than those of Herodotus, and most true to nature; but their lyrical composition is more adorned, and develops a rich and animated conception of the life of nature. It might almost be said that one single Psalm (104) represents the image of the whole Cosmos . . . We are astonished to find in a lyric poem of such limited compass the whole universe . . . Similar views of the Cosmos occur repeatedly in the Psalms, and most fully, perhaps, in the ancient, if not ante-Mosaic book of Job. The meteorological processes which take place in the atmosphere, the formation and solution of vapor according to the changing direction of the wind, the play of its colors, the generation of hail and of the rolling thunder, are described with individualizing accuracy; and many questions are propounded which we, in the present state of our physical knowledge, may, indeed, be able to express under more scientific definitions, but scarcely to answer satisfactorily . . . When the feelings died away," continues the great Prussian savan, "which had animated classical antiquity, and directed the minds of men rather to a visible manifestation of human activity than to a passive contemplation of the external world, a new spirit arose. Christianity gradually diffused itself; and wherever it was adopted as the religion of the state, it not only exercised a beneficial influence on the condition of the lower classes, by inculcating the social freedom of mankind, but also expanded the views of men in their communion with nature. The eye no lorger rested on the forms of the Olympic gods. The Fathers of the Church, in their rhetorically correct, and often poetically imaginative language, now taught that the Creator showed himself great in inanimate, no less than in animate nature; and in the wild strife of the elements, no less than in the still activity of organic development. It was thus the tendency of the Christian mind to prove, from the order of the universe and beauty of nature, the greatness and goodness of the Creator; and this tendency to glorify the Deity in his works gave rise to a taste for natural observation. And although the ancient world is not abruptly separated from the modern, modifications in the religious sentiments and tenderest social feelings of men, and changes in the special habits of those who exercise an influence on the ideas of the mass, must give a sudden predominance to that which might previously have escaped attention.

Incidental as is the testimony here rendered by the venerable philosopher of Berlin to the important truth we are exhibiting, it could scarcely be more striking or more significantly to the point had his special object been to establish that truth. He finds the Scriptures and their great disclosures actually producing, on a scale no less than grand, the very effects we have ascribed to them;

placing the human faculties in a new relation to the phenomena of nature, and starting mankind in a direction sure ultimately to lead to a true philosophy and an all-conquering science.

But that the reality of this influence may be more fully appreciated, let us glance at some of the decisive facts in the history of ancient, middle, and modern ages.

In the earlier civilizations, Hindoo, Chinese, Chaldee, Persian, and Egyptian, not immediately moulded by Divine revelation, whatever else may be said of them, it is certain that there were no approaches toward the beginning of a process which might place the powers of nature in the hands of men. In evidence, we adduce that land of tombs and pyramids where the native tendencies of humanity worked themselves out so soon and so signally. The calculating and contriving faculties of the mind were, doubtless, exercised by a class in that remarkable country with very considerable success; and the more obvious movements of the heavenly bodies were noticed more accurately, perhaps, than elsewhere. Nor would we by any means underrate such attainments. As trophies of intellectual vigor, they are undoubtedly entitled to respect. And when we find Egypt resorted to by such students as Thales and Pythagoras, Plato and Archimedes, as a university for all the learning then to be acquired, we may readily admit that, in the comparative quiet of the Nile valley, men must very early have made no despicable progress in certain departments of thought and certain exercises of skill. Still it is undeniable that, save in the one direction of abstract mathematics, the world became not one whit the wiser. As to awakening a single influence calculated to evolve at last a true philosophy of nature, or to suggest to mankind a true method of inquiry, it all amounted to absolutely nothing. Of this, the proof is entirely conclusive, even in the single specimen already given from Aristotle of preposterous ingenuity and labored nonsense. For that philosopher had at command all the lore of Egypt and of the East, as well as of his own more favored classic land.

Of Grecian culture, and its relation to physical investigations, the illustration that has been given may readily spare us the necessity of saying much. That culture, admirable as it was in the mere aspect of mental power and polish, and memorable as will ever be its products of imaginative beauty and speculative genius, furnished not one hint that might help humanity to a conquest over nature. While the earth bears upon its bosom intelligent creatures, emanations will reach them from "the blind old bard of Scio's rocky isle," to delight; from the brilliant intellect of the sage of the Academy, to instruct; and to arouse and animate, from the fervid glow of that unrivaled orator

> . . . "Whose resistless eloquence
> Wielded at will the fierce Democratie,
> Shook th' arsenal, and fulmined over Greece
> To Macedon and Artaxerxes' throne."

And so long as calculating faculty finds exercise in the essential relations of abstract quantity, the works of Euclid and Archimedes, Apollonius and Diophantus, will remain the recognized foundation of the mighty structure of mathematics. But all this avails nothing in man's actual relation to the intricacies of the external world. Nay, so far from lighting him through these to the hiding-place of truth, such culture, by the very direction in which it set the mind, and the false confidence it engendered, hopelessly despoiled man of his earthly heritage. The traveler gazing upon the clouds misses the diamond that sparkles at his feet. And the occupant of a stately hall, charmed with its artistic adornment, loses the glorious prospect of mountain and streamlet, and all the sweetness of earth and sky, that may be spread around in richest profusion.

And if deficiency so signal as to any sure principle of science pervaded all Greek civilization, that latter evolved on the banks of the Tiber only served to perpetuate and increase the evil. Intense action, personal and public, was the very life of Roman progress. Born in strife, cradled in armor, and nurtured amid conflicts, the people of Romulus took it as their mission to subdue the world. And the spirit thence issuing could not but tell alike upon their passions and their policy. No retreat was left for patient wisdom with her ceaseless researches. Of the immolation of truth on the altars of ambition and cruelty by imperial Rome, her armies and her amphitheatre tell the sad story. "The peace establishment of Hadrian and his successors," we are informed by the celebrated author of the "Decline and Fall," "was composed of no less than thirty formidable legionary brigades, and most probably formed a standing force of three hundred and seventy-five thousand men." And with this gigantic array bloody pastime well accorded.

"Here the buzz of eager nations ran,
In murmured pity, or loud-roared applause,
As man was slaughtered by his fellow-man.
And wherefore slaughtered? Wherefore, but because
Such were the bloody circus' genial laws."

Could wisdom find, even under the auspices of a Tully and a Pliny, a home where multitudes were thus incessantly
Butchered to make a Roman holiday?

No wonder Gibbon has himself to tell us, that native philosophy there had not being. This is his decisive testimony: "The authority of Plato and Aristotle, of Zeno and Epicurus, still reigned in the schools, and their systems, transmitted with blind deference from one generation of disciples to another, precluded every generous attempt to exercise the powers or enlarge the limits of the human mind." And this continued till, as decline progressed, he adds more emphatically, "the Roman world was indeed peopled by a race of pigmies, when the fierce giants of the North broke in and mended the puny breed."

With the final extinction of the Roman empire of the West, about five centuries after the Christian era, and when the victorious Northern tribes had become established in the countries of Western Europe, came into permanent operation those influences which conducted the people there settled through the dark and stormy night of the middle ages to the dawn of modern civilization. And of the agencies thus operating, Christianity undeniably occupies the position of supreme control. Nay, without its tranquilizing and transforming power, no credulity can conceive that from a deluge of barbarism so destructive could have emerged a brighter intelligence, and a more healthy social system, than the world had ever known. Gibbon himself, strangely hateful to him as was the thought of a Divine revelation, and restlessly ingenious as he was to make occasions for discrediting it, if possible, in the eyes of mankind, is obliged to admit this. In his own words:—

"The progress of Christianity has been marked by two glorious and decisive victories; over the learned and luxurious citizens of the Roman empire, and over the warlike barbarians of Scythia and Germany, who subverted the Roman empire, and embraced the religion of the Romans. This introduced an important change in the moral and political condition of the conquerors. They received, at the same time, the use of letters, so essential to a religion whose doctrines are contained in a sacred book; and while they studied the divine truth, their minds were insensibly enlarged by the distant view of history, of nature, of the arts, and of society. The version of the Scriptures into their native tongue, which had facilitated their conversion, must excite among their clergy some curiosity to read the original text, to understand the sacred liturgy of the church, and to examine, in the writings of the fathers, the chain of ecclesiastical tradition. These spiritual gifts were preserved in the Greek and Latin languages, which concealed the inestimable monuments of ancient learning. The immortal productions of Virgil, Cicero, and Livy, which were accessible to the Christian barbarian, maintained silent intercourse between the times of Augustus and the reigns of Clovis and Charlemagne. The emulation of mankind was encouraged by the remembrance of a more perfect state; and the flame of science was secretly kept alive, to warm and enlighten the mature age of the Western world. In the most corrupt state of Christianity, the barbarians might learn justice from the law and mercy from the Gospel; and if the knowledge of their duty was insufficient to guide their actions, or to regulate their passions, they were sometimes restrained by conscience, and frequently punished by remorse. But the direct authority of religion was less effectual than the holy communion which united them with their Christian brethren in spiritual friendship, and gradually produced the similar manners and common jurisprudence which have distinguished from the rest of mankind the independent and even hostile nations of modern Europe."

Testimony like this, from one so unfriendly to religion, is surely doubly significant.

Even more decisive is that of a writer scarcely less distinguished, but of very different character, whom we shall now quote. M. Guizot uses this language:—

"It was the Christian church, with its institutions, its magistrates, its authority, which struggled so vigorously to prevent the interior dissolution of the empire, which struggled against the barbarians, and which, in fact, overcame the barbarians. It was this church, I say, that became the great connecting link, the principle of civilization, between the Roman and barbarian world. Had not the Christian church at this time existed, the whole world must have fallen a prey to mere brute force."

And again, after a wider survey, he proceeds:—

"'The church has exercised a vast and important influence upon the moral and intellectual order of Europe, upon the notions, sentiments, and manners of society . . . Notwithstanding all the evil, all the abuses, which may have crept into the church, notwithstanding all the acts of tyranny of which she has been guilty, we must still acknowledge her influence upon the progress and culture of the human intellect to have been beneficial; that she has assisted in its development rather than its depression, in its extension rather than its confinement."

This is undoubtedly just. So far as she departed from the sacred guidance that had been left her in the Scriptures, the church, beyond question, impaired her influence for good. Abuses did thus creep in. Acts of folly and tyranny were perpetrated by her in the name of the All-wise and All-righteous. But still, the divine truth which she held, and in considerable measure promulged, illuminated and moulded the world with unrivaled power.

And among other benefits conferred on mankind by revelation, even as impeded by the errors of the church, and tending to that intellectual revolution which liberated modern mind, first in the Reformation, and then in the birth of Science, may be mentioned the two important facts, that *all the schools*, and *nearly all the authorship*, of this period, were due to influences derived from the Scriptures. In illustration of this remark, the writings and the institutions of the great Alfred may be referred to. With a devout Christian spirit, and a wise executive energy, he applied himself efficiently to such measures as might revive that learning in England which the incursions of the Danes had sadly impaired. And to this end he became both a distinguished author and an extensive founder of seats of learning. The influences under which he did this, may be seen in one of his extant letters, written to the bishop of London of his day. "Calling to mind what benefit had been derived by all nations from the translation of the Greek and Hebrew Scriptures, first into Latin, and then into the various modern languages," he concludes, "therefore I think it better that we also translate some books the most necessary for all men to know, that we may all know them; and we may do this with God's help very easily, if we have peace; so that all the youth that are now in England, who are freemen, and possess sufficient wealth, may for a time apply themselves to no other task." In such a spirit he is said to have re-established many of the old monastic and episcopal schools, in various parts of the kingdom. Asser, his biographer, expressly mentions that he founded a seminary for the sons of the nobility, to the support of which he devoted no less than an eighth part of his whole revenue. And this is believed to have been the foundation of the illustrious University of Oxford.

Under influences very similar, and in nearly the same age, were established the schools which, in a few generations, matured into the magnificent Universities of Bologna, of Paris, and of Cambridge. And of their effect in promoting liberal learning in Europe, at the time when the enthusiasm of the Crusades gave place to the enthusiasm of study which succeeded them, some idea may be formed from the fact that, at the beginning of the fourteenth century, "there are said to have been thirty thousand students at the University of Oxford, while that of Paris could boast the attendance of a still vaster multitude."

That the Arabian conquerors of Spain, by their peculiar manifestation of activity, contributed to the mental impulse thus received, is not to be denied. And the service which they especially rendered to European mathematics, by the introduction into the West of the old Eastern numerals, should be candidly acknowledged. Still it is to be remembered, that the potent element in their incomplete civilization was but a reflex of the Jewish and Christian revelations; that their highest culture was really derived from sources which the Christian church had preserved; and that their system, so far from being able to infuse vitality into other forms of human society, carried in itself the seeds of a sure and early decay.

Thus was it that Christianity, through many struggles, moulded the mind and formed the genius of Europe, in its transition age, and prepared the way for that double regeneration which ultimately purified religion and unbarred nature.

To two great men, indeed, it was given to inaugurate that revolution. Luther was doubtless, in some sense, the prophet sent for the purification of the church, and Bacon was the ordained herald of a true philosophy of investigation. But they were both, in fact, only the exponents of that intellectual maturity to which, chiefly by the ramified influences of His word, the Almighty had providentially conducted the European races. And had no "Brother Martin" appeared, or "Baron of Verulam," the same age, or one near at hand, would have witnessed a revolt both from Rome and from Aristotle, a Protestant church and a Novum Organum.

Wickliffe (1324-1384) had already appeared as the morning star of the Reformation; and Roger Bacon (1214-1292) as the pioneer of experimental science. And the mere juxtaposition of a few leading names will show how that light was diffusing, which on us beams in full day from an open Bible and an unvailed universe.

Copernicus appeared in 1473, and gave publicity to his astronomical conclusions in 1543.

Luther was born in 1483, and published his theses in 1517.

Kepler lived between 1571 and 1630.

Galileo from 1564 to 1642.

And Bacon's great work appeared in 1620-21.

Thus we find coexisting in about one century the great leaders in the mighty twofold movement of modern mind. Some of them breathe the same air and look upon the same skies. And not a generation intervenes between the first and the last. Surely this simple fact speaks volumes as to the common influences which evolved them all; and exhibits almost to the eye the actual birth of modern science, in the transforming agencies so long exercised by revealed truth upon European mind.

And the principle thus exhibited, we may now see expanding into wider compass. That branch of the great European family, whose whole character has been most thoroughly imbued with the lessons of the Bible, takes conspicuously the lead in every department of physical science. The scientific labors of other nations have certainly been in some instances exceedingly brilliant. The pure and mixed mathematics of France must especially be so characterized. And yet in physics it is undeniable that with the exception of here and there a happy thought, as in the memorable discovery of Volta and Galvani, scarcely more has been done elsewhere than extend English researches and verify English theories.

In physiology, the two greatest discoveries ever made were by philosophers of the British isle. (See these and other facts forcibly urged in an able "Discourse on the Baconian Philosophy," by Samuel Tyler, of the Maryland bar.) Harvey, the contemporary and friend of Bacon, detected the circulation of the blood as early as 1628. And Sir Charles Bell, nearer our own times, distinguished between the nerves of sensation and those of motion. Sydenham laid the foundation of medical science, and John Hunter that of comparative anatomy. And Jenner evoked that simple but wondrous secret of vaccination, which has disarmed the direst disease, perhaps that ever afflicted humanity.

In chemistry, also, Britons have taken the lead. Dr. Black, of Edinburgh, a hundred years ago, as already mentioned, astonished mankind by the discovery of *carbonic acid gas*, and soon after by announcing the mysterious but important doctrine of *latent heat*. And at the beginning of the present century, Dalton, of Manchester, explained the admirably adjusted law of *chemical equivalents*. Priestley, the discoverer of oxygen gas, Watt and Cavendish, who ascertained the composition of water, and, above all, Davy, the unrivaled analyst and founder of agricultural chemistry, were all Britons; as was Grey, who first generalized electrical phenomena.

But, far more than all, that land of Bibles and of churches gave to the world that wonderful man, the enthroned prince of all the philosophers, to whose patient and persuasive hand the bright sunbeam yielded the secret of the painted bow and of all the sweet colorings of earth; and to whose calm, attentive eye the invisible cords revealed themselves which bind together the material universe.

And while such has been the unparalleled progress of physical research there, on our side of the Atlantic, under similar auspices of Bible Christianity, we behold like results, on a scale to attract the attention of mankind. Our Franklin has disarmed the clouds. Our Fulton has bridged the ocean, and freighted every river. Our Maury has fenced the highways of the sea and written finger-boards upon the fitful atmosphere. Our Brooke has fathomed the great deep, and uncovered the monuments of its ancient dead. And our Morse, skillfully applying the electro-magnetic discoveries of our accomplished Henry, has taught the earth, with lightning speed, to whisper messages from city to city and from continent to continent.

And this is all, directly or indirectly, the fruit of that simple, humble, observant philosophy, which, from disordered faculty in a complex world, could receive no being; to which neither Egypt, nor Greece, nor Rome, and far less India or China could give existence, but which, born in that sacred land where God spake with men, was nurtured through the ages on the bosom of Christianity.

Now, what arithmetic can calculate the debt due from mankind to the Scriptures of truth for this single service? Take them away; go back through the centuries, and obliterate all records of heaven's glad tidings, leave man only to himself and the impenetrable mysteries around him; then see Egypt buried, Greece in ruins, Rome engulfed in a dark, destructive deluge, and naught remaining but the wild roar of angry elements, without one tranquilizing breath, one ark of refuge, one ray of hope; and tell us where were all our boasted science and successful philosophy? Hopelessly gone! Lost in boundless, irremediable night! But not so. He whose ways with man are wise and merciful, had sent a messenger that could, with silent yet controlling voice, speak to the tempest of human passion, "Peace, be still!" had constructed a life-boat that, safely riding the surging billows, should bear onward to a stable resting-place the hopes of the world; had provided a diffusive balm for the healing of the nations; had issued that word, whose first, last, and every utterance is with power, "Let there be light!"

Hence the existence and the character of modern civilization, the development of true philosophy, the emancipation of human intellect, the success of well-directed investigation, and the multiplied triumphs of advancing science.

Then let no delusive pride of intellect mislead the votaries of scientific progress into irreverent depreciation of that venerable volume, whose pregnant hints and significant suggestions contain the germ of all physical discoveries, and whose transforming power has enabled regenerated society to achieve those discoveries, and with them comfort and power.

But science has also, as we have said, reciprocated the service thus received from religion. She has rendered honor to the source of her being; to adorn and defend which, indeed, she has gathered materials from all the recesses of creation. And though in some instances the earlier disclosures seemed to threaten discredit rather than confirmation to sacred truth, yet in proportion as research has been complete in every department of physical inquiry, the result has been to elucidate and corroborate, often most surprisingly, the records of revelation.

The first example we adduce is furnished by the science, which deals with the most obvious yet most remote of all objects of contemplation, and which is perhaps the most universally interesting, as it was the earliest considered department of human inquiry. It is true that the Scriptures and Astronomy have not many points of contact, whereby agreement or disagreement between them may be tested. But they have some. And these furnish very striking indications. At first, indeed, through a contracted interpretation given by some in authority, to that simple and truthful *language of appearance*, employed in sacred as in common narrative, men, "knowing neither the Scriptures nor the power of God," feared lest Galileo's telescope should reveal things in conflict with the Divine Word. And that fear was the parent of much wickedness as well as of much folly. But as mankind must credit the evidence of their senses; and as the sphere of vision now enlarged by the tube of the old Tuscan seer, placed before the eyes of men demonstration evident of those celestial motions, which reflection had taught Copernicus to embody in theory, the petty dogmas which ignorance attempted to chain upon the Bible had to be given up; and a more comprehensive view of certain grand indications, which the unrivaled Book had always offered to notice, much more than vindicated the superhuman wisdom of the ancient record. While the absurd systems, like, that a specimen of which has been adduced from Aristotle, laboriously constructed by speculative genius in early ages, have, with advancing discovery, been more and more signally exposed, it has been found that the Scriptures, on the same subjects, so speak as that every additional disclosure in the heavens lends greater significancy to their language on the whole. Do they point to the glorious luminary of day as the appropriate symbol of the Sun of Righteousness? Forthwith they exhibit this Spiritual Sun as the center around which revolves the entire system of Christian truth, and life, and blessedness. And are not those great discoveries of Kepler and Newton, which show a mighty array of planets and satellites moving forever round the sun, here shadowed forth? At the same time does not the grandeur of order and power in this mechanism of worlds, wondrously expand, to human appehension, the significance of the spiritual system, and glorify Him, who is at once its bond, its light, and its life?

Does the Bible propose to men the inquiry, "Knowest thou the ordinances of heaven?" And are there not intimated in the words, realities of settled order and universal law, the fullness of which human faculty, astonishing as may be its achievements, can never explore? And when, with magic mirror, the Herschels, Lord Rosse, and kindred explorers, have read the secrets of the stellar spaces, have they not seen written there this very question put to old Job? When they have tracked revolving sun-worlds, at distances that figures refuse to tell, and light itself almost fails to traverse, and have resolved innumerable patches of scattered *star-dust* and floating *star-cloud* into myriads of *sun-systems*, regulated by laws which the Calculus of Leibnitz, in the hands of Laplace, forever declines to reveal, have they not read in that question a still grander significance? And when, by certain way-marks in the sky, they have reckoned that incredible motion of nearly *half a million of miles per day*, which is bearing our sun, with all his retinue of planets, toward an unknown point in or near the constellation Hercules, how or why, save to suggest it as a general result of universal gravitation, wildest conjecture dares not answer, have they not learned, by a teaching never to be forgotten, that after his last achievements in the stars, man, as the Bible had told him it should be, knows only in part the ordinances of heaven? But this, too, they have learned, just as the sweet Singer of Israel so long ago chanted, though peradventure with a sublimity of meaning even beyond that which had been caught by his enraptured spirit, and a sublimity ever heightening as more is known: "The heavens declare the glory of God!"

Thus does astronomy interpret and establish the Holy Scriptures.

And no less striking, while still more numerous, are the explanations and confirmations of the sacred record furnished by that science which evokes from the bosom of the earth her buried secrets. Here, too, rigid and restricted system had narrowed to a hand-breadth the mighty meaning of the grand old documents. And a timid faith, feeble because fearful, dishonored the very cause it professed to serve, by distrusting its ability to stand every test, and protecting its trembling belief by embittered denunciation. But again, mankind must credit their senses. And the history of pre-Adamite ages, found written on the uncovered rocks, enforced a more candid and comprehensive reading of the entire Scriptures; and then was seen, in all the astonishing precision and fullness of its meaning, that marvelous series of intimations which the Bible had all along given of ante-human cycles of being; and with which some of the old fathers had been so deeply impressed. Does Moses speak of successive intervals in the progress of creation? It is the most conspicuous fact in all geology. Does he describe a certain order of advance in organized forms, from "the herb yielding seed after its kind," to "the creeping thing that had life," and "the great sea-monsters," and "winged fowl," and from these to the "great beasts of the earth," and "cattle after his kind," and then lastly to man, the crown and lord of all? Geology, with precision truly wonderful, displays altogether the same advance, and in exactly the same order. Here are seen characterizing lower formations, certain simple botanical species and low animal forms, amplifying upward into the enormous carboniferous flora and its accompaniments; then the huge fish, reptiles, birds, and other egg-bearing creatures, during many ages; next, the mighty mastodon, and mammoth and gigantic beasts of various kinds, and, lastly, existing flower and fruit-bearing plants, and the animal forms associated with man, and himself latest and highest of all. Assuredly this correspondence between the strata of geology and the narrative of Genesis is one of the most surprising confirmations conceivable of the Divine verity of the Mosaic history.

But again, do the Scriptures, in repeated instances, speak so remarkably of the *creative ages* in the sense of *worlds*, as if there had been a succession of forms given at different times to the same world; and do they variously repeat the idea, by grand allusions to an unmeasured antiquity, and a transformed earth? Geology finds those prodigious ages, those extended and recurring periods, and those successive transformations, indelibly recorded in the monumental rocks. And more instructively still, if possible. Does the Bible continually exhibit those interpositions of immediate agency, on the part of the Almighty, which modify the general course of natural laws, and which we designate Providence; nay, does it, in fact, consist of a history of such interpositions in regard to mankind? And what more conclusive illustration of special agency, precisely similar in principle, can be imagined, than the fossil history furnishes? Here is seen occurring, again and again, what no general laws have ever produced. A whole universe of living creatures disappear, buried beneath the sands of the seas in which they have sported, or the ruins of the hills on which they have roamed; and races appear, not only unlike, and of altogether different species, but absolutely opposite in almost every attribute of being. How is this? There is, certainly, by natural law, no transformation of species. It can only occur by immediate creative power. If physiological research has settled any point beyond controversy, it is, that such are the universal laws of vegetable and animal life, that no one distinct species can ever, by mere natural agencies, be transmuted into another. As well might the earth be expected, merely by the operation of gravity and other like properties, to clothe itself with a resplendent ether, and send forth controlling powers of light and life upon a new system of worlds, as that from the ruins of primeval ferns should have sprung our forest oaks; our eagle, soaring to the sun, from the insect that sipped some humble flower in the early world; or man, with all his faculties, from some groveling reptile of a past existence. These changes, then, revealed by geology, these destructions and reproductions, these burials of old, and creations of new races, exhibit in a light which science fully recognizes, that very direct agency of God in the government of the world, the history of which, in its relation to mankind, constitutes the great burden of Scripture. So that, never has the human mind been called to contemplate a more signal confirmation of truth than is furnished to the Scriptures by the accumulating developments of geology.

So, again, is it in the department of meteorology. Lieut. Maury, after all that research has disclosed concerning the phenomena of the atmosphere, sums up his conclusions in these emphatic words: "The Bible tells it all in a single sentence! 'The wind goeth toward the South and turneth about unto the North: it whirleth about continually; and the wind returneth again according to his circuits.'"

Nor are such testimonials rendered alone by the sciences separately. There are surprising relations between different branches of science, which no less strikingly elucidate and corroborate the Bible. For instance, all readers have remarked how very characteristic are certain repetitions of numbers, in the Scriptures, as 7, 10, 12, 40, etc. And there have not been wanting those who were ready to regard this feature of the sacred books as a sure mark of human contrivance in the narrative. But many sciences at once appear, bearing concordant testimony to the existence of a numerical adjustment, precisely similar, in the heavens, in the earth, and among all creatures. In the planetary motions, Kepler's third law has long since announced a double multiplication of times in constant proportion to a triple multiplication of distances. In botany it is found that the leaf appendages of all plants are arranged according to the numerical series, 1, 2, 3, 5, 8, etc., in which any two consecutive numbers, added together, make the next succeeding. And in physiology it is ascertained that 10 marks the digits of all creatures with hands or divided feet, and 7, the number of bones in the neck of all mammalian vertebrata, whether whale or giraffe, elephant or human subject. Chemistry tells us that there is not a breath of air that trembles in the great atmospheric ocean, nor a drop of spray that sparkles on the briny deep, nor a particle of any compound substance on the globe, which is not constituted according to a definite law of numbers. And optics assures us that there is a like numerical constancy in the colors of heaven's beauteous bow. Thus has general science, to such inquirers as Kepler and Newton, and Cuvier and Dalton, and De Candolle, revealed, as pervading all nature, a numerical system precisely analogous to that which constitutes so remarkable a feature of the Bible. And such principles of co-ordination in the word and works of God, we can readily perceive to be admirably adapted to the constitution of man's mind. It is an arrangement in each case exactly suited to finite intelligence. It lends distinctness to the association of facts; it helps the intellect to grasp truth, and the memory to retain it. It strikes the fancy of youth, interests the mature mind, and so wraps salutary recollections around the decaying faculties of age as to lighten its burdens and irradiate its gloom.

One other instance we adduce, of peculiar correspondence between the teachings of Scripture and the conclusions of general science. The inspired history, as is familiar to all, affirms that "God made of one blood all nations that dwell on the face of the earth;" that however now diverse in feature, color, and other subordinate characteristics, and of speech, how various soever the human tribes that people the globe, they all constitute but one family, descended from a common ancestry. This, scientific research in its earlier and partial stage seemed to discredit, by the apparently radical and irreconcilable differences of structure, capacity, and language, between extreme races, which it exhibited. Nor were there wanting those who eagerly seized, as some indeed still do, such indications, as a pretext for indulging a relentless enmity against the moral system of revelation. But just in proportion as investigation has been complete in every branch of inquiry bearing upon the question of national or tribal origin, as the whole range of *ethnology* has become really scientific, its testimony has proved thoroughly corroborative of the Scripture doctrine. It is a wide field, embracing in its scope applications of almost every branch of human knowledge. But ably has it been explored. Nor is there left a shadow of doubt, as to the truth, on the minds of the first men of the world, in every department of the investigation. Comparative anatomy and physiology through their great high-priests,

Cuvier and Owen, have spoken with oracular voice, "Man is one." Travel, custom, and minutely verified archæology, as traced by the admirable Prichard, have delivered the same declaration. And monumental history has, with response precisely accordant, replied to the interrogatives of the Humboldts and Lepsius, Bunsen, Schoolcraft, and Gallatin.

And particularly striking is the evidence furnished by that branch of monumental history which is contained in language. The scientific methods by which this has been elicited, first suggested by the sagacious mind of Leibnitz, have, within our generation, been pursued with an enthusiasm and success second to that exhibited in no other pursuit. It has been but a few years since a Russian grammarian, the heroic Castrén, (see seq. *Human Family*, p. 81,) although in delicate health, left his study, traveled for months alone in his sledge through the snowy deserts of Siberia, coasted along the borders of the Polar Sea, lived whole winters in caves of ice, or in the smoky huts of greasy Samoieds, then braved the sand-clouds of Mongolia, passed the Baikal, and returned homeward by the frontiers of China; that he might, in so vast a sweep, gather materials for the expanding science of comparative philology. From such an instance, we at once perceive with what zeal this branch of knowledge has been recently pursued. And the result is thus glowingly sketched by a distinguished German scholar:—

"If, now, we gaze from our native shores over that vast ocean of human speech, with its waves rolling on from continent to continent, rising under the fresh breezes of the morning of history, and slowly heaving in our own more sultry atmosphere, with sails gliding over its surface, and many an oar plowing through its surf, and the flags of all nations waving joyously together; with its rocks and wrecks, its storms and battles; yet reflecting serenely all that is beneath, and above, and around it; if we gaze, and hearken to the strange sounds rushing past our ears in unbroken strains, it seems no longer a wild tumult, or 'ανήριθμον γέλασμα, but we feel as if placed within some ancient cathedral listening to a chorus of innumerable voices, and the more intensely we listen, the more all discords melt away into higher harmonies, till at last we hear but one majestic trichord or a mighty unison, as at the end of a sacred symphony.—Such visions will float through the study of the grammarian, and in the midst of toilsome researches his heart will suddenly beat, as he feels the conviction growing upon him, that men are brethren in the simplest sense of the word, the children of the same father, whatever their country, their color, their language, or their faith."

This, from Professor Müller, is the latest utterance of linguistic science.

Thus it is that the heavens and the earth, the atmosphere and the ocean, and all the processes of life, and all the monuments of history, return, in answer to the calm, sagacious, impartial cross-questionings of scientific inquiry, one clear, full, harmonious, decisive testimony to the truth, grandeur, and preciousness of Divine revelation.

But this is not the only tribute received by religion from advancing science. It is the untiring scribe, with magic finger, to copy for all the tribes of earth, in their several tongues, the messages sent them by their Maker. And it is the dauntless colporteur, of swift foot and unflagging energy, to bear those recorded messages to every isle of the ocean and every land of the globe.

Such, then, are the relations which the Scriptures and Science sustain toward each other and to the welfare of mankind. The one is the mighty moral, the other the great material element of human progress. The one is primary and essential, the other subordinate, but greatly subsidiary. The one, though mainly designed as man's guide to a higher and more blessed existence, has, by direct suggestion, and by a regulating influence over disordered faculties, placed reason in a position to grapple with the problems of the world. The other, in solving those problems, has not only evoked from Nature's treasure-house, and placed in human hands, vastest appliances for efficiency and enjoyment, but has brought from every corner of creation lights to illuminate the sacred pages, voices to swell the chorus of praise to their Divine Author, and hands to bear to the remotest habitation of our planet the venerable records of revelation. By the one, is opened the way to spiritual, by the other, to natural good. That tells us of our unseen but gracious Father in heaven, and of a future glorious home with Him. This shows us tokens of His greatness and goodness, in the wondrous structure of our probationary dwelling-place. Upon the dark mystery of mortality the revealed Word sheds a blessed light. In tones of authority it bids into submission wayward and unhallowed passion. It whispers peace to the troubled breast, and on the anxious, trembling spirit, binds the wings of eternal hope. It takes the soul into the very presence of that "Friend who sticketh closer than a brother," and kindles in the heart that flame of love which is earth's sweetest blessing and heaven's highest bliss. To our children it gives the first, best, and grandest lessons, while over all domestic joy it casts a sacred shield. It secures our sabbath rest, and charges with sweet music every breeze that wafts the sound of the "church-going bell." Of all wholesome law it is the strength, and of all social order the guardian. It is the pledge of gladness in the bridal scene, and at the bedside of death the only voice of comfort. It sweetens all existence, and surrounds even the grave with bright visions of faith. Unhappy the people, and most wretched the man, to whom the Divine word is not thus wisdom and life! But without the triumphs of Science, too, there is amazing loss. By these are opened the portals of nature's mighty temple, and men behold there mirrored forth the glory of their Maker. By these fire and air, earth and sky, winds and waves, with energies exhaustless, are made willing servants to human creatures. By these we have victory over darkness and distance, over Arctic frost and tropical drought, and over sterile soils and unpropitious seasons. These minister to the hungry, food; covering to the unclothed; and to the houseless, shelter. Here heart and intellect may find exercise in a boundless field, and heroic enterprise can gather richest rewards. Here wealth immeasurable is poured into the lap of civilization, and the church finds multiplied without limit the means of fulfilling her Lord's last command to "preach the gospel to every creature."

And since this is the real truth of the case between Science and Religion, since they actually sustain relations so significant toward each other and toward Heaven's benign purposes for mankind, we may certainly conclude, in the language of so sound a thinker and so forcible a writer as Dr. McCosh, that—

"It is, assuredly, no useless or profane work that is engaged in by those who would, with proper humility, endeavor to remove jealousies between parties whom God hath joined together, and whom no man is at liberty to put asunder. . . . We are not lowering the dignity of science when we command it to do, what all the objects it looks at and admires do, when we command it to worship God. Nor are we detracting from the honor which is due to religion when we press it to take science into its service. . . . Let not science and religion be reckoned as opposing citadels, frowning defiance upon each other, and their troops brandishing their armor in hostile attitude. Each has its own foundation. These let them unite, and the basis will be broader, and they will be two compartments of one grand fabric reared to the glory of God. Let the one be the outer and the other the inner court. In the one let all look, and admire, and adore; and in the other let those who have faith kneel, and pray, and praise. Let the one be the sanctuary where human learning may present its richest incense as an offering to God; and the other the holiest of all, separated from it by a vail now rent in twain, and in which, on a blood-sprinkled mercyseat, we pour out the love of a reconciled heart, and hear the oracles of the living God."

DISCUSSION II.

THE HUMAN FAMILY.

THE scientific determination of an actual family relationship among all varieties of human beings, has been briefly stated in the foregoing essay. On a subject, however, of such importance, an additional discussion, simple and yet full, clear but condensed, may be useful. Especially in view of the strenuous claims in behalf of the diversity theory, put forth before the American, and particularly the Southern public, within the last few years, and urged with triumphant confidence, alike in winged pamphlet and ponderous quarto, under cover of an immense parade of boasted science; and recently sanctioned, though with apologetic caution, by at least one of the writers admitted to the dignified associations of the "Smithsonian Contributions to Knowledge." (See vol. viii. pp. 1, 105, 159.)

In the present essay, therefore, we propose to investigate with some thoroughness the issue thus presented; to examine the subject in several aspects; and to indicate the general considerations and the special scientific processes by which such great master-models of vast and accurate research as the Humboldts, Prichard, Chevalier Bünsen, and Professors Lepsius and Owen, have been brought to the conclusion, fully agreeing with the established sentiment of Christendom, that men, under all varieties, are but of one stock; that the human race is, in fact, one family from a common ancestry.

The alternative to this doctrine, proclaimed in the recent publications referred to, is sufficiently distinct. Their authors contend that "*men were created in nations*, and not in a single pair." (Types of Mankind, p. 82.) That they have no common original nature, no essentially agreeing rational constitution, and no comprehensively designed merciful arrangement for their general improvement in the present life and for their joint participation of a higher future existence. That some are absolutely, and unconditionally, "*inferior*," and not only "born to be ruled," but "destined to live and prosper," merely, "till a superior *destroying race* shall come *to exterminate and supplant them*, and that no philanthropy, no legislation, no missionary labors, can change this law." (pp. 79, etc.)

That these sentiments are seriously in conflict with the admirable moral tone of the Scriptures, the equitable spirit of modern civilization, and the benign energy of Christian heroism, need scarcely be suggested. And it must be acknowledged that if scientific processes, fairly conducted, do really, in this instance and in this manner, utterly break up the moral fabric which the wisdom of ages has sanctioned, and put a final extinguisher upon the best motives and highest hopes of humanity, it is not only a "new thing under the sun," but a most strange and portentous anomaly in the course of human experience.

For this controlling reason, then, at the outset, we are constrained to distrust the conclusions now referred to, as unsound, and the methods by which they are reached as not genuinely scientific. And here we are reminded of what, with his accustomed felicity, a distinguished author characterizes as *a species of superstition attached to the notion of science*, as if it were an indescribable magical something, different in itself from accurate and classified knowledge systematically deduced from unquestionable principles and established facts. A moderate acquaintance with the habitual tendencies of the superficial, though so-called scientific speculation of the day, may satisfy any mind of the justness of this profound remark.

Science, it should be remembered, is a very humble as well as calm and patient laborer; whether with Newton gathering pebbles on the shore of the great ocean of truth, or with Bacon seeking admission to the kingdom of nature, as it is said a higher kingdom must be sought, with the docile spirit of a simple-hearted child. When, therefore, we find large claims proudly put forth in the name of science, tending to revolutionize the practical moral convictions of mankind, and to annihilate the benignant sympathies and actuating motives of humanity, the very incongruity of the procedure brings it at once into suspicion as erroneous and unreliable.

In addition to this general consideration requiring the most serious questioning of the proposed theory, we have a further special but kindred reason, in its bearing upon our peculiar Southern institution, for meeting it with distrust and subjecting it to unconfiding scrutiny.

The sacred code which guides the conscience of Christendom, and which is, beyond question, incomparably the surest directory to duty, in all human relations, is at once our authoritative reply to all misguided assailants of our position as providentially in charge of a form of servitude every way remarkable, and our acknowledged standard of the obligations connected with that position. And so long as we abide by the sanctions of this code, whatever deluded enthusiasts and corrupt agitators may pretend, we have with us not only the decisive voice of constitutional law, but the undisturbing acquiescence, if not the full approval, of the enlightened Christian mind throughout the world. Right-minded people may indeed believe that the golden Christian rule tends toward the abatement of asperity and the remedying of oppression in all human relations, and cherish the pleasing hope that as the spirit of Christianity more and more prevails, equity and kindness will more and more ameliorate, everywhere, the condition of the more burdened portions of society. But they cannot on any scriptural ground believe in a wild theory of absolute personal equality, destructive of social order, and rushing headlong into universal anarchy. Nor, despite the fervid declamation and fiery denunciation so much indulged within the last half century, can they believe that the Creator sanctioned sin, when he legislated for slaves, in old Abraham's house, and under the Jewish commonwealth. (See Genesis, xvii. 12; Exodus, xxi. 21, etc.) And when he caused to be recorded in the New Testament such reiterated injunctions to masters to treat their slaves considerately and kindly and to servants religiously to

6*

obey, even under the severest species of bondage. (See Eph. vi. 5; Col. iii. 22; 1 Tim. vi. 1; Titus, ii. 9; 1 Peter, ii. 18, etc.

It is a striking and instructive fact that the fierce assailants of the South, and its institution so peculiar and so effective in elevating the negro race, should have found it necessary to direct their batteries against the Sacred Scriptures, either in the way of insane transcendentalism, with one class of contestants, or of *"higher-law"* atheism and *"irrepressible-conflict"* instigation, with another, or of atrocious blasphemy, with a third, or with perhaps a still more numerous assemblage, of pious sentimentalism conjoined with applauded falsehood, treason, and murder.

Thoroughly satisfied, as we are, by the intrinsic and extrinsic evidences attending the sacred code—evidences profoundly reverenced by the giant intellects of Bacon, Newton, Milton, and Locke, and unhesitatingly admitted by the common sense of the leading portion of mankind—that the sanctions of that code rest on an immovable basis of truth, we cannot deem it right or wise or becoming, and we cannot consent, that the defenses of our position be transferred from this foundation of rock to the shifting quicksands of less than doubtful theories. It is in our view wholly untrue, and we will not even tacitly allow ignorance and prejudice the moral advantage of representing, that Southern servants are held only as a higher race of ourangs, not really contemplated in the authoritative precepts on which the morality of Christendom is founded.

The question, then, as presented, is one which does not admit of indifference, on account of its obvious bearing upon our special position as Southerners, as well as upon the moral and higher relations of men everywhere.

At the same time, however, it is very far from necessary to mingle in its treatment passion and prejudice. Indeed, under various conditions has it been again and again examined by naturalists, with entire dispassionateness, as a general matter of scientific interest; and although, in the progress and result of these inquiries, "we observe," as remarked by Dr. Morton, (Crania Americana, p. 2,) "that diversity of opinion which is so frequent in human researches," yet has the investigation been, for the most part, conducted as a fair search after truth,—Virez supposing he had ascertained *two* species, Desmoulins *eleven*, Borey *thirteen*, and others a still greater number of original kinds, among men; while Linnæus, Blumenbach, Cuvier, and other distinguished students of nature became settled in the conviction of a strict unity in the human family.

Among investigators in this department of research, the celebrated Dr. James Cowles Prichard stands unrivaled as a model of freedom and fairness of mind, associated with virtuous reverence for everything good, cautious examination conjoined with discriminating sagacity, and the most amazing accumulation of intelligence covering the whole field of inquiry. Setting out with full confidence in the great principle, that "truth can never be found ultimately in opposition to truth," he devoted the energies of a sound mind, sustained erudition, and the persistent endeavors of a long life, to exploring the wide range of fact in all branches of knowledge affecting his ultimate problem, physical, physiological, psychological, historical, and philological; and after the most copious induction of this kind, under the requirements of an inexorable logic, he was brought to a result thus announced in the closing words of his last work: "We are entitled to draw confidently the conclusion, that all human races are of one species and one family."

"Prichard," says Bünsen, "will not be forgotten in the annals of history. His works contain the best and clearest discussion of all the elements of natural philosophy which bear upon the great question of the unity of the human race. His ethnological inquiry is conducted on the basis of a clear geographical and ethnological exposition, in which the critical reforms introduced by Ritter, Klaproth, and others, are adopted with independent judgment. In the linguistic portion he availed himself, generally, of the most thorough critical researches, and made use of the best materials which continental and English glossaries and observations offered to him. He had sound knowledge of Greek, Latin, German, etc., and good taste in selecting and naming his authorities. But his great merit is his excellent good sense and sound judgment. . . . As it stands, his work is the best of its kind. . . . Up to the present moment, (1854,) there is no book which treats the question with equal depth and candor."

These characteristics of Prichard's mind, method, and conclusions, we wish to be particularly marked: his "excellent good sense, and sound, independent judgment;"

his care to collect the most abundant "observations," and avail himself of "the most thorough critical researches;" his substantial "knowledge," the "depth" of his convictions," the "clearness" of his thoughts, and, above all, the "candor" of his spirit.

It is in association with precisely this style of character, this order of mind, and this reliable application of the inductive philosophy, that genuine scientific results are to be looked for in the future, as they have been displayed in the past.

And it is with unfeigned regret that we find ourselves constrained to remark upon the characteristics, so opposite to these, of certain industriously circulated and insidiously indorsed (see Smithsonian Contributions to Knowledge, vol. viii. p. 81,) publications of the last year or two, which, especially as the production in part of Southern talent, we had very much rather find worthy of unqualified commendation. In these, for the most part, there are not only blemishes of the most serious nature, but improprieties of tone and purpose so marked and so extensive as unavoidably to weaken, if not actually to neutralize, their claims to scientific authority. Prejudice and passion are stamped too conspicuously on their pages to be overlooked by the most casual observer; and it must always be in vain for the noble triumphs of science to be claimed by authors who exhibit such tokens of disturbed or clouded reason. In proof that we censure thus not unadvisedly, and that the cause of truth requires these traits to be understood, we adduce a few specimens.

One of these writers, Dr. Patterson, in his memoir of the distinguished naturalist, Dr. Morton, thus mingles intense feeling with philosophical discussion; alluding to an instance of violence by one of the Western tribes, in which a valuable life was lost, he says: "We have had too much of sentimentalism about the red man. It is time that cant was stopped now. Not all the cinnamon-colored vermin west of the Mississippi are worth one drop of that noble heart's blood." Here is stereotyped passion in the terms "cant" and "vermin."

In like manner, and in reference to a higher subject, another, Dr. Nott, gives vent to a spirit of no little bitterness: "On former occasions we had attempted to conciliate sectarians, and to reconcile the plain teachings of science with theological prejudices. In return, our opinions and motives have been misrepresented and vilified by self-constituted teachers of the Christian religion. We have, in consequence, now done with all this; and have no longer any apologies to offer, nor favors of lenient criticism to ask. The broad banner of science is herein nailed to the mast. Even in our own brief day, we have beheld one flimsy religious dogma after another consigned to oblivion, while science, on the other hand, has been gaining strength and majesty with time."

Abusive epithets are here accumulated with an angry energy that almost pants in its eagerness. *"Sectarians," "theological prejudices," "vilified," "apologies," "favors," "flimsy religious dogmas,"* bespeak an excitement of mind manifestly inconsistent with the self-possession of reason, the composure of philosophy, and the dignity of science. A calm, clear intellect, assuredly is indispensable to trustworthy scientific investigation. And though we may not absolutely hold that your true philosopher is

> "A man whose blood
> Is very snow-broth; one who never feels
> The wanton stings and motions of the sense,
> But doth rebate, and blunt his natural edge
> With profits of the mind, study, and fast;"

yet must he be in general, and doubly in reference to great questions he professes to elucidate,

> "Free from gross passion."

Another individual, less distinguished but more notorious than the writers already quoted, makes arrogant mockery, profane jesting, and boastful denunciation the chief staple of his contributions to ethnology, as if they were legitimate adjuncts of scientific inquiry. And he has actually had the fatuity to stamp upon his own pages with his own hand the brand of a revengeful and belligerent temper. "It has so happened," says Mr. Gliddon, on the last page of his book, "that my surname has been frequently made the target for indiscreet allusions on the part of certain *theologastii*, without any provocation having been given on my side, through a single personality, in the course of ten years' lectureship upon Oriental Archæology in the United States. To treat such in any other manner than with silent indifference, would have been unbecoming, as well as at the moment of each offense unavailing. I preferred my own convenience, and in the foregoing pages I have indicated an easy way of 'carrying the war into Africa.'" Whatever may be said of this in other aspects, no one can question that it indicates a most unreliable state of mind for a man who professes to deal scientifically and destructively with the most important verities embraced in the range of human intelligence.

Nor are these the only *prima facie* reasons for distrusting the processes and conclusions of the class of works under consideration. In them all there is implied, and in some avowed, discipleship of the phenomenal atheistic philosophy of Comte, known as *positivism*. And this necessarily throws the theory of "creation in nations" into the category of Lamarck's development hypothesis, and the speculations of the "Vestiges of Creation." Since it is clear, that, if no Creator is acknowledged, there can be no "creation" meant in any true sense. And the notion, after all, involved in the scheme really is, that in some inexplicable, inconceivable way, men merely appeared in nations, without having been created at all. They only *happened* —without a true causation—or waked up from sleeping stocks, unaccountably animated, or grew out of ourangs, which had grown out of frogs, which had been developed from eternal monads under the blind decrees of a Dead Fate.

The issue of the theory—that every region had originally its tribal autochthons—in some such absurdity as this, might, indeed, have been inferred from the consideration that such theory is directly in conflict with the relations of means and ends involved in any economy of creation and providence. It being well-nigh incredible that a presiding intelligence would, in the act of endowing an order of creatures with energies and impulses adapted to endless self-multiplication, produce them in countless numbers.

But though the Lamarckian hypothesis might thus have been inferred as involved in the indefinite autochthon theory, it is the avowal of atheism under the guise of Comte's phenomenal scheme, which converts that inference into something of an acknowledged conclusion.

A conclusion, however, so universally rejected by the common sense of mankind, as well as thoroughly refuted by the demonstrations of logic and the proofs of science, (see the admirable discussions in Sir Charles Lyell's Elements of Geology, and in Hugh Miller's Footprints of the Creator,) is not of course willingly and fully confessed. And it is, perhaps, but justice to the parties, to admit that they have not fully considered the relation between their theory and the atheistic philosophy to which some of them have committed themselves. This is the less unlikely, from the indications they give that their acquaintance with Comte's system is derived mainly from the meagre and partial synopsis contained in G. H. Lewes's "Biographical History of Philosophy." This is the only exposition of positivism which they quote. If fully aware, moreover, of the position they were assuming, they could hardly have ranged themselves so complacently among those whom a well-informed reviewer (North British Review, May, 1854,) so justly characterizes as "a cohort of narrow-minded enthusiasts and half-believing admirers, who, on the authority of Mill and Lewes, are taking the atheistic positivism as their creed, while it is unnoticed by the profoundest minds of the age."

Nor could they have claimed, with such supreme satisfaction, to have passed, under Comte's leadership, "beyond that undeveloped stage of the reasoning faculties classified as theological," and to have taken their place "among the educated who are *creating new religions* for themselves," had they not been ignorant of the pregnant fact, that the latest development of their master's system, and of the vaunted process of education toward "creating new religions," is an actual return to the very lowest form of "theological" folly. That Comte himself, the denier of a God, under the desolation of bereavement, when Madame Clotilde de Vaux, the object of his love, was torn from him by death, sought relief for an aching heart in the most absurd Fetischism of his own construction; human beings, and the higher beasts, in the aggregate of their vitality, constituting his god, and Madame Clotilde, under some fanciful notion, a supreme goddess.

Whether, however, aware or unaware of all this, these writers are, by the simple fact of giving it unconditional indorsement, more than abundantly discredited as trustworthy explorers of truth. If in possession of the whole case, they have deceived; if not so possessing it, they have trifled with their readers. And in either event there is most culpable unfairness. Authors who venture to deal destructively with the practical groundwork of human convictions, and to substitute what they are bold enough to proclaim a better system, which, notwithstanding, they have not half examined, are egregiously misleading, and may be fatally deluding all who accept their proffered guidance.

In all these improprieties of tone, manifestations of temper, and proofs of prejudice, which we are compelled to notice as pervading the discussions connected with the diversity doctrine in its latest phase, we find inevitable considerations of conclusive cogency, forbidding any ready acceptance of that doctrine. And these considerations, superadded to the associations which it involves, as we have seen, with the absurdities of Lamarck's hypothesis—and to its injurious bearing, previously indicated, upon the moral code of Christendom—and the securest sanctions of our Southern social organization, make out so strong a case of *prima facie* practical impossibility against the theory, that every right-minded man may at once feel justified in setting it aside as satisfactorily shown to be untenable and untrue.

This mode of reaching the conclusion, however, though doubtless sound, and perhaps satisfactory to those everywhere-to-be-respected individual minds whose determinations are governed by the seldom-erring practical logic of common sense, may not suffice as an ultimate exposition for that class of inquirers who look to a scientific solution of the important problem. We shall therefore need no apology for going more thoroughly into an analytical examination of the entire question, to the full extent, indeed, of the moderate limits we believe best adapted to usefulness.

Our method will be, to scrutinize the principal considerations relied upon by the advocates of the diversity theory; and then to adduce, in order, the chief evidences which establish, in our judgment conclusively, the specific unity and organic identity of all varieties of the human family.

The first proposition urged in support of the diversity doctrine is, that *some very marked and otherwise unaccountable relation exists, throughout the habitable globe, between the flora and fauna of different districts, as grouped by nature, independently to a great degree of climate, and the distribution of human varieties.* This proposition rests mainly upon the authority of Professor Agassiz, a gentleman for whose abilities and attainments we, in common with all who are even partially acquainted with the scientific achievements of the age, entertain very high respect, but whose suggestions on points touching the natural history of man must be regarded as far from conclusive. Partly because his special range of study has lain in another field; partly because he has exhibited in this department a fanciful and fluctuating genius, now inclining to one and now to another opinion; and partly because in the very act of lending his name and influence to the doctrine that men "were created in nations," he admits an enduring doubt as to an original diversity at all. "*I still hesitate,*" are his words, in the very paper announcing the proposition now in view, on "Provinces of the Animal World, and their Relations to the Types of Man, 1854," "*I still hesitate to assign to each (variety) an independent origin.*" To appreciate the force of this doubt, we must take it in connection with a favorite and eloquently urged conviction of this eminent zoologist. "We recognize," he says, (Christian Examiner, January, 1850,) "the fact of the unity of mankind. It excites a feeling that raises men to a most elevated sense of their connection with each other. It is but the reflection of that divine nature which pervades the whole being. It is because men feel thus related to each other, that they acknowledge those obligations of kindness and moral responsibility which rest upon them in their mutual relations. Where the relationship of blood has ceased, do we cease to acknowledge that general bond which unites all men of every nation? By no means. This is the bond which every man feels more and more the farther he advances in his intellectual and moral culture, and which in this development is continually placed upon higher and higher ground—so much so, that the physical relation, arising from a common descent, is finally lost sight of in the consciousness of higher moral obligations. It is this consciousness which constitutes the true unity of mankind." Nobly said, certainly, in vindication of oneness of nature in all men, and in inconsistency, most sound-judging persons will think, with strenuous advocacy of diversity of origin. For, why the needless multiplication of miracle in giving being to a prolific creature, indentical in nature, in a thousand, or a hundred, or ten simultaneous or successive different pairs, or "nations," in so many regions of the earth? Such expenditure of special power is assuredly not in accordance with the analogies of Providence. No wonder the distinguished philosopher "hesitates to assign to each human variety an independent origin." To his main proposition, therefore, sustaining the idea of manifold autochthon tribes, no great weight can be attached, nor to the particulars supposed to establish it.

The exact words of Agassiz, in stating his thesis, are: "*That the boundaries within which the different natural combinations of animals are known to be circumscribed upon the surface of our earth, coincide with the natural range of distinct types of man.*" Here, at the outset will be noticed an immense fallacy, under the single phrase "*natural range,*" which vitiates the entire proposition. It either involves the assumption of an original starting up of earth-born nations, each in its own "natural" district, a doctrine about which the learned professor declares that to the end he "hesitates;" or, it asserts some other fixed relation between regions and races, irreconcilably in conflict with the plainest facts. If it be meant that Europe, for instance, had native clans anterior to the immigration of Teutons, Celts, etc., or their earliest wandering predecessors, and that our Indian tribes sprang up in their several "natural ranges," without connection with other parentage, then what is it but the most obvious *petitio principii*, the merest taking for granted the very thing sought to be proved through the laborious processes of massive volumes, without at last dispelling the mists of doubt from this very leading mind? But if this be not what is meant, then may it be unanswerably urged, what original and fixed relation England and its flora and fauna sustain to the present Anglo-Saxon population, or to any other people that have entered the island from abroad? And what is the "natural range" of the spreading population of the United States?

But not to dwell upon this radical unsoundness of the proposition in question, let its alleged supports be examined. They are such affirmations as these: "Among the animals which compose the fauna of a country, we find types belonging exclusively there, and not occurring elsewhere;" "the grand divisions of the animal kingdom are primordial, independent of climate." And upon these affirmations, in connection with the general proposition of coincident human types and zoological groups, it is sweepingly alleged, "that the laws which regulate the diversity of animals, and their distribution upon earth, apply equally to man, *within the same limits, and in the same degree.*"

Now, granting, as is undoubtedly true, that instances occur of very restricted existence of certain classes, alike in the vegetable and animal kingdoms, and that, apart from human agency, neither plant nor animal of any one kind can be found indiscriminately scattered through every region where it could exist; yet, is it not plain that the fact bears directly against the assertion, that men are controlled *within the same limits, and in the same degree,* as other living things, by the laws which regulate diversity? And that it bears also very strikingly in favor of an original creation of men in only one centre? Why, it may be confidently urged, should it be supposed that unlimitedly migratory man was "created in nations," the world over, when the unwieldly walrus is confined to the Arctic shores, the awkward kangaroo, under whatever varieties that exist, to the arid wastes of Australia, and the scarcely locomotive sloth to a limited district of Southern America? And how did it happen that not a horse, cow, sheep, goat, hog, dog, or cat, of all the numerous varieties of these creatures elsewhere domesticated by man, was found in 1492, existing on the American islands and continent, in companionship with the men there supposed to have once waked up "in nations" out of dust, or metamorphosed lizards, or something of that sort? Why, if the laws which regulate diversity apply equally in the same limits and degree to man and to the lower creatures, did not the "nations" that happened to rise up somehow in America, find, on rubbing their eyes and looking about them, some of these very useful, voiceless servants at hand, which they might tame and turn to good account? The instinctive sagacity of a sound mind at once determines these questions against the diversity theory. An inference from analogy is immediately suggested, that if other orders of animals were originally given being in only one locality, so, probably, was man. That if the lower creatures, so universally adapted to his use, had not their "natural range" in America, in the sense of being created there, neither had he, but that he found his way thither by routes which admitted not of their transfer. A conclusion, which, as will be presently seen, is remarkably confirmed by Lieut. Maury's discoveries respecting air and ocean currents, and by linguistic and other facts copiously furnished in the valuable national work edited by Dr. Schoolcraft.

The statement that the grand divisions of the animal kingdom are altogether independent of climate, cannot be maintained in any sense subsidiary to the notion of like "primordial" diversities among men. It is no doubt true that climate alone did not determine the original positions assigned different classes of plants and animals, and yet is it equally certain that every organized form does sustain a very marked relation to climate. "The migration of quadrupeds from one part of the globe to another," observes Sir Charles Lyell, (Elements of Geology, vol. iii. p. 16, etc.) "is prevented by uncongenial climates, and the branches of the ocean which intersect continents. . . . Where the continents of the Old and New World approximate toward each other on the North, the narrow straits which separate them are frozen over in winter, and the distance is further lessened by intervening islands. Thus a passage from one continent to another becomes practicable for such quadrupeds as are fitted to endure the intense cold of the Arctic circle; accordingly the whole Arctic region has become one of the provinces of the animal kingdom, and contains many species common to both the great continents. But the temperate regions of America, which are separated by a wide extent of ocean from those of Europe and Asia, contain each a distinct nation of indigenous quadrupeds." Yet man is there, under only "such variation of form, color, and organization," remarks the same widely-informed, unprejudiced, and coolly-judging author, "as has been convincingly proved to be perfectly consistent with the generally received opinion of an origin from a single pair." And, continues the same philosophic investigator, "*were the whole of mankind now cut off with the exception of one family, inhabiting the Old or the New Continent, or Australia, or even some coral islet of the Pacific, we might expect their descendants, though they should never become more enlightened than the South Sea Islander, or the Esquimaux, to spread in the course of ages over the whole earth, diffused partly by the tendency of population to increase, in a limited district, beyond the means of subsistence, and partly by the accidental drifting of canoes by tides and currents to distant shores.*"

With this unmistakable announcement, by one admitted to have no superior in this department of science, might safely be left the refutation already given of the notion, that well-defined distinctions between human races coincide with corresponding limits of definitely circumscribed zoological realms, independently of climate, and only explicable on the theory of original diversities.

But there are other facts of so striking a character, in irreconcilable conflict with that notion, that it is scarcely allowable to pass on without listening a moment to their decisive utterance. One of these facts is the established unity of the whole American race, notwithstanding immense diversities of form, color, and appearance, from the misshapen and miserable occupants of Terra del Fuego, to the lordly Iroquois, whom our fathers found so formidable, and the half-torpid Esquimaux still gorging themselves with blubber on the Arctic coasts. To this fact the venerable Mr. Gallatin, so long and so remarkable an investigator of the Indian dialects, bears the following testimony, in perhaps the last public document penned by his hand: "*The several languages of the aborigines of America, as far as they have been examined, seem to leave no doubt of the unity of that race.*" (See Letter in Dr. Schoolcraft's Work, vol. iii. p. 97.) To the same fact, Dr. Morton also, in the last paper ever prepared by himself for publication, and the completion of which was even prevented by his death, thus bears witness: "A certain sameness of organization among such multitudinous tribes seems to prove, in the geographical sense, the origin of one to have been equally the origin of all." (Paper in Schoolcraft, vol. ii. p. 316. And even Agassiz does not deny this fact; on the contrary, he assumes the American race, in its totality, as one of the *eight* originally "created nations," which he arbitrarily adopts for his purpose; though other authors claim a different, and some an indefinite, number of such "nations." Now with this great fact of human oneness throughout so vast a region, there is plainly no reconciling the learned professor's asserted sameness of localities for groups of animal species and types of men. Such reconciliation is attempted indeed by sweeping into one group the endlessly diversified, and in some instances irreconcilably dissociated classes of animals between Labrador and Cape Horn. But such classification is too manifestly a forcing of facts to suit a theory to be other than worthless.

When the formidable grisly bear of the Rocky Mountains, and the bison multitudes of the Northwestern prairies, with their associated fur and feather clad companions, are discovered dwelling beneath the same skies as the ferocious jaguar of Brazil, the strange ant-eater and sloth, and the gorgeous feathered tribes of inter-tropical America, then, and not till then, can anything like a unity of animal species be affirmed as coinciding with that of the human variety pervading the continent.

Another fact of the same character, and conducting to the same conclusion, is the unity also established of the human families, dwelling in the broad area between the delta of the Ganges, the Pillars of Hercules, and the shores of the Baltic. Comparative philology, of which in another connection we shall adduce the testimony, has placed this fact beyond all question. In the language of one of Bünsen's coadjutors, in his great work, Christianity and Mankind, vol. iii. p. 180, "there was a time when the ancestors of the Celts, the Germans, the Sclavonians, the Greeks and Italians, the Persians and Hindoos, were living together beneath the same roof." Yet who has ever heard of animal forms in the wilds of Scotland and Scandinavia analogous to the tigers and their associates amid the jungles of Bengal?

Still another circumstance, controverting in just the opposite way the notion of coterminous human types and animal groups, is the very extensive coexistence of Papuan and other varieties of negroes, and nations of totally different characteristics, in the great Malayan range of Poly-

nesian Oceanica. "Black, woolly-haired people, resembling
in their features and color the negroes of New Guinea, are
widely spread in the Indian Archipelago. They inhabit
the interior of many islands, from New Guinea, New
Britain, and New Ireland, northward to the Philippines,
and eastward to the Hebrides," (Prichard's Nat. Hist. of
Man, p. 346;) while the Malayans occupying other portions of the same islands, and in Tahiti and other districts
of the Polynesian Paradise, improved into some of the
finest specimens of physical man, reaching round in an
immense circuit, are found furnishing residents to the
African islands of Madagascar, as proved by Humboldt.
(*Ibid.*, 341.) Any one who will turn to the portrait of a
Nigrito boy, given by Commander Wilkes, of the United
States Exploring Expedition, vol. v. p. 306, as a specimen
of that race in the Philippines, will at once recognize a
head and face the counterpart to which may be seen by
scores on any Southern plantation. Yet the true Polynesian tribes of the same islands, especially the Irogotes
and Pampagnons, are represented by Wilkes as a fine
race.

Now, either these two varieties of men must be admitted
to be not both autochthons of that sweep of islands, or it
must be acknowledged that human varieties are not coterminous with certain localities and zoological realms. It
matters little which horn of the dilemma be chosen by the
advocates of the diversity theory. Either way the fact
bears directly against their hypothesis, that all the more
marked varieties of men belong strictly to regions where,

in common with coincident groups of plants and animals, they were originally developed.

All these facts, and they might be almost indefinitely extended, prove, beyond question, that the accomplished Agassiz has permitted himself to yield to the temptation, offered, by a certain facility of escape from difficulty, in this adjustment, to arrange an arbitrary classification of human varieties, on the one hand, and, on the other, a fanciful grouping of animals into realms, so as to force them into a semblance of agreement, on his artificial plan, which is actually denied in the distributions of nature. No wonder, we repeat, he "*hesitates*" about the doctrine of original diversity, aware, as he cannot but be, of such radical unsoundness in the theory of distribution which he has been persuaded to throw off from a most ingenious and versatile mind. We have deemed it proper, on account of the influence of his name as a naturalist unsurpassed in his peculiar department, thus to indicate the total inconclusiveness of his speculations concerning the origin, distribution, and varieties of mankind. We close the refutation of those speculations with another extract from the well-nigh decisive judgment of Sir Charles Lyell.

"It is unnecessary," he says, (Elements of Geology, vol. iii. pp. 17, 121,) "to accumulate illustrations in order to prove that the stations of different plants and animals depend on a great complication of circumstances, on an immense variety of relations in the state of the animate and inanimate worlds. Every plant requires a certain climate, soil, and other conditions, and often the aid of many animals, to maintain its ground. Many animals feed on certain plants, being often restricted to a small number, and sometimes to one only; other members of the animal kingdom feed on plant-eating species, and thus become dependent upon the conditions not only of their prey, but of the plants consumed by them. . . . The possibility of the existence of a certain species in a certain place, or of its thriving more or less therein, is determined not merely by temperature, humidity, elevation, and other circumstances of the like kind, but also by the existence or non-existence, scarcity or abundance, of a particular assemblage of other plants and animals in the same region. . . . Whereas the power of existing and multiplying in every latitude, and in every variety of situation and climate, which has enabled the great human family to extend itself over the habitable globe, is partly the result of the physical constitution, and partly of the mental prerogative of man. If he did not possess the most enduring and flexible corporeal frame, his arts would not enable him to be the inhabitant of all climates, and to brave the extremes of heat and cold, and the other destructive influences of local situation. Yet, notwithstanding this flexibility of bodily frame, we find no signs of indefinite departure from a common standard. And the intermarriages of individuals of the most remote varieties are not less fruitful than between those of the same tribe."

The distinct judgment expressed in the latter portion of this quotation, concerning the specific oneness of the human family—under all the endlessly varying gradations of form, occasioned, within certain limits, by the operation of climate and other influences, on an original extraordinary flexibility of constitution — furnishes a suitable point of transition from one of the main propositions of the diversity advocates, to its other leading affirmation — concerning a pristine, well-defined, non-transitional, unchangeable distinction of species, in the diverse portions of our world's human population. The several statements embodying this affirmation may be expressed in the following proposition, derived from Dr. Nott's Synopsis, Types of Mankind, p. 465 :—

"*There exists a genus Homo, embracing many primordial types or species, which have remained permanent, and untransitional, through all recorded time, and despite the most opposite moral and physical influences.*"

The stress of this proposition lies obviously in the asserted *definiteness and permanence* of the types spoken of. If there be, as alleged, clearly-marked boundaries between unlike races, allowing of no intermediate gradations, which seem by insensible blendings to affiliate them, according to the diversified conditions of climate, habit, etc.; and if adequate proof be furnished, that such distinctions have existed since man appeared upon the earth, then it must be conceded that the proposition is not only plausible, but probably sustained. But if there be any failure of evidence as to either of these subordinate elements, the proposition at once, be it noted, loses its claimed position as a truth scientifically established. For if there be any insensible blending of grades between the extreme varieties, so that no line of division can be truly drawn between one and another, then the affirmed non-transitional distinctness of types is immediately shown to be a merely arbitrary assumption, not authorized by the facts of nature. Or, supposing such separate, ungradational, clearly-defined diversities of race to be made out, and that they have existed for a very long time; still, if the whole term of human existence be not clearly embraced in the evidence —if there occur any gap in the testimonies of time— if any ancient period be left to doubtful conjecture—then again is the proposition vitiated. Since no one can in that case allege the impossibility, or even improbability, of the introduction of strongly-marked varieties into one family, by some such secondary divine appointment as that of Genesis, ix. 25-27, to which the prevalent impression of a very remarkable tri-partition of human destiny is commonly, and with reason, attributed.

Now, the question is, can either of these two branches of the main proposition be fairly made out? We are well assured, after very careful examination, that they cannot— that there exists indeed an absolute impossibility in the way of such proof, as to each of the points involved— that it is altogether, and in the nature of the case, impracticable, with any certainty to trace cranial relics, or monumental delineations, or historical records, those of revelation being excluded, up within any definite approximation of man's primeval age—and consequently impossible to trace diversities of race up to the beginning; that it is equally impracticable to point out races of men the most extreme in diversity, which have not, ranging between them, indefinite varieties so closely approximating either limit, as to constitute an insensibly blending gradational series, with no break in the progression, no interval admitting of a natural line of demarkation; and that consequently it is doubly impossible scientifically to establish the proposition, in support of which crania are piled on crania, and diagram on diagram, in the multiplied pages of massive volumes.

Let us, however, examine the argument under each head, and see if the general allegation be indeed sustained by facts.

We take up the point of absolute, definitely bounded types without interblending varieties. Is it established? Is it true? Does nature so speak?

Let the types, as they are called, be looked at separately, and then collectively. And here it occurs to remark upon this delusive term in a professedly scientific discussion. *Types* are marks, figures, modes; *species*, in the scientific sense, are classes intrinsically distinct. And although, like almost all other general terms, this may be, and has been questioned as to its exact scope—whether it embraces sameness of parentage as well as correspondence of governing qualities—yet is its meaning sufficiently agreed upon to make it the best general designation, in such inquiries. Whereas, the introduction of another term, and one apparently indicating a fallacious mode of determining specific diversity, viz., by a few superficial marks, is calculated to embarrass instead of elucidating the question, and seems, indeed, to involve a sort of tacit admission that at last the differences contended for as existing among men, are not exactly of the same kind as these scientifically admitted in determining species among lower creatures. Not, however, to dwell on this. We summon the American type. Agassiz assumes this to be a unit. Mr. Gallatin declares, "no doubt is left of its being one race." Dr. Morton affirms "the origin of one to have been equally the origin of all." Yet what are the facts as to some of the most striking peculiarities which characterize varieties of men? The very marked differences between the warlike hunting tribes, that disputed inch by inch with our fathers the possession of this great country, and the more compactly settled, and therefore more artificially cultivated but less vigorous people so cruelly oppressed and butchered by Cortez and Pizarro, who has not had occasion to notice? Now, Dr. Morton testifies of the old Peruvians, "that they possessed a *brain* no larger than that of the Hottentot and New Hollander, and far below that of the barbarous hordes of their own race: 155 crania gave but 75 cubic inches for the average bulk of the brain. . . . Of 22 Mexican crania the mean capacity was 79 cubic inches, 4 above that of the Peruvians. . . . While of 161 crania belonging to the nomadic tribes of North America, the average was 84 cubic inches, 5 above that of the Aztecs and 9 beyond that of the Peruvians." (Dr. Schoolcraft's Work, vol. ii. p. 329.)

Here, then, is an item of structure on which all advocates of specific diversity lay great stress, as strongly marking different types. Yet the highest authorities in this case testify that it is not specific or primordial, but only circumstantial, and incident to habits of life. This is Dr. Morton's account of the matter. (Schoolcraft, vol. ii. p. 239.) "We know that the government of the Incas was of the kind called paternal, and their subjects, in the moral and intellectual sense, were children, who seem neither to have thought or acted except at the dictation of a master. Theirs was an absolute obedience that knew no limit. Like the Bengalese, they made good soldiers in their native wars, not from any principle of valor, but from the mere sense of passive obedience to their superiors. But the condition of the savage is wholly different. His life is a sleepless vigilance, a perpetual stratagem; and his brain, always in a state of activity, should be larger than that of the docile Peruvian, even though it ceased to grow after adult age."

Again, as to *shape of head*, it is of a certain general standard, only "in greater or less degree," says the same eminent comparative physiologist. And it has exceptions; "a more elongated form being seen among the Missouri tribes, and among the Iroquois and Cherokees."

In *stature* there is a like deviation, *e.g.*: "Some of the tribes of Patagonia embrace a remarkable number of tall men, and perhaps their average stature exceeds that of any other of the affiliated natives;" while "whole tribes which possess a comparatively low stature exist in South America."

In *color* there are still wider differences. "The Charroas, (*ibid.*) on the southern shores of the Rio de la Plata, are *almost black*, as are some of the California tribes; while the Batocudys of Brazil and the Borroas of Chili are examples of a comparatively *fair tint*. And we are told that, among the islanders of St. Catharine's, on the coast of California, young persons have a mixture of white and red in their complexions, presenting a singular contrast to the inhabitants of the adjacent mainland. . . . The fairness of the Mandans of the Upper Missouri is proverbial." "There are many of these people," says Catlin, (Customs of North American Indians, vol. i. p. 94,) "whose complexions appear as light as half-breeds; and among women especially there are many whose skins are *almost white*, with the most pleasing symmetry and perfection of features, with hazel, with gray, and with blue eyes."

With regard to *hair*, Mr. Catlin also states, concerning that of the tribe just mentioned, that it is generally "as fine and as soft as silk," while the usual characteristic of this appendage to the Indian *ensemble*, is its long, black, and coarse texture. And even conceding to the microscopic observations of Mr. Browne of Philadelphia an authority altogether discredited by later and fuller researches, this variation in the head-covering of the red men may still be noticed. A circular section is exhibited by Mr. Browne as generally belonging to the Indian hair, while the slightly oval marks that of the European, and the flattened ellipse that of the negro; yet specimens are given by him of the oval section from the Indian head, and of a measurement not exceeding that exhibited in the best Caucasian blood, *e.g.* the two diameters of the oval section of a hair from the head of a Choctaw Indian, are given as respectively $\frac{1}{304}$ and $\frac{1}{390}$ of an inch; and the corresponding measurement of a hair from the noble head of Washington $\frac{1}{312}$ and $\frac{1}{416}$. (Schoolcraft, vol. iii. p. 383.) Nor can it be doubted that the soft and silken locks of the Mandans, described by Catlin, correspond, in minute structure, with the auburn tresses of our own bright beauties.

Here, then, is a single race of men presenting in itself a very wide range of variation in almost every one of the great features regarded as marking one type from another, indefinitely approximating, on the one hand, the structure and appearance of well-developed Europeans, and on the other, those of the more degraded, unintellectual, and swarthy portions of the human family. The first support of the diversity proposition under review seems fairly to break down under the pressure of this one fact.

But the great Indo-European family exhibits a precisely similar scene of almost endless variation. Who is not familiar with the characteristic features of the sons of Erin, in contrast with those of the countrymen of Kosciusko, and those of the kinsmen of Palafox? London and Paris, Naples and Athens, St. Petersburg and Madrid, present each its own standard of a great human variety; and yet how widely different are they all from the ancient people of Sanscrit speech in that vast peninsula of Southern Asia, where

"The rich soil,
Washed by a thousand rivers, from all sides
Pours on the nations wealth without control!"

"The inhabitants are swart, and in their locks
Betray the tint of the dark hyacinth."

So, again, with the prodigious multitudes of ever-varying human creatures spread over the immense area from Finland and Hungary, through the wide tract of Northern and Central Asia. These, all that can be included under the general appellations of Finns, Hungarians, Tartars, Turks, Samoieds, Mongolians, and Tungusians, have been shown, by the untiring researches of Rask, Schott, and Castrén, into their speech, to constitute one great family of men. "After studying," says Castrén, "for a long number of years, Finnic, Samoiedic, Turkic, Mongolic, and Tungusic dialects, it seems, as far as I can see from my own researches, that there exists between them both a formal and a material congruence, . . . and that they belong to one class or race." (Bünsen, vol. iii. p. 278.) Yet, who that looks upon the specimens of these various tribes, as rudely given in our common illustrated modern geographies, but must be struck with the interminable gradations with which they blend into each other, between extreme limits, which themselves blend, on the one side, into the highest European, and, on the other, into the lowest form of broad-cheeked, narrow-headed, low-statured, fish-eating barbarians!

Passing over the great Malayo-Polynesian range, already alluded to, of blended varieties, between limits approximating the Caucasian in Tahiti and elsewhere, and the dark, crisp-haired Hawaiians and others verging negroward;

and the Shemitic stock, varying between the traits of the fair daughters of Judah and those of the black Bedouins of Arabia; we next view the generally tanned and often woolly-haired, but still endlessly varied inhabitants of Africa, undistinguishably blended between the Berber and Egyptian of one extreme, and the Guineans, Hottentots, and Caffres of the other. The following is the strong testimony of so thoroughly informed a witness as Professor Lepsius: "You speak," he says to the authors of Types of Mankind, p. 233, "of a *gradation* in the people of the continent of Africa, from the Cape to the North. It is a very curious fact that the languages of the Hottentots and Bushmen ... bear some characteristic traits, which are found in the tongues of Northeastern Africa. ... The whole African continent had, in my view, within a certain time a parent population, and its languages were consequently analogous. I understand what you designate a negroid type in the Egyptian figures, and I have nothing against that observation. But the fact does not interfere with their principal character being Asiatic." So also Mr. Birch, of the British Museum, (*ibid.*:) "You are quite right as to the intermediate relation of Egypt to the Asiatic and Nigritian races."

In connection with the above expression of Lepsius, we quote from him a still more striking fact, (Letters from Egypt, xxvi.) "I have prepared the grammar and vocabulary of the language of the Bischaribas, inhabiting the eastern portion of the Soudan, ... and both with reference to its grammatical construction, and its position in the development of languages, *it proves itself to be a very remarkable member of the Caucasian stock."*

"Moreover," says Bünsen, (vol. iii., p. 185,) the roots of the Egyptian language are, in the majority of cases, monosyllabic, and on the whole identical with the corresponding roots in Sanscrit and Hebrew."

Here, therefore, entering Africa by the valley of the Nile, we find that early civilized and intelligent, though strangely idolatrous people, so much dealt with by the Scriptures and the old classic writers, blending, by language and many physical and intellectual characteristics, with the Japhetic and Shemitic stocks. Passing southward, the same race is tracked, by the sure guidance of affiliated tongues, through Soudan and Abyssinia. The predominant color of the ancient Egyptians is represented, as is well known, on their monumental tablets, etc., as of a peculiar *red*. And all the Nubians of the Nile, or Berberines, are, for the most part, (Prichard's Nat. Hist. Man, p. 285,) "of a red-brown complexion, sometimes approaching black, but still different from the ebony hue of the negroes proper. Their hair often frizzled and thick, yet not precisely similar to that of the negroes of Guinea." Of the Abyssinians, Baron Larrey says, (*ibid.*, 287,) "that they belong to the same general class with the Berberines and Egyptians: countenances full, without being puffed; eyes beautiful, clear, almond-shaped, languishing; cheekbones projecting; noses nearly straight, rounded at the ends; nostrils dilated; mouth of moderate size; lips thick;

teeth white, regular, and scarcely projecting; beard and hair black and crisp; and complexion the color of copper."

"Connected with the Abyssinians are the Gallas, a race extensively spread in eastern inter-tropical Africa, and one of those holding an intermediate place between the Arabian on the one side and the negro on the other."

"Their countenance," says Dr. Ruppell, "is rounder than that of other Abyssinian nations: noses straight, but short; lips thick, but not yet like those of the negroes; hair thick, and strongly frizzled, and almost woolly." (*Ibid.*, pp. 285-87.)

From the lower Nile, tracing westward the Mediterranean border of Africa to the Straits, we note various Berber tribes, spread over the region of ancient Lybia. Here the Tyrian colonists of old found both fixed and desert-roving tribes—

> "Hinc Getulæ urbes, genus insuperabile bello,
> Et Numidæ infreni cingunt, et inhospita Syrtis;
> Hinc deserta siti regio, lateque furentes
> Barcæi." . . . .

And here African chiefs—

> . . . . "Iarbas,
> Ductoresque alii, quos Africa terra triumphis
> Dives alit——"

deemed themselves fit suitors for fair Dido's hand.

These Berbers are described as "in general of a swarthy color, with dark hair; but those who inhabit the mountains of Auress, or Mons Aurarius, though they speak the same language, *are of a fair and ruddy complexion, and their hair is of a deep yellow.*" (*Ibid.*, p. 265.) The Tuarik Berbers, consisting of many different tribes spread through all the habitable part of the great plain of Sahara, are especially remarkable, since they are found to "differ from each other most strikingly in physical traits, according to the climates where they dwell: being in some parts white, in others black, but without the features of negroes." (*Ibid.*)

Southward, to the mountain chain which ranges nearly parallel to the equator and at a distance of some 10° therefrom nearly bisecting the continent, including all that can be occupied of the vast sandy sea, is an immense expanse over which are spread a still greater variety. Some of the people of the interior are described as "very handsome;" the nations of Haiissa, for example, whom Mr. Jackson declares to "possess a peculiarly open and noble countenance, with prominent noses, and expressive eyes." (*Ibid.*, p. 294.) While others, for instance the Barnawi, are reputed to be more like the ideal negro. And as to the intellectual capacities of these tribes, the description which the celebrated Mungo Park gives of Lego, the capital of Bambarra, may serve as an illustration. "The view of this extensive city, numbering some 30,000 inhabitants, with its flat-roofed, two-story houses; its mosques seen in every quarter; the ferries conveying men and horses over the Niger; the numerous canoes upon the river; the crowded population; and the cultivated state of the surrounding country, formed altogether a prospect of civilization and magnificence which I little expected to find in the bosom of Africa." (*Ibid.*)

Toward the Atlantic extremity of the great equatorial mountain chain are found still other varieties of men. On the northward slope range the Mandingoes, one of the most powerful, numerous, and intelligent of the African races. Golberry affirms of them that "they resemble the blacks of India more than those of Africa." (*Ibid.*) Though Park states that they are not so handsome as the Joloffs, who are the most beautiful and at the same time the blackest people in Africa, and with hair of the kind termed completely woolly. The color of the Mandingoes is a yellowish black. Some of them, according to Major Laing, resemble the ancient Romans in many of their customs.

On the western declivity of the Hong chain occur in power the Fulahs, a people identical with the conquering Felatahs in Central Africa. The intelligent French traveler, M. Golberry, describes them as "fine men, robust, and courageous; possessing a strong mind; cautious and prudent; understanding commerce, and traveling in the capacity of merchants even to the extremity of the Gulf of Guinea." "Their women," he says, "are handsome and sprightly. The color of their skin is a kind of reddish black. Their countenances are regular, and their hair is longer than, and not so woolly as, that of the common negroes. Their language also is more elegant and sonorous than are those of the nations by whom they are surrounded." (*Ibid.*) From their appearance, and other circumstances connected with the Felatahs and Fulahs, M. d'Eichthal, in an elaborate memoir, maintains that they are an offset from the Polynesian race.

On the southern slope of the great range of mountains which terminates in the Sierra, and reaching round through a vast circuit of maritime country, to the inner angle of the Bight of Benin, are found the people presenting the negro traits in full development. Upon these it is needless to dwell, familiar as they are to almost every resident in the United States.

The interior of Africa south of the equator has of course been less satisfactorily explored than its northern expanse; still, reliable researches have also been here made, and especially have the recent discoveries of Dr. Livingstone thrown important light upon the geographical, ethnological, and kindred questions connected with this part of the continent.

Professor Ritter had, some time since, after the fullest investigation then practicable, represented the great plateau of Southern Africa as rising in every part at no great distance from the coast, supported on each side by a mountainous border, which offers an immense barrier in front of the surrounding ocean. "This elevated basin, it is believed, like all other regions so situated, contains vast lakes and immense mountain plains, a theatre where mankind must have formed themselves into peculiar races, during immemorial times, as they received the impress which physical agents were fitted to produce. In a country so analogous in its conditions to the high regions of

Eastern Asia, we should expect to find some points of resemblance in the tribes of people to the inhabitants of the last-named region. Accordingly, in the nations of South Africa there are many points, both in their physical and moral character, which bear a comparison with the great nomadic tribes of Mongolia and Daouria." (Prichard.)

These conclusions, though in part modified by Dr. Livingstone's discovery, that "the interior of Southern Africa is a vast, fertile, watery plateau of less elevation than flanking hilly ranges," (see Livingstone's Trav. and Res. in S. Africa, pp. 287 and 539,) are much more than confirmed by his observations on the characteristics of the various tribes spread over this region.

We can only glance at the peculiarities of these Southern races. The Hotentots, like our Indians, have deteriorated and dwindled before the devastations of a vitiated civilization. They were a pastoral people, active and courageous, though, under a peculiar patriarchal government, mild and contented. Now, through severe treatment, they have become the most degraded of men.

Their descendants, the miserable Bushmen, as described by the missionary Bonatz, are "of small stature, dirty-yellow color, prominent forehead, much depressed nose, and thick projecting lips. Their constitution is so much injured by dissolute habits, and constant smoking of duhra, that both old and young look wrinkled and decrepit." Dr. Knox testifies, from abundant personal observation, that the face of the Hottentot resembles that of the Kalmuc, except in the greater thickness of the lips; and he sets them down as a branch of the Mongolian race. In some important points their crania resemble those of the Northern Asiatics, and Esquimaux. (Prichard.)

"The people," says Livingstone, p. 366, "who inhabit the central region of South Africa are not all quite black in color. Many incline to that of bronze, and others are as light in hue as the Bushmen, who, it may be remembered, afford a proof that heat alone does not cause blackness, but that heat and moisture combined do very materially deepen the color. Wherever we find people who have continued for ages in a hot, humid district, they are deep black.... The Batoka who live in an elevated region, are, when seen in company with the Batoka of the rivers, so much lighter in color that they might be taken for another tribe."

The Caffres, north and east of the Hottentots, are thus described by Professor Lichtenstein: "The universal characteristics of all the tribes of this great nation consist in an external form and figure, varying exceedingly from the other nations of Africa. They are taller, stronger, and better proportioned. Their color is brown; their hair black and woolly. They have the high forehead and prominent nose of the Europeans, the thick lips of the negroes, and the high cheek-bones of the Hottentots." (Prichard.) This, Dr. Livingstone not only confirms, but extends. Of the entire central southern region, he says, p. 408: "All the inhabitants have a certain thickness and prominence of lip, but many are met with in every village in whom thickness and projection are not more marked than in Europeans. All are dark, but the color is shaded off in different individuals from deep black to light yellow. As we go westward, we observe the light color predominating over the dark, and then again, when we come within the influence of damp from the sea air, we find the shade deepen into the general blackness of the coast population. The shape of the head, with its woolly crop, though general, is not universal. The tribes on the eastern side of the continent, as the Caffres, have heads finely developed and strongly European."

Of a tribe in the very centre of the southern plateau, about south latitude 10°, and east longitude 19°, he adds, p. 486: "The people in these parts seemed more slender in form, and their color a lighter olive, than any we had hitherto met. Several were seen with the upward inclination of the outer angle of the eye. The mode of dressing the great masses of woolly hair which lay upon their shoulders, together with their general features, reminded me of the ancient Egyptians."

Ascending northward along the Eastern coast, are people analogous to the Caffres, and speaking cognate tongues. "The farther our travelers advanced from the coast," says Captain Owen, "the more they observed the natives to improve in appearance. Of those of Moroora, some are perfect models of the human form; their hair is not woolly, but grows long, turns in slender curls, and is neatly plaited." (Prichard.)

In his "Researches," Prichard has shown that there are strong grounds for concluding that all the nations known to inhabit Africa, south of the equator, with the exception of the Hottentots, speak idioms, which, if not dialects of one mother tongue, may be considered as belonging to one family of languages. And the exception thus noticed will be at once associated with the fact, before quoted from Lepsius, that the dialects of the Hottentots and Bushmen are of the same family with those of Northeastern Africa. Here again later exploration has confirmed and extended such well-grounded conclusions. "The dialects spoken in the extreme south," says Livingstone, p. 367, "whether Hottentot or Caffre, bear a close affinity to those of the tribes living immediately on their northern borders; one glides into the other, and their affinities are so easily detected that they are at once recognized to be cognate. If the dialects of extreme points are compared, as that of the Caffres and those of the tribes near the equator, it is more difficult to recognize the fact, which is really the case, that all the dialects belong to but two families of languages."

We have thus made a rapid circuit of the vast African continent; glancing at its multitudinous tribes, some of whom deviate more widely from the fine European standard than perhaps any other human varieties, the negroes of Australia possibly excepted, who are allied to those of New Britain, etc., and originally derived, most probably, as will be seen, from Africa. And in the whole range we discover the same endless variations, and gradational blendings between the widest extremes, exhibited by all the other people of the earth.

In *color* they vary through every shade, between the

appropriate European that sometimes appeared in Egypt, and still exists in the neighborhood of Mount Atlas, and the polished ebony of the thoroughly dyed negro. In *physiognomy*, they range between the elegant Grecian outline and the exaggerated monstrosity of prognathous development. In texture, etc. of *hair*, they exhibit every grade, from the soft Asiatic, and even auburn locks of some Egyptians, and of the Aurarian Berbers, through the long and plaited ringlets of the Moroorian Caffres, the short and crisp curls of the Nubian Berberines, the thick and frizzled half wool-like covering of the diffused Galla, and the still more woolly head-growth of the sagacious Fulahs, and of most of the southern races, to the thoroughly developed negro tufts of the Guinea tribes.

In every important particular that marks varieties of men, the inhabitants of Africa vary with such indefinite blendings of one grade into another, between the Caucasian standard and the lowest negro specimen, that it is impossible to draw a line of divison at any point of the scale, and affirm here one type ends and another begins.

This, then, is the decision of America, of Europe, of Asia, of Oceanica, and of Africa. There are no absolute, definitely bounded types of men, without undistinguishably interblending varieties; no such unconditionally fixed boundaries, circumscribing precisely marked families, separating them from all others, and allowing of no transitional instances, as assumed in the diversity proposition; and consequently the first postulate of that proposition neither is, nor can be sustained.

We pass therefore to its other affirmation, *permanence of type* through all time. And here it is of course to be noticed, that with the evidence just adduced full in view, so entirely discrediting the assumption of definitely bounded, unblending varieties of men, we can only use the term type in this connection as designating an ideal model, supposed to be more or less approximated by individuals through some indefinite range. The point alleged, however, we wish distinctly and fairly to examine. It is, not only that there have been negroes in the world from the beginning, as well as Hindoos and Europeans, Mongolians, Samoiedans, and North American Indians, but that Greek, Roman, and Celt, Scandinavian, Saxon, German, and Sclave, etc., and indeed almost every traceable people on the globe, are now, without change, save perhaps a little increase, just such as they were when first waking up to conscious being.

"*Nothing short of a miracle*," is the strong and bold assertion, (Types Mankind, p. 89,) "*could have evolved all the multifarious Caucasian forms out of one primitive stock.*" And attempts are seriously made to extort from history some support for the idea, that each tribe always had been what it subsequently was. So extravagant a doctrine, however, directly in the teeth of the most commonly known historical facts, and totally disproved by undeniable linguistic affiliations, is not worth considerate refutation. It is immediately set aside by its own absurdity. Nor is this all; the earnest advocacy of a notion so obviously untrue, carries with it something more than suspicions for the whole theory. How can authors who blunder so seriously on points open to universal apprehension, be relied upon as "knowing whereof they affirm," in matters of more recondite character?

But not to take advantage of this extravagance in detail, we accept the question in its more prominent features, and candidly meet the inquiry concerning human forms the most widely separated. Has it been made out documentally, monumentally, craniologically, or in any other way? can it be made out, that the white race has remained unchanged, and the negro race unvarying, through all time, "in spite of all the climates of the globe?"

The first consideration on the subject that at once occurs is, if it be so, it is a very wide departure from the general laws of specific existence. The following, says Lyell, may be admitted as laws prevailing in the economy of animated nature: "First, that the organization of individuals is capable of being modified to a limited extent by the force of external causes; secondly, that these modifications are, to a certain extent, transmissible to their offspring; thirdly, that there are fixed limits, beyond which the descendants from common parents can never deviate from a certain type; fourthly, that each species springs from one original stock, and can never be permanently confounded, by intermixing with the progeny of another stock." (Elements of Geology, vol. ii. p. 433.) If, then, it can be shown of the white race, or of the black, that no modification of organization has ever been produced by extremes of climate, food, and other commonly operative influences, that can be demonstrated concerning them which can be exhibited in no other extensively distributed species of animals on our planet.

But the advocates of this theory, discerning the bearing of analogy against their scheme, very positively repudiate it as a legitimate element of scientific investigation, notwithstanding the implied necessity of relying on analogy at the very basis of every inductive method. "The diversity of races must be accepted by science as a fact," they say, (Types, p. 65,) "independently of theology, and of all *analogies* or reasons drawn from the animal kingdom." This is said, be it remarked, as a sort of preliminary to a most elaborate discussion, aiming to disprove the Bible, and show that "men were created in nations," and at last so utterly failing in the proof, that the leading scientific mind engaged, in spite of fanciful tendencies and strong partialities, pleads guilty to final doubt on the subject.

But, passing by analogy, we address ourselves to the alleged evidence of facts. The Jews are adduced as a specimen of permanence. They certainly do stand marvelously among the nations, unabsorbed, unobliterated, untransformed—a fossil people in the deposits of time. But the Christian derives from this instance what he justly deems a vastly better lesson than that suggested. And the physiologist finds influences kept in operation on the Jewish mind and habit, well calculated to react upon the physiognomy and preserve some of its marked features, under considerable changes of other kinds which the people are known to have undergone in different regions.

Stress is also laid upon the correspondence between the crania gotten from ancient places of sepulture, and the modern heads of races in the same locality, supposed to be descended from those there buried. This, however, is plainly inconclusive to the purpose, since, in such cases, the former and the recent have existed under conditions too similar to necessitate a wide deviation.

The main evidence, after all, relied upon, is the existence of negro delineations on the monuments of Egypt. And we frankly acknowledge there is, at first view, something in this circumstance apparently favoring the asserted original existence, even from the very first, of negro races; but it is only on a superficial view, and merely in appearance.

Nobody knows how many years or centuries elapsed between the creation of man, or the flood of Noah, and the construction of those monuments. There may have been abundant time for the Nisus Formativi, or constitutional vital tendencies, severally imparted to the sons of one father, to be developed, under circumstances favorable to the introduction and transmission of the forms contemplated in such imparted tendencies, to a very extreme degree. It by no means necessarily requires a very enormous period for peculiar influences to work out, in a species possessing some special tendencies, the extreme results which they are capable of producing. "It follows," says Sir Charles Lyell, (Elements of Geology, vol. ii. p. 464,) "from many facts, that a short period of time is generally sufficient to effect nearly the whole change which an alteration of external circumstances can bring about in the habits of a species."

It may very well have been, therefore, that the descendants of one son of a family, who had received a certain constitutional tendency, according to a great providential plan, passing into Egypt, occupied the rich valley of the Nile, and, after a moderate period, multiplying greatly, spread themselves to the southward, and experienced, under the operation of causes adapted to develop it, the evolution in varying measure of that general tendency they had inherited; until, ere long, the diversified grades of dark skin, crisped hair, and prominent lips were produced, terminating in the extreme of thorough negro peculiarities. And that individuals of the race thus developed should, in the course of no great number of centuries, considering the course of the Nile valley and the general relations of the country, be introduced into Egypt by curiosity, trade, or war, could hardly be otherwise than inevitable.

Of this probability, some very remarkable confirmations are furnished in certain of Dr. Livingstone's late discoveries. First, that the sources of the Nile occur, it seems, not in a lofty mountain region, difficult of access, but in the elevated, humid, southern plateau between south latitude 6° and 12°. (See Livingstone's Trav. p. 514.) Second, that the peculiar customs of flour and bread making, and of spinning and weaving, which he met with in the heart of Southern Africa, are the exact counterpart of processes delineated in the old Egyptian sketches. (See those sketches, as given from Wilkinson by Livingstone, pp. 213 and 434.)

Now, it is worthy of remark, in this connection, that while Bünsen and Lepsius, certainly the best Egyptologists of this or any other age, from the monuments assign to the old Egyptian monarchy an antiquity reaching back to 3893 B.C. (See Egypt's Place in Univ. Hist., *passim*.) Even the industrious propounders of the permanent-type doctrine, after scrutinizing the records from Memphis to Meroe, *can find no negro delineation more ancient than "the twenty-fourth century* B.C." (Types, p. 239.) It is true these authors claim the right to "*infer* that these Nigritian types were contemporary with the earliest Egyptians." But it is manifest that an inference filling so prodigious a gap as *sixteen centuries*, is the mere substitution of bold assumption for non-existing evidence. Science no more allows such random leaps to conclusions, than justice would sanction the procedure of a jury hastening to consign a perhaps innocent fellow-creature to the gallows, by bridging with inferential guesses vast chasms in testimony.

The truth is, the utter absence of all negro representations, from the oldest Egyptian monuments, through a period, as yet ascertained, of sixteen hundred years, is a most significant fact in contravention of the very inference and theory of absolute original contemporaneousness. The very occurrence of a negroid form in those sketches, only at the end of a considerable period, during which the delineating art was practiced, is a striking indication that not till then had these forms become familiar in Egypt, a singular confirmation of the view entertained by Lepsius and Bünsen from their own researches, and of the probabilities we just now exhibited on independent grounds, that the African races were developed only in the course of ages from Egypt downward.

In arguing thus, from the Manetho-monumental chronology, we neither admit nor deny its absolute correctness. It may be generally true. It may be partially erroneous. But we are authorized to suppose that through its entire range it is proportionally the one or the other So as, in either view, to leave the argument entirely valid.

Nor, in conditionally admitting the most extended Egyptian chronology, or even some reasonable indefinite period between its farthest limit and the Noachian deluge, do we intend the slightest disrespect to the time-calculations heretofore founded on the genealogical lists of the Bible. While believing with Bünsen (Egypt's Place, etc., p. 160,) and Lepsius (Letters from Egypt, p. 361,) that the Old Testament, as well as the New, was designed for practical religious benefit, and not by revelation to convey a full account of ancient chronology, or any other branch of mere human knowledge; and with Michaelis and Prichard, that the genealogical lists between Noah and Abraham may be incomplete, as indicated by a comparison of Genesis, x. 24, and Luke, iii. 36; 1 Chronicles, vi. 1–4, and vii. 23–27, we also believe with them all, that there is in the world no other history so truthful, and, where it professes to give a complete, unbroken narrative, so accurate as that of the Bible.

10*

Egypt and its monuments furnish, then, no reliable evidence for the contemporaneousness and permanence, *ab initio*, of the white and black varieties of men, or of primordial specific distinctions between them. How else, indeed, should the most recent and most consummate Egyptologists be among the most earnest advocates, in the history of science, of a strict unity in the human family?

Another weak support for the primitive and ever-continued diversity doctrine is derived from ancient human relics variously exhumed, and referred not only to a very remote age, but to races diverse as those now existing. For instance, a supposed Indian skull dug up from among buried stumps, etc., some sixteen feet below the surface, at New Orleans, and by a most credulous calculation assigned to an imaginary date 57,000 years ago. Of such instances and their bearings we shall have more to say in our discussion of "the age of mankind;" here it is sufficient to make a single remark. Inferences, founded on a fanciful scheme so totally in conflict with the known progress of history and of human development; with the mature convictions of Lyell, Murcheson, and the most accomplished geologists, at least up to a very recent period, to be noticed in the sequel; with the candid admission of so able a sympathizer in the diversity doctrine as Dr. Jos. Leidy, (see his letter in the preface to "Indigenous Races of the Earth," 1857,) *"that no satisfactory evidence has been adduced in favor of this early appearance of man;"* with the comparatively recent dates of the oldest recorded astronomical observations, the most ancient of which ever heard of, Laplace tells us in his Systeme du Monde, are some rude Chinese notices of eclipses 2000 years B.C., and the first that can be relied on at all only 1100 years B.C.; and with the limited range of even Egyptian chronology,—are too preposterous to require serious refutation.

One other statement, adduced in behalf of unchangeable permanence and primordial distinction of races, remains to be considered, viz., that the negroes in America have not improved, and are not improvable, save in some lower particulars scarcely worthy of notice.

The remark of Sir Charles Lyell, that they are undergoing a manifest improvement, is pronounced "an unscientific assertion." "One or two generations of domestic culture," it is affirmed, "effect all the improvement of which the negro organism is susceptible."

Respecting this, as a question of fact, most readers in the United States, certainly all residents of our Southern section, have some means of judging from personal observation. Such observations, it is true, embrace too brief a period to furnish any satisfactory solution of the question; still, they may give an impression entitled to some credit, as to the tendencies in the case, and especially when the observed characteristics of our blacks are compared with descriptions or delineations of the traits still prevalent in Guinea. Our own impression, derived from such sources and from life-long familiarity with Southern plantation-life, and intimate acquaintance with hundreds of the race, some of whom, as known by us in infancy, were natives of

Africa, is, that Lyell was not so much mistaken on this point; and that, notwithstanding exaggerated specimens of the lowest standard not unfrequently to be seen, there is on the whole, and apart from all suggested suspicions of mixed blood, a very marked improvement of the race— physically, intellectually, and morally.

The accomplishment of such a result, indeed, may be regarded as among the final causes by which the destiny of that race in America has been determined. A principle which Southerners may, on the most solid basis of truth, triumphantly maintain against all opposers, in vindication of their moral position, as part of a vast scheme of an all-wise and benign Providence. Nay, the benefit has been incalculably beyond the improvement mentioned. For thousands, even millions, of these otherwise degraded heathen, have, in this peculiar situation, become, to all human appearance, partakers of the highest blessings of the everlasting gospel. This, indeed, is no excuse for the covetousness and cruelty commonly involved in their original capture and transportation, but it is, in connection with the lessons of Scripture already referred to, a full vindication of the general beneficence of this system of bondage, as in existence, and of the Christian virtue of those pious masters, who, holding their servants as under Divine sanction, endeavor faithfully to discharge the duties of their station under a sacred sense of responsibility to their "Master in heaven." (Col. iv. 1.)

But in thus giving our impression on the particular point of a considerable degree of actual elevation, already effected, and to be still more accomplished for the race, through their experience in our Southern country, we are by no means committing ourselves to a general theory of possible upward development in this or any other race. Elevation and degradation are very opposite processes, in individuals, families, and races. The one, according, as it would seem, to a prevalent constitution of nature, is for the most part comparatively easy to be effected, and soon consummated. The other, even when practicable, as often it is not, is extremely difficult and of slow attainment. Nor does it at all follow that because one set of influences rapidly evolves a deteriorating tendency to its lowest limit, influences of an opposite character can fully, if at all, restore the depreciated individual or class. A constitution seriously impaired by exposure or excess can seldom be by any means completely renovated; and the taints of blood, fixed by repeated transmission, under circumstances adapted to the tendency, are sometimes ineradicable by any remedial measures. As the converse of a proposition is not necessarily true in logic, so the reverse of a deteriorating process may not be attainable in nature. The divine plan, though having admitted, under given conditions, a downward deviation from a stock coincident with the best Shemitic or Japhetic, to the lowest negro, may not, even under opposite conditions, admit a complete return to such coincidence. A very extensive range of improvability, indeed, in creatures of almost every class, under favorable influences, must be admitted as a general law of nature. And such instances as the Mandan Indians, the Malayans of Tahiti, the Aurarian Berbers, etc., actually exhibit that improvability in varieties of men of very marked character, and on a scale to which no low limit can be justly assigned. So that there is good reason to expect, under the continuance of favorable influences, a very considerable elevation of the negro race. It is our belief, moreover, that such improvement is to be wrought out very much through their relation to our own Southern States. Still, we know not that it is other than an unauthorized assumption to suppose that they can, under any combination of circumstances, ever be restored to the physical, intellectual, and social condition of the highest European standard. And hopeful as we are concerning the gradual elevation of the masses of mankind, of all varieties, under the great ameloriating agencies of Christianity and modern civilization, till this, and every other race shall attain the best standard of which it is susceptible, we have little expectation of their fully recovering the structural symmetry, cuticular texture, complexional beauty, and ornamental locks, which, in their pristine state, distinguished, we may believe,

"Adam the goodliest man of men since born
His sons, and fairest of her daughters Eve."

But, however this may be, it is clear that observations are altogether too incomplete to authorize dogmatism either way in this incidental point. And it is still more obvious that even if negroes should in the future, however by favorable influences elevated in the human scale, always continue negroes, it will furnish no necessary proof that they always have been. They may have been developed downward, and yet never be allowed in all respects to redevelop upward. The possibilities of the future, apart from revealed sanctions, constitute however a mere speculation, with which it is no appropriate concern of scientific investigation to amuse or perplex itself. Its proper sphere is the *actual*, and in that sphere the hypothesis of absolute permanence of type through all past time finds no support. Facts abundant, in the phenomena of variation among lower animals, and in the history of human varieties, and even significant tokens in the early Egyptian monuments, array themselves invincibly against the notion of unvarying continuance of the white and black, and all other races, as they now are, from the very dawn of human existence.

And nature, in reply to the interrogatory of science, returns a distinct negative to each branch of the unvarying primordial type proposition.

Having thus scrutinized, as proposed, the main arguments adduced by the supporters of the diversity doctrine, and found them unsubstantial and delusive, we proceed briefly to present the chief considerations which satisfy us of the specific unity of the human family. Such considerations, in addition to many already incidentally adduced, are, first, affiliations of language; second, discernible processes of distribution; third, physical, physiological, and psychological correspondences among men of all varieties; and, fourth, the doctrines of the Bible. Our limits admit of the merest sketch of evidence under these several heads.

The proof from affiliated language, in spite of extraordinary suggestions to the contrary thrown out by Agassiz and others, is really decisive of the question of the common origin of the tribes of our race,—it being plainly incredible, that, among the infinitely diversified combinations of sound of which the human organs are everywhere capable, systematic coincidences in the structure of words and sentences, among different people, should endlessly occur by mere accident. It is vain also to attribute this agreement to the natural tendencies of organs similarly constructed. No unprejudiced man, in his senses, can be made to believe that while the Greek machinery for utterance evolved the word "αρτος," to express what the English and American speaking apparatus denotes by "*bread*," and the Latin organs of sound suggested by "*panis*," all widely distinct, and especially the last utterly unlike the other two, the French mouth should have developed, solely by the correspondence of its structure with that of the old Roman, the articulation "*pain*," for the identical thing. Every mind immediately discovers that the French word is really the Latin, adopted and slightly changed; and so in a thousand instances.

The occurrence of a few such coincidences in any two tongues shows manifestly some connection between the people speaking them; and the appearance of a great many proves a very close connection, as in the case of the Italian, French, etc., with the Latin. But, when, besides corresponding words, the very mode of arranging the elementary sounds to produce words is found coincident in two languages, and the method of varying words in expressing the relations of things is discovered to be mainly the same, not only is a close connection between these nations indubitably proved, but it is distinctly shown that their two classes of utterance are pervaded by a common contrivance, and therefore emanated from one mental influence,—that they are in fact parallel streams flowing from the same source. The radical consonantal arrangements so extensively prevailing, for instance in the Latin and Greek, and the diffused parallelism of their declensions and conjugations, constitute the most reliable historical documents concerning their common ancestry. So in like manner with the French and English. Such exactly agreeing modes of expressing thought as "*L'homme-de-guerre,*" and "*The-man-of-war,*" pervading the two languages, are but part of the family likeness transmitted from the same parentage.

Thoroughly to explore the tongues of the earth is, then, the true way to determine the great question of *origin*, as a scientific question. But this is a laborious process, not to be pursued without untiring patience, accumulated efforts, and vast erudition. No wonder it is depreciated by the impatient, superficial, and unlearned theorists, claiming to be scientific, who can so easily substitute for it a few half-observed appearances, a crude hypothesis, a bold utterance, and an abundant amount of dogmatism and denunciation; and by dint of defiant assertion palm it upon the prejudiced, the busy, and the credulous, as *science.*

"Languages," says Baron Humboldt, (Kosmos, vol. ii. p. 471,) "compared together, and considered as objects of the natural history of the mind, and when separated into families according to the analogies existing in their internal structure, have become a rich source of historical knowledge; and this is probably one of the most brilliant results of modern study in the last sixty or seventy years. From the very fact of their being products of the intellectual force of mankind, they lead us, by means of the elements of their organism, into an obscure distance, unreached by traditionary records. The comparative study of languages shows us that races now separated by vast tracts of land are allied together, and have migrated from one common primitive seat; it indicates the course and direction of all migrations, and, in tracing the leading epochs of development, recognizes, by means of the more or less changed structure of the language, in the permanence of certain forms, or in the more or less advanced distinction of the formative system, *which* has retained most nearly the language common to all who had migrated from the general seat of origin."

"The largest field for such investigations into the ancient condition of language, and consequently into the period when the whole family of mankind was, in the strict sense of the word, to be regarded as *one living whole*, presents itself in the long chain of Indo-Germanic languages, extending from the Ganges to the Iberian extremity of Europe, and from Sicily to the North Cape."

"The same comparative study of languages leads us

also to the native country of certain products, which from the earliest ages have constituted important objects of trade and barter. The Sanscrit names of genuine Indian products, as those of rice, cotton, spikenard, and sugar, have, as we find, passed into the language of the Greeks, and, to a certain extent, even into those of Shemitic origin."

"From these considerations, and the examples by which they have been illustrated, the comparative study of languages appears an important rational means of assistance by which scientific and genuinely philological investigation may lead to a generalization of views regarding the affinity of races, and their conjectural extension in various directions from one common point of radiation."

The processes thus indicated, originating in the sagacious intellect of Leibnitz, have been since pressed forward, and especially within the last two generations, with amazing industry and ability by the leading scientific linguists of the world. Adelung and Vater, Schlegel and Bopp, Rask and Guinon, William Von Humboldt and Lepsius, Gyarmathi and Schott, Furst and Delitzch, Müller and Bünsen, etc., and, most memorable of all, that unrivaled martyr to learning, already mentioned, Alexander Castrén, "who, after his prodigious tour of exposure and labor in pursuit of linguistic knowledge, returned to his duties as professor at Helsingfors, to die, after he had given to the world but a few specimens of his rich treasures." (Bünsen's Christianity and Mankind, vol. ii. p. 274.)

Some of the results reached by these thorough explorers,

and attested by such sure witnesses, have been already referred to; we add a few others of striking character.

"The evidence of language," says Professor Max Müller, (ibid.,) "is irrefragible, and it is the only evidence worth listening to, with regard to ante-historical periods. It would have been next to impossible to discover any traces of relationship between the swarthy nations of India and their conquerors, whether Alexander or Clive, but for the testimony borne by language. What authority would have been strong enough to persuade the Grecian army that their gods and their hero ancestors were the same as those of King Porus, or to convince the English soldier that the same blood was running in his veins and in those of the dark Bengalee? And yet there is not an English jury now-a-days, which, after examining the hoary documents of language, would reject the claim of a common descent and a legitimate relationship between Hindoo, Greek, and Teuton."

But the results of such investigations extend very far beyond the obvious affiliations in the several branches of the great Iranian stock.

"The heads," says Bünsen, (vol. iii. p. 172,) "of the critical Hebrew school, Gesenius and Ewald, had thrown out a hint that, by the reduction of the tri-literal Hebrew roots to bi-literal ones, (proposed already in the seventeenth century,) we might find strong reason to suspect a radical affinity between Hebrew and Sanscrit. Klaproth had pronounced, without reserve, that it was so. And, in 1838–40, two masters of the Hebrew tongue—Furst, of

Leipsic, (himself a Jew,) and more especially Delitzch, of Halle—accepting the method adopted by Indo-Germanic scholars, maintained and exemplified the constant and undeniable analogy between Indo-Germanic and Sanscrit roots. . . . . And Lepsius and Dr. Charles Meyer have established the fact beyond all doubt, that there exists an undeniable community of living roots between the two families. They have further shown that, in many instances, the Egyptian roots present the intermediate links between both, as well in words as in forms."

From his own researches into the Babylonian, Egyptian, and other tongues, Bünsen adds, (ibid.) :—

"If the Indo-European languages exhibit undeniable proof of the gradual extension of these races from the eastern part of Central Asia, the Shemitic tongues present no less striking evidences of their being derived from the western part of the primitive seat of mankind. The range of the Shemitic branch is less extended than that of the Iranian, but it forms a more compact and not less interesting mass. The Shemitic tribes never extended into Europe, except by temporary incursions. They have, however, not lost their ground in Asia, Armenia excepted, and have penetrated into Africa, at various epochs, even in the historical times, in which, assuredly, no traces of Japhetic origin are discernible. It is a fact which can be philologically proved, that the Shemitic formation constitutes the ground-work of African languages, from the Mediterranean coast of Africa into the interior of that mysterious country even beyond the equator, in an uninterrupted line."

This remark may be extended through a statement, by William Von Humboldt, of singular interest in connection with the Nigrito races of Polynesia and New Holland, already spoken of.

"To judge correctly," he says, "of the negro races in their pure form, we must always commence with the inhabitants of the great southern continent; as between these and the brown races no direct contact is conceivable, and, according to their present condition, it is difficult to conceive any kind even of indirect connection. The remarkable fact, however, still remains, that many words in the languages of these races, although we certainly possess only a few of them, bear an evident likeness to words of the South Sea Islands."

The languages of the latter are, from critical examination, classed by Müller, Bünsen, etc., in that vast circle of non-Iranian and non-Shemitic dialects, to which they give the general name Turanian. This, it will be remembered, is the immense sweep of kindred families, to the investigation of whose tongues Castrén so heroically devoted himself.

Of this great assemblage, Müller, after a most elaborate analysis, affirms: "Two nuclei may be distinguished, a Northern and a Southern; and of these, still farther back, a coalescence in one common form. Here," he adds, (Bünsen, vol. iii.,) "where the differences between the Turanian languages cease, the first stamina of the ancient Shemitic and Arian are found to converge toward the same centre of life. Radicals applied to certain definite but material meanings in common by all Turanian dialects, belong to this primitive era, and some of them can even now be proved the common property of the Turanian, the Shemitic, and the Arian branches."

Among the numerous dialects comprehended under the general term Turanian, spoken by more than a third of the human race, may be reckoned the Chinese, and cognate, so termed, monosyllabic tongues. The peculiarities which these present have been much dwelt upon by diversity authors, as supposed to offer insuperable difficulties in the way of scientific critical affiliation with other forms of human speech. (See Mr. Maury's paper, on the classification of tongues, in Nott and Gliddon's Indigenous Races.) Nor have explorers holding different views been indisposed candidly to admit more or less of difficulty in those peculiarities. So late as 1847, Bünsen, in his celebrated paper of that year before the British Association for the Advancement of Science, said: "The difficulties are immense. . . . Nor do we undertake to answer the question whether that wreck of the primitive language, that monument of inorganic structure, the Chinese, can be linked, by any scientific method, to the other families of human speech, and thus, directly or indirectly, connected with the great tripartite civilizing family of mankind, Shem, Ham, and Japhet. But we add, there is no scientific proof that it cannot. . . . There is a gap between that formation (Chinese) and all others, and that gap corresponds probably to that caused in the general development of the human race by great destructive floods, (we pause not to notice questions here suggested,) which separate the history of our race from its primordial origins."

Later and fuller researches, however, exhibited in Bünsen's more recent and important work, Christianity and Mankind, have removed some of the difficulties before admitted, and have shown undeniable bonds of affinity between the Chinese and cognate languages and the other tongues of the earth. (See Max Müller's masterly exposition of "the last results of Turanian researches," especially his chapter on the relation of the Taï to the Lohitic languages, and their connection with the Bhotiya class and Chinese. Bünsen, vol. iii. pp. 390–402.)

"As to the formal elements, or the grammatical growth of language," he maintains, "no difficulty exists in considering the grammatical system of Sanscrit, the most perfect of the Arian dialects, as the natural development of Chinese—an admission made even by those who are most opposed to generalizations in the science of languages."

He further insists: "These two points comparative philology has gained—

"1. *Nothing necessitates the admission of different independent beginnings for the* MATERIAL *elements of the Turanian, Shemitic, and Arian branches of speech; nay, it is possible even now to point out radicals which, under various changes and disguises, have been current in these three branches ever since their first separation.*

"2. *Nothing necessitates the admission of different beginnings for the* FORMAL *elements of the Turanian, Shemitic, and Arian branches of speech; and, though it is impossible to derive the Arian system of grammar from the Shemitic, or the Shemitic from the Turanian, we can perfectly understand how, either through individual influences, or by the wear and tear of grammar in its own continuous working, the different systems of grammar of Asia and Europe may have been produced.*"

"Translated into historical language," he continues, in accordance with the convictions of Humboldt, "these grammatical conclusions establish the following facts:—

"The first migration from the common centre of mankind proceeded eastward, where the Asiatic language was arrested at the first stage of its growth, and where Chinese, as a broken link, presents to the present day a reflection of the earliest consolidation of human speech," etc., etc. (*Ibid.*, pp. 479-480.)

With these important facts and conclusions, Bünsen, by means of the abundant data furnished in Schoolcraft's elaborate collection, has been enabled, in the most undoubting manner, to connect the dialects of the North American Indians. "The linguistic data," he declares, "thus furnished, combined with the traditions and customs, and particularly with the system of mnemonic writing, (first revealed in Schoolcraft's work,) enable me to say that the Asiatic origin of all these tribes is as fully proved as the unity of family among themselves."

Thus are all the languages of the earth, however at first view apparently dissociated and incongruous, traceable to one source; and, by consequence, all human tribes have proceeded from one centre and descended from one parentage.

And the unity thus traced, as justly and eloquently remarked by the copiously furnished author last quoted, "is not simply a physical, external one; it is that of thought, wisdom, arts, science, and civilization. By facts still more conclusive than the succession of strata in geology, comparative philology proves what our religious records postulate—that the civilization of mankind is not a patch-work of incoherent fragments, not an inorganic complex of various courses of development, starting from numberless beginnings, flowing in isolated beds, and destined only to disappear in order to make room for other tribes running the same course in monotonous rotation. For beyond all other documents, there is preserved in language that sacred tradition of primeval thought and art which connects all the historical families of mankind, not only as brethren by descent, but each as the depository of a phasis of one and the same development. In language are deposited the primordial sparks of that celestial fire which, from a once bright centre of civilization, has streamed over the inhabited earth, and which now already forms a galaxy round the globe—a chain of light from pole to pole." (Vol. iv. p. 112.)

Immediately connected with these demonstrative utterances of scientific comparative philology, are the indications of the same general truth furnished by the traceable processes of human distribution. The relation of many of the tongues of the earth to each other constitutes, as we have seen, a very sure guidance to some of the otherwise undiscoverable traces of paths along which tribes of men have trod, in wandering from their primitive Asiatic home to distant regions. There is much in the affiliation of dialects, and in the observed relative development of speech, to indicate, in the words of Baron Humboldt, "the course and direction of all migrations." These, however, are not the only means by which man may be traced in his farthest rovings.

There are highways on this globe, constructed by higher than human art, whose courses, though definite as a planet's path, have remained as undetected till mapped by modern skill, and that chiefly under the guidance of one of our distinguished countrymen, an American, and a Southerner. And those highways give tokens, engraved by a finger whose marks are equally ineffaceable and undeniable, of the human travelers they have conducted to remotest climes.

The great streams that flow unceasingly through the ocean constitute such highways; and the great atmospheric currents above the sea furnish an additional and unerring locomotive power, for transportation, more ancient than the human race.

This is the testimony of Lieut. Maury, in reply to certain queries proposed by Dr. Schoolcraft. Alluding in the first place to the use made by Colonel Hamilton Smith, in his "Natural History of the Human Species," of the Mexican legend of "*seven caves*," communicated by Montezuma to Cortez, in relation to a traditionary connection between the Aztec race and the nations of the Old World:—

"The colonel had a stronger case than he imagined, in

conjecturing that the Chichimacs might have been Aleutians, and that *'caves,'* if not denoting islands, might have referred to canoes. The Aleutians of the present day actually live in caves or subterranean apartments. They are the most bestial of the species, in their habits copying after the seal and the whale."

"These islands grow no wood. For their canoes, fishing implements, and *cave*-hold utensils, the natives depend upon the drift-wood which is cast ashore, much of which is *camphor* wood. Another link in the chain, which is growing quite strong, of evidence which for years I have been seeking, in confirmation of a gulf stream, near there, and which *runs from the shores of China over toward our Northwest coast.*"

Next, in reply to the question whether the Pacific and Polynesian waters could have been navigated in early times:—

"Yes! if you had a supply of provisions, you could run down the trades on a log.

"There is no part of the world where nature would tempt savage man more strongly to launch out upon the open sea, with his bark, however frail; then, there is the island in the distance to attract and allure; and the next step would be to fit out an expedition. . . . The native finds a hollow log. This is split in two, and a dam made across either end with knead of clay. He puts in a few cocoa-nuts, a calabash of water, breaks a green branch thick with foliage, sticks it up as a sail, and goes before the wind at the rate of three or four miles the hour. I have seen them actually do this, their little fleets, like 'Birnam wood coming to Dunsinane,' by water. But by some mishap, in the course of time this frail bark misses the island or falls to leeward; the only chance then is to submit to the wind and waves to go where they will bear.

"But the South Sea Islander would soon get above vessels with clay bows and mud sterns. As fissures in bread-trays, in negro-cabins of the South, are sewed up with white-oak splits, so the Marquesas Islanders make large canoes out of little slats of wood sewed together with cords of cocoa-nut fibre, the holes being puttied up with clay. These canoes will sometimes hold twenty rowers."

"In the Pacific, between 25° and 30° south, it is easy for such vessels to sail in any direction between north round by west to southwest; and north of the equator, to the 25th or 30th parallel, it is likewise easy for such rude vessels to sail in any course between northwest round by the west to south. It is difficult to get to the eastward within the trade-wind region."

Again, in reply to the inquiry whether, before the invention of the compass, long voyages were possible:—

"Such *chance* voyages were not only possible, but more than probable. When we take into consideration the position of North America with regard to Asia, and of New Holland with regard to Africa, and with the winds and currents of the ocean, it would have been more remarkable that America should not have been peopled from Asia, or New Holland from Africa, than that they should have been."

"Captain Ray, of the whale-ship Superior, fished two years ago in Behring's Straits. He saw canoes going from one continent to the other.... Along the course of the 'Gulf Stream,' from the shores of China, already alluded to, westerly winds prevail; and we have well-authenticated instances in which these two agents have brought Japanese mariners in disabled vessels to the coasts of America."

"In the Indian Ocean an immense surface of water is exposed to the heat of the torrid zone, without any escape, as it becomes expanded, but to the south. Accordingly we have here the genesis of another 'gulf stream,' which runs along the east coast of Africa, bearing to the south of New Holland."

"There was then, in the early ages, the Island of Madagascar to invite the African out with his canoe, his raft, or more substantial vessel. There was this current to bear him along at first, at the rate of nearly, if not quite, one hundred miles a day, and by the time the current began to grow weak, it would have borne him into the region of westerly winds, which, with the aid of the current, would finally waft him to the southern shores of New Holland. Increasing and multiplying here, he would travel north to meet the sun, and in the course of time he would extend himself over to the other islands, as Papua and the like."

"When we look at the Pacific, its islands, the winds and currents, and consider the facilities there that nature has provided for drifting savage man, with his rude implements of navigation, about, we shall see that there the inducements held out to him to try the sea are powerful. With the bread-fruit and the cocoa-nut, man's natural barrels there of beef and bread, and the calabash, his natural water-cask, he had all the stores for a long voyage already at hand." (Schoolcraft, vol. i. p. 23.)

Upon the first part of this, and other particulars of like character, the learned American Archæologist remarks: "Thus we have traditionary gleams of the foreign origin of the race of North American Indians. . . . They point directly to an Oriental origin. Such has from the first been inferred. At whatever point the investigation has been made, the eastern hemisphere has been found to contain the physical and mental prototypes of the race. Language, mythology, religious dogmas, the very style of architecture, and their calendar, as far as it is developed, point to that fruitful source of nationality and dispersion." (*Ibid.*)

In relation to other points suggested by Maury, bearing upon the question of the diffusion alike of men and of the lower animals, much information is given by Lyell. We make room for only a single fact. "Kotzebue, when investigating the coral isles of Radak, and the eastern extremity of the Caroline Isles, became acquainted with a person by the name of Kadu, who was a native of Ulea, an isle fifteen hundred miles distant, from which he had been drifted with a party." (El. of Geol., vol. iii. p. 92.)

Such are the paths along which population has been conducted to our globe's remotest extremity. Thus—

> "Wise to promote whatever end he means,
> God opens fruitful nature's various scenes."

And thus has he conducted to every region children of Adam, and diffused

> "Soul, passion, intellect; till blood of man
> Through every artery of nature ran;
> O'er eastern islands poured its quickening stream,
> Caught the warm crimson of the western beam;
> Beneath the burning line made fountains start
> In the dry wilderness of Afric's heart;
> And through the torpid north, with genial heat;
> Taught love's exhilarating pulse to beat;
> Till the great sun, in his perennial round,
> Man, of all climes, the restless native found."

This is not merely poetry; it is sound philosophy. And it opens at once the next branch of evidence respecting the family relationship between the most widely separated tribes of men; that presented in the mental phenomena and physical characteristics of every variety of human kind.

On the latter and lower, but in some respects more obviously presented point, the most searching investigations, in spite of all the circumstantial diversities urged by a certain class of observers, have issued in what amounts in fact to a strict demonstration of human unity.

Facts connected with the phenomena of hybridity approach very closely this demonstrative character. Questions, indeed, are raised respecting these phenomena, and assertions not a few most energetically advanced. But facts will yield neither to perplexed speculation nor to headlong boldness: still less, can they be expected to submit, when the challenging parties are themselves at issue.

Dr. Van Evrie and Dr. Nott, recent controversialists on this subject, agree in maintaining that mulattoes are strictly hybrids; but they differ quite widely in regard to the general laws of nature respecting hybrids. The latter contends that in the hybridity which takes place between proximate species, as he holds varieties of men to be, although the earlier generations appear more delicate, yet "*prolificacy is unlimited.*" (Types, p. 376.) The former affirms, (Essay, p. 29,) with characteristic but unverified confidence, "*the mulatto of the fourth generation is as sterile as the mule of the first.*" These opposite statements, which it is almost self-evident neither of the learned gentlemen could on his own side substantiate, they may be left to reconcile; meanwhile, the long-admitted and unquestionable fact remains a patent verity, that mixed races of men, as the Griquas of South Africa, descended from the Dutch and Hottentots; the Cafusos of Brazil, and similar mestizoes elsewhere, from negroes and Indians; the Papuans of New Guinea, etc., from negroes and Malayans; and the mulattoes and creoles of the West Indies and of our own country, not only exist in great numbers, but, according to wide observation, continue, wherever circumstances permit, rapidly to multiply. From our last census returns we find that "the mulattoes in the United States, numbering, in 1850, 405,751, are about *one-eighth* as numerous as the blacks, and the free mulattoes are *more than* half the number of free blacks." (Census Rept., p. 82.)

It is one thing then, and may serve a purpose, to speak

of mulattoes as "mules," but it is altogether a different thing scientifically to establish their hybridity. And even if something approaching it could be proved, it would be nothing more than might be expected, under the wide deviation from the white standard, so early developed and so long perpetuated in the negro, and would be therefore no satisfactory evidence of specific diversity. But real hybridity in the case cannot be proved. The fact quoted from our last census is of itself decisive. But further:—

"If we search the whole world," says Prichard, (Nat. Hist., p. 12,) "we shall probably not find one instance of an intermediate tribe produced between two distinct species, *ascertained to be such.*"

"I cannot share the opinion," says M. de Candolle, (Essai Elementaire, 8me partie,) "that between species of the same genera hybrid species may be found."

"I have never yet seen a hybrid plant," says Mr. T. A. Knight, (Observations on Hybrids, p. 253,) "capable of affording offspring, which has been proved, with anything like satisfactory evidence, to have sprung from the originally distinct species."

"There is no satisfactory proof," says Lyell, (Elements of Geology, vol. iii. p. 14,) "that a single permanent species has ever been produced by hybridity."

And Professor Wagner, of Germany, is said to have shown that the sterility of hybrid animals is generally secured by an organic impediment.

It is plain, indeed, that such a law in nature is needed, toward preserving the order of the organized creation.

Since, in the language of Prichard, "if hybrid races were produced and continued without impediment, the organized world would soon present a scene of universal confusion."

Facts, then, are all against the notion of mixed races among men being hybrids. They are but intermediate varieties. Physiologically, man is really proved to be one. This is the latest utterance of perhaps the master physiologist now living—Professor Owen. (Lect. before Brit. Association for Adv. Science, Liverpool, Sept. 1854.)

"With regard to the number of known species of apes, it is not without interest to observe that, as the generic form of the quadrumana approaches the bimanous order, they are represented by fewer species. The unity of the human species is demonstrated by the constancy of those osteological and dental characters brought to view in investigating the corresponding structural particulars in the higher quadrumana. Man is the sole species of his genus, the sole representative of his order, and, in reference both to the unity of the human species and to the fact of man being the latest as he is the highest of all animal forms upon our planet, the interpretation of God's works coincides with what has been revealed to us, as to our own origin and zoological relation, in his word."

It is not, therefore, too much to say, in the words of Professor Müller, "From a physiological point of view, we may speak of varieties of man, but no longer of races. Man is a species, created once, and divided into none of its varieties by specific distinctions. In fact, the common origin of the negro and of the Greek admits not of a rational doubt."

The mental phenomena to which we have alluded, if furnishing proof less palpable to the senses, are, in their specific correspondences, when carefully examined, equally decisive of essential oneness in mankind.

Vast as is the interval between the towering intellectual proportions of a Shakspeare, a Milton, a Bacon, a Newton, or, beyond these, of a Paul, and those of the groveling creatures known as Esquimaux or Fuegans, Hottentots or Guineans, there are not only countless links binding them to the same common kind, but certain great psychological features making manifest their family relationship.

A ratiocinative and logical faculty marks man wherever he is found, and a creative genius varying with circumstances. On every soil and beneath every sky is he characterized by the sense of responsibility which renders government possible, and binds him to the moral system of the universe. The outworking, too, of this element of his being, in some form of religious belief and custom, is coterminous with his diffusion.

Against this it is vain to urge, as indicating specific difference, the favorite allegation of diversity advocates, that the brain of the Indian, etc., is comparatively small, and that no instance can be adduced of a negro who has made high attainments in literature or philosophy.

Dr. Morton himself teaches, in an extract already given, that the Indian brain has, by peculiar habit of exercise, been in some tribes considerably enlarged. A fact, indeed, falling in with the commonly observed tendency of all human tissues to enlargement, within moderate limits, through a given process of action. Size of brain, however, at any rate, is no final test of mind. The quality of material must surely be quite as important as its quantity. Dr. Wyman testifies that other heads in Boston were notoriously larger than Daniel Webster's.

To demand instances of superior intellect among races long degraded is, then, plainly unreasonable, and amounts in truth to a begging of the question, by the opponents of unity. Can they furnish such instances among the forty or fifty millions of native Sclavonian serfs spread over the vast plains of European Russia?

Instances can certainly be adduced, though they are rare, of pure-blooded negroes making very considerable attainments in high learning. J. H. B. Latrobe, Esq., of Baltimore, has described one whom he knew, who became a quite profound mathematician. The census returns also exhibit some singular statistics, as to the education and employment of many negroes, alike in New Orleans and New York. And the sound judgment, good feelings, and steady principle which observant masters so often discover in their well-trained servants, certainly speak favorably of their position in the extended scale of humanity. Our laws themselves, moreover, by assuming the rational and responsible nature of the negro, and regulating him by such serious sanctions, bear testimony incontestible to a universal conviction on the subject.

The truth unquestionably is, that while habit and other

causes have greatly modified and extensively degraded the one mental as well as the one bodily constitution of the greater part of mankind, not only are the lowest tribes improvable in the latter respect as well as in the former, but the mind, in its most degraded state, by unmistakable movements, vindicates its high connections. How strikingly does the emotional nature of man everywhere respond to the stroke of grief or the touch of delight! Smiles and tears, laughter and groans, may be witnessed equally in the hovel and the palace, in the ice-burrow of the oil-fed Samoied and the star-canopied sand-home of the half-starved Bushman. And there is something in this single fact more convincing than whole volumes of materialistic speculation. The great poet of mankind has fitly celebrated, in words that can never die, this instinctive demonstration of the heart—

"One touch of nature makes the whole world kin."

To this entire argument from nature, conclusive as it is, the Bible sets the seal of revealed verity. It not only affirms, in plainest terms, that God "hath made of one blood all nations of men for to dwell on all the face of the earth," (Acts, xvii. 26,) but it traces them down from one created pair, and one preserved household. It not only makes known, as its supreme, all-comprehending disclosure, one "Son of man," at once the "Second Adam," and "the Lord from heaven," mysteriously accomplishing a great scheme of mediation for mankind, but it addresses its encouragements and admonitions, its precepts and promises, with undiscriminating benignity, and, with universal comprehensiveness, commands them to be conveyed to every variety and every grade of human creatures—as constituting one great brotherhood, children of one vast family. So thoroughly, indeed, is the doctrine of one actual blood relationship between all human beings interwoven with the highest announcements and most practical inculcations of revelation, that it must be pronounced impracticable to reject the one and retain the other. It certainly is not possible to admit ordinary fairness, far less inviolable veracity, in the fundamental lessons of Scripture, and yet reject their uniform teaching concerning the co-ordinate relations of men toward each other, and to their common Father and one Mediator.

Accordingly, we find the most frivolous air of levity, the bitterest tone of mockery, and the fiercest spirit of hostility directed against the belief of anything supernatural in the Bible, associated with the diversity theory. At the same time, with strange inconsistency, the attempt is made to represent the issue, so far as revelation is concerned, as a mere question of interpretation, like those involved in the solution of astronomical and geological facts, scripturally described under their phenomenal instead of their scientific relations.

This alternative is prudently urged by some of the more considerate claimants of diversity, and it is even in part mingled by others with their dire denunciations. But it cannot be admitted. Man, his relations, his duties, his prospects, his origin, and his destiny, constitute the essential, the all-pervading topic of revelation. And there is no interpretation that can change these in the manner proposed, without rending to its base the whole fabric and scattering to the winds its dishonored fragments.

In the Bible, as in common parlance, there is no necessary connection between incidental mention of natural events, according to their appearances, and the scientific realities of the case. Not so, however, with its account of the position and relations of the human family. If its historical, preceptive, and spiritual exhibitions, on this ground so distinctly conveyed, be not reliable, it is discredited throughout. There is, in fact, nothing left to credit.

Could science necessitate such interpretation, it would really prove Christianity a fable, and revelation an imposture; Bacon a dupe, Newton a driveler, and the sober judgment of the Christian world an insane infatuation or a childish delusion.

Of all this, however, there is, as we have seen, happily not the remotest possibility. Science really speaks here, as everywhere, in harmony with Scripture. And truth, now as heretofore, is found like its Author, One.

DISCUSSION III.

THE CHRONOLOGY OF CREATION.

THE era of our world's creation is a question, in our time, by the progress of knowledge, invested with an interest which it has not heretofore possessed. Geological science has now reached a position from which it claims to pronounce with confidence, respecting the prevalent time-interpretations of Genesis i., that they cannot be true. And the enlightened Christian student, at once trustful toward genuine science, as the heaven-lit lamp by whose radiance human reason is to trace in nature the orderings of an All-perfect mind; and reliant on Scripture, as attested divine revelation, full of all that is most precious for mankind, finds himself constrained to review those interpretations. He remembers that the doctors of Salamanca, however much in earnest, were equally in error, when they urged their view of certain expressions in the Bible, against the geography of Columbus; and that vastly wide of the truth was that infallible tribunal, which so grievously condemned the immortal old Tuscan and his grand astronomical discovery, as at war with what they pronounced the meaning of the sacred records. Nor had the divine Author of the Holy Book committed it, he is well persuaded, to a false astronomy, though the learned Turretin and other Protestant theologians could find in such passages as Ecclesiastes, i. 5, "*The sun also ariseth, and the sun goeth down,*" and Psalm xciii. 1, "*The world also is established that it cannot be moved,*" what was to them complete disproof of the Copernican system.

Of the evils occasioned by errors of this kind, the considerate inquirer is well aware. How they prejudice men of mere science against the Bible, and men of exclusive piety against science; and furnish the excuse of perplexity to the uninformed and indifferent on either side. To guard against such harm, therefore, he deems a duty of supreme importance. Hence, in the great question, now pending between the record of creation as read from the rocks and that given in Genesis, as commonly understood, he regards it as a serious obligation to trace, if possible, the whole truth, that its harmony may be discerned, and its excellence vindicated. What, then, the monumental masses beneath his feet, freely and fairly examined, and what the inspired narrative, thoroughly studied, really do teach, severally and unitedly, respecting the antiquity of our world, and the course of its pre-Adamite changes, becomes to him an inquiry of deep significancy.

The very nature and history of the question at once satisfy him that its adequate solution is not to be reached by any superficial views, hasty conclusions, vague generalizations, or arrogant dicta as to the meaning of Scripture, or of the rocky archives of the world. A faithful and large induction is, he well knows, the only key that can open the secrets of the earth's primeval history. Everything short of this, therefore, he promptly rejects. The

Scripture language, he also sees, must be phenomenal, in order to be true always and for all men, since the great appearances appeal to all senses alike, while philosophic expression must vary with degree of culture; yet so constructed must that language at the same time be, he cannot but judge, since truth cannot be at war with truth, as essentially to violate no ultimate disclosure of science. To trace under the phenomenal from this deeper construction, so as to find the true meaning, as evinced in its being every way consistent, is a task not to be performed, he is sure, by an imperfect, unfurnished, or fanciful mind. From such guidance he instinctively turns in seeking the truth. He sees the largest, freest, best furnished men mainly agreed respecting the rank and conclusions of geological science. The Cuviers and Brogniarts, the Chalmerses and Pye Smiths, the Bucklands and Lyells, the Sedgwicks and Murchesons, the Mantells, Sillimans, Agassizes, and Hugh Millers, most of them equally eminent as Christians and as explorers of natural truth. Individuals of less calibre and attainments, he finds, either admitting their own ignorance while depreciating geology, or exhibiting in extravagant schemes of reconciliation between it and assumed meanings of Scripture, strange deficiency of knowledge and judgment. To the dicta of these, however positive, his mind cannot satisfactorily yield. He is obliged to look for something more clearly and consistently adequate. And the question recurs with redoubled force, What is true on the subject? What is the consistent and reliable explanation of the petrified and of the inspired documents?

The simple answer is, in our judgment, contained in the *period-day* reading of Genesis i. We believe that the six periods (Heb. *Yoms*) of the creative history, are really intended to be read not as "*days*," but as "*ages*." This reading is, we are satisfied, beyond comparison, most accordant with the entire range of facts that have been elicited from the monumental records within the earth, and with the structure of the sacred history, as well as with striking intimations in other parts of the Bible. Reasons for this judgment we shall briefly give, using, as occasion requires, some of the best authorities on both branches of the argument, the biblical and the scientific.

The question is not only of grave importance as connected with a supposed issue between the scientific and the scriptural chronology of creation, but it is suggestive of some very curious facts in the history of associated theological and geological opinion.

The rigidly literal mode of Scripture interpretation, already referred to, by which the grand ideas of Columbus and of Galileo were in their day opposed, has, by not a few, and up to a date quite recent, been insisted on, in regard to geology. All animal forms, and their rock-entombed remains or effigies, are, by this class of judges, pertinaciously referred to an origin only a day or two ante-dating that of man. And our whole mundane system is held, under the same principles of construction, to be only of about the age of the human race; that is, some six thousand years, or a few decades of centuries more. Here one supposition is, of course, that multitudes of the fossil forms were original creations. That the rocks containing them were simply thus called into being, by an instantaneous divine fiat. But a wild assumption of this nature, without a particle of support in Scripture or reason, setting aside the whole observed order of Nature and Providence, and frustrating forever all rational investigation, were now scarcely worthy of mention. Seriously to oppose it were like arguing against the fancies of a patient in delirium. An alternative hypothesis, on this chronological plan, refers all the phenomena of strata and fossils directly or indirectly to the deluge, however rationally inexplicable they may be on such grounds, nay, by the clearest induction absolutely discrediting any such explanation. Even the learned Kirby could be so imbued with the infatuation of this kind of scriptural application as to quote Ps. xliv. 19, "*Thou hast sore broken us in the place of dragons, and covered us with the shadow of death,*" in proof of the existence now, of some subterranean home where multitudes yet survive of those monstrous saurians, specimens of which, in skeleton, have been so abundantly discovered in certain ancient formations! A mode like this of dealing with the dignified wisdom of recorded Revelation is really so unworthy of a sound and reverential mind, that we cannot but experience in the contemplation of it a painful sense of human weakness.

The once favorite idea of this class of constructionists, that all the thousand traces of ancient submergence under water, observed all over the globe, were to be referred *directly* to the deluge, has become at the present day so absolutely untenable in the light of abundant facts, as to be given up, we believe, on all hands. But a modified form of the theory is still held, the deluge being supposed *indirectly* to explain the facts of geology. The hypothesis is, that between the dates of creation and of the flood, vast accumulations of sediment were borne from time to time by streams and inundations, from the land into the sea; and that the upheaval of all this, at the time of the deluge, and the corresponding subsidence of what had been the land, buried all that had previously been occupied by terrestrial creatures, and provided, as their home from that date, the variously compounded surface over which the antediluvian sea had rolled. But this indirect diluvial hypothesis, though in some respects more plausible than that once prevalent, which supposed the mere passage of the Noachian waters over the continents to have left all the aqueous traces noticed by geologists, is in fact not more credible, in the light of modern discovery; while it is directly at war with certain historical details of the Scripture itself. In Genesis ii. 10–14, we read of the rivers which watered Eden. And the continued existence of two at least of them, the Hiddekel or Tigris, and the Euphrates, to this day, fully disproves the imagined subsidence of that part of the earth. Geological facts, which we shall incidentally exhibit, will be found even more thoroughly to discredit this theory.

Here, however, we meet a prejudice by which good and otherwise well-informed men are, on this subject, altogether blinded. Without having fairly examined the case, they insist that what is claimed for geology as a science cannot be admitted. That it is merely a crude mass of speculations, and not a coherent system of results, carefully reached by a large induction of facts. "We deny their facts," say these opponents of the scientific geologists. "Grant them their facts, and of course they will make good their theory." Grant them their facts! A concession, truly, from persons who almost boast that they know little or nothing of the subject! Deny their facts, indeed! The blind obstinately persisting to all around them, "we believe nothing you allege about the sun. No doubt if we admit your facts, you can make good your solar theory." Something requiring a much stronger characteristic designation than "*unreasonableness*," is evident here. How quickly would these worthy but prejudiced deniers of authenticated truth perceive, and how deeply feel, the weakness and unworthiness of a course the counterpart of their own, though in relations more solemn, were unbelievers to reply to their Christian appeals, "we deny your facts," and then refuse candidly to examine the evidences by which they are authenticated!

Even, then, if none of the more important geological facts were patent to our own eyes, if we were simply dependent upon the testimony of such men as Lyell, and Humboldt, and Miller, as to the particulars traced by themselves in the strata of the earth,—just as the vast majority of even the cultivated are dependent on the Keplers and Herschels for the details of astronomic observations,—it were most unreasonable, and at variance with all the sound principles of evidence for which we in other things contend, for us to talk about denying their facts. Cautious and sagacious men, whose well-disciplined faculties have through long years been devoted to a minute, methodical, and extensive examination of the soils and rocks, caves and cliffs, mines and mountains, yet explored on the globe, may surely be believed capable of describing what they have discovered, and what they really know in the case. And when we are certain that, whatever their scientific enthusiasm, they have, for the most part, no conceivable motive for misrepresenting appearances or perverting truth, it would really seem something worse than folly to say, "we deny your facts."

But, as in the case of controlling truths of astronomy, which are sufficiently obvious to all intelligent and observant minds to furnish a basis of undoubting confidence in the testimony, borne by accomplished explorers of the heavens, concerning the wonderful results they have verified,—so facts, the most striking and convincing, in the structure of our earth's crust, are so commonly noticeable, as not only to claim the attention of all reasonable men, but to furnish a secure basis for proper reliance upon the achievements of able and faithful investigations in this department of research.

The truth is, almost every man may discover for himself, alike in great utterances of the Bible, and in strange tokens everywhere presented by the earth's strata, much more than enough to discredit every form of the six-thousand-year hypothesis. And this is one of the instances in which liberal inquiry has done essential service to the one cause of truth, by manifesting the grand harmonies between Nature and Revelation.

The Bible, in not a few passages, indicates, as impressively as do the monumental rocks themselves, that the earth is incalculably older than the human race. In Psalm xc., entitled in our version, "a Prayer of Moses, the man of God," we read: "Before the mountains were brought forth, or ever thou hadst formed the earth and the world, even from everlasting to everlasting, thou art God." Here the inspired writer, laboring apparently with the idea of boundless past duration, expressed by the phrase "from everlasting to everlasting," introduces, as an aid to the mighty conception, the period since the mountains were brought forth and the earth and the world were formed. Its very introduction, by way of comparison, for such a purpose, conveys, perhaps more strikingly than any form of statement could have done, his own impression of the immensity of that period. Still more significant, if possible, to the same effect, is the remarkable personal address of "Wisdom," in Prov. viii. 22–30: "The Lord possessed me in the beginning of his way, before his works of old. I was set up from everlasting, from the beginning, or ever the earth was. When there were no depths I was brought forth; when there were no fountains abounding with water. Before the mountains were settled, before the hills, was I brought forth; while as yet he had not made the earth, nor the fields, nor the highest part of the dust of the world. When he prepared the heavens, I was there; when he set a compass upon the face of the depth; when he established the clouds above; when he strengthened the fountains of the deep; when he gave the sea his decree, that the waters should not pass his commandment; when he appointed the foundations of the earth; then I was by him, as one brought up with him." Here the highest descriptive power seems taxed to the utmost in carrying the mind back toward the era of the going forth of creative wisdom. And the period since our planet was called into being is again employed, as, by its vastness, the only fit term of comparison in such an estimate.

Intimations like these are not rare, and they seem to render altogether insignificant, under the mere aspect of extent, the past term of human existence, in the great chronology of creation.

On that vast chronological scale there are, as we have intimated, natural marks even more specific and not less impressive. So various are the aspects in which these may be exhibited, that the chief difficulty in offering them to view, within a moderate space, is so to group them as that some adequate effect on the mind may be produced. We select, however, a mode suggested by objects that meet the eye at one of the most interesting spots on the globe.

The intelligent observer who is permitted to feast his higher being on the grand scenes of Niagara, finds his mind wondrously impressed, and borne on to great thoughts, by the sublimities of time no less than by those of dimension and of power. He cannot, indeed, address the mighty torrent, in words so beautifully applied to the hoary ocean it hastens to meet:—

"Time writes no wrinkle on thine azure brow;
Such as Creation's dawn beheld, thou rollest now;"

for time has furrowed there a thousand seams. But the very marks so indelibly registered speak of ages rolled away, no less surely than does the tracery beneath whitened locks reveal the ravages of threescore years and ten.

There is the yawning chasm, in rock exceedingly hard, hundreds of feet in depth, and extending in length not less than eight miles; and there are the recent ruins of the slowly-receding wall, which tell of the process by which the enormous scooping has been effected. And when the agency and its *observed* results are compared with the total achievement, the period for such wear and tear is found really to baffle calculation.

But there are, at this instructive spot, traces of a chronology that was already inconceivably old when the bosom of Erie was laid bare, and the waters of that emerald current began to cut a passage through the limestone. The attentive visitor finds imbedded in that rock numberless effigies of creatures that once tenanted the waters of a free ocean; beings that in their time, longer or shorter, passed through the various stages of sentient existence which we observe to characterize animated forms. And their fossils, thus brought to light, tell the simple story of ancient vicissitude, and unregistered ages. They make known, not only the extended lifetime of such creatures, but the gradual advance of calcareous deposit in which those denizens of the deep were entangled and entombed, at all depths, through a range of more than hundreds of feet. They speak of the enormous pressure which could convert so immense an accumulation of mud into rock of hardest texture. And then, their elevation to the light of day, and their final exhibition to human eyes, tell of those unknown times of internal throe and progressive upheaval, which eventuated in rolling elsewhere the briny waves, for other service, and establishing the conditions under which lake and cataract have been since performing their part in the magnificent phenomena of nature.

But immensely distant as is the past age to which these facts and these inductions have borne the thoughtful observer, he is not permitted to stop there. Tokens are at hand, apart from the special character of the stone, and supposing it of a kind elsewhere prodigiously developed in connection with such indications, of an earlier and protracted period, claiming his attention. Issuing with the jet of a cool and gentle stream from a fissure in the rock, near the margin of the Canadian bank, and on its upper reach, he finds a ceaseless current of inflammable gas, precisely analogous to that which modern skill has educed from coal and bitumen for the illumination of our cities. Following, then, this current of combustible air, as Theseus the thread of Ariadne, he treads securely the hidden pathway along which that subtle fluid has traveled, till, far beneath the tombs of ages, over which the mighty waterfall forever reverberates, he enters a world of wonders, incalculably more ancient than all he has left behind. Here is before him one of the vast storehouses in which compact fuel for unborn generations has, for countless centuries, been piled away, in masses well-nigh immeasurable. And these masses bear a registry of events that transpired long before depths were opened there for the ocean, in which those creatures were born, lived, died, and were put away in marble, whose history tells so much of the ages that preceded the beginning of the cataract's evasive power. Here he reads of a vegetation that, at an epoch fancy herself reaches only on tired wing, burdened the warm and steaming earth,—a vegetation characterized by gigantic proportions and exhaustless abundance, such as no soil or climate belonging to these later times, not even the nutritive alluvium of the Amazon under the stimulating blaze of an equatorial sun, can parallel. Here he finds recorded notices, not only of the foundation of fertile land already provided for the matted roots of great tree-ferns and greater forest-pines, and of the heated, misty air that ministered to their luxuriance, but also of the flood-seasons, which tore these mighty growths from their stations, and bore them onward to some great estuary, and laid them there in vast heaps, to be heavily covered, in the progress of centuries, by sediment derived from adjacent shores, and thus be preserved under conditions preventive of wasteful decomposition, but admitting such change of elements as might, in an extended period, convert fibrous into *quasi*-mineral fuel. The same registry sketches for him an outline of other events, succeeding these in series that years cannot measure, ere yet preparation was made for that sea in which the great formation was deposited which now constitutes the bed and barrier of the splendid cascade; movements in the frame-work of the globe, convulsive perhaps, like those which yet at times cause a continent to tremble; or gradual, like those which are in our day slowly but surely lifting the coast of Norway and depressing that of Greenland; alternate heavings and sinkings, as it were, of the bosom of our "Alma Mater;" beatings of her vital pulse; throbbings of her mighty heart. Thus at length the great sea-cavity is adjusted, above the storehouse of future flame, where may settle the wafer-layers of that calcareous paste, which after-generations of an uncounted age look upon as enormous piles of imperishable rock.

Thus do the stupendous gorge, the mighty masses of fossil-marked stone, and the carbureted exhalation of "the burning spring," to one but moderately acquainted with the authenticated and generalized facts of geology, and visiting this unrivaled locality, speak, with a distinctness that can scarcely be mistaken, of the long ages registered in the carboniferous formation, and of those succeeding periods of animated tribes, sedimentary deposit, petrifying process, subsequent upheaval, and prolonged erosion, evidences of which, in other places, have been so often traced by sagacious observers.*

---

* In principle this time-argument is strictly true. In fact it is true only by accommodation. The Niagara rock belongs not, as supposed in our illustration, and as for any known physical reason to the contrary it might have done, to a formation above, and lower than the great coal deposits, but to a member of the lower

That the conclusions thus grouped may be seen to be altogether different from fanciful speculations, some of the evidences substantiating the main points may be briefly brought to notice.

Great grooves, channeled, like the lower Niagara bed, in hardest rock, may be seen marking some part of the course of almost all large rivers. And the ruins thus appropriated by the waters, and borne onward in their flow, are found, in many cases, to be gradually packed away in alluvial accumulations, of which the deltas of the Mississippi, the Ganges, and the Nile are well-known instances. Now, of these accumulations, there are some tokens that, in a general way, mark the rate of increase. Such are certain fixed objects, connected with the outlet of the Egyptian stream, to which the ancient and the modern condition of the delta may be referred. The whole term of these deposits is, by such criteria, found to reach very far back of our historical period.

But above the river beds lie terraces of diversified configuration, composed of those outspread heaps of soil, sand, clay, and gravel, that so generally constitute the terrestrial surface on which we tread, and which, when laid open by some natural or artificial cut, we find for the most part to consist of adjusted layers, evidently deposited in succession, at a remote date, from water in which, from time to time, they were borne. This general process was manifestly long

---

and older vast Silurian system. So that the carbureted gas there appearing must, in all likelihood, be referred to some very partial and exceptional store of bituminous matter.

anterior to that of the river alluvium. Its greatly higher antiquity is indicated, not only by all the circumstances of position, but by the enormous extent of the beds, as ascertained, in some cases, by boring and by the evidence which the pebbles furnish of prolonged attrition previous to burial. Already, then, we are here conducted, probably, far beyond the human era. (See in the "Smithsonian Contributions to Knowledge," vol. ix., 1857, an important paper, by Professor Hitchcock, on "Surface Geology.")

Now, however, additional marks of age claim attention. Indurated strata, marked by perfectly definite and characteristic peculiarities, present themselves to notice. They are found everywhere to constitute a vast framework of variously-textured rock, sometimes underlying plains, sometimes swelling into hills, sometimes piled in huge mountain-ridges, or shooting up into towering pinnacles. This rocky frame of our world has also been, by nature and art, in many places exposed to observation. And it is proved to consist, not of one jumbled mass, but of very distinct layers or beds of different kinds, and sometimes of immense thickness, lying one above another, in a regular order, ascertained to be mainly the same all over the globe, and reaching down to prodigious depths. In no one place, it is true, have many of these layers been exposed to view at once. Nor has any natural chasm or artificial cut penetrated at all near the depth to which these strata may, by other means, be traced. And yet, tilted up as the strata are, by violent heavings from within, especially in the neighborhood of mountains, one may be seen showing itself at a considerable distance behind and under another, as, in a pile of books, one may rest on

another. And although *a*, *b*, *c*, and *d* may not be all seen at one view, yet *c* being found to rest on *d*, whenever they occur together, *b* on *c*, and *a* on *b*, the actual order of the whole is known.

By a great number of observations, over a vast extent of the earth, the relations of upper and lower strata have thus been ascertained, and designated in about this order downward: 1, *Alluvium* and *diluvium or drift;* 2, *tertiary* series, a partially indurated system reaching down as low as the chalk; 3, *secondary*, from the chalk, through the oölite, to the new red sandstone; 4, *paleozoic*, from the coal-beds to the slates. And while the uppermost layers of rock give tokens of an antiquity greatly exceeding that of the unindurated beds overlying them, those that are lower furnish abundant evidences of still greater age, in proportion as they are farther down.

Although no human search has yet reached into the earth half a mile below the surface of the sea, yet these various rocky formations may be traced, by methods well-nigh as reliable as those of astronomy, to their profoundest depths. London, for example, rests on a great bed of clay, belonging to the class of accumulations designated the *tertiary* system; but, underlying that clay is found, by repeated borings, at depths from 200 to 600 feet, the remarkable chalk concretion which, at certain points on the north and west of the great metropolis, appears at the surface, and again on the south rises into the Surrey hills. Now, supposing the *dip* of the chalk strata to be accurately ascertained at both the northern and southern points of emergence, and the distance between these points to be known, it is obvious that *data* will be possessed for calculating, with trustworthy precision, the greatest depression of the chalk basin. It is a case of simple trigonometry.

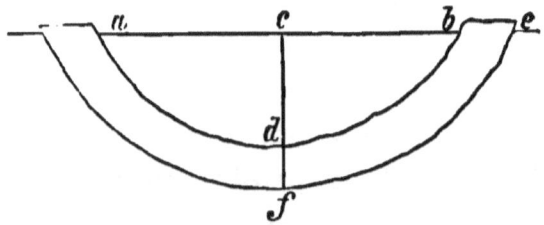

The distance *a b* being known, and the angles of depression at *a* and *b*, to find *c d*. It will also be seen, from this example, not only how the continuity of a formation is proved by its reappearance, but how a measurement of its edge *b e*, at the surface, is an approximate criterion of its lowest thickness *d f*. The thickness of the chalk is, by such process, as well as by measurements in some cases more direct, found to be about 1000 feet.

Estimates of this kind may be, and have been, applied to the vast oölitic and liassic formation found to underlie the chalk in the London basin; and equally well to the saliferous or later red sandstone strata, on which the lias rests, and to the great coal deposits below the saliferous sandstone. Of these last, says Baron Humboldt, (Kosmos, vol. i. p. 158,) "I have found, after repeated examinations, that the lowest coal-stratum which is known in the vicinity of Duttweiler, near Bettingen, northeast of Saarlouis, must descend to depths of 20,000 to 22,000 feet below the level of the sea." Under the coal lies the old red sandstone. And beneath that the great Silurian limestone beds, lower than which again are the slates and gneiss. Last of all, the original granite is reached, at a total depth of perhaps as far below the lowest coal, as that is beneath the surface. Thus the strata may be measured to a depth of from eight to ten miles. And gradually formed, as they obviously were, who shall measure the enormous periods employed in their production?

A general idea of the whole may be gotten from a simple diagram.

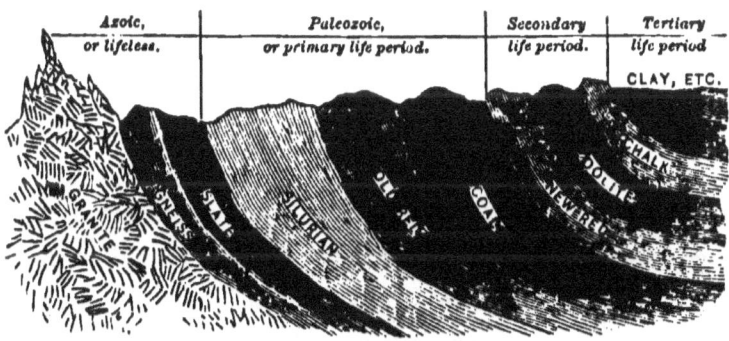

Besides the unmeasurable ages indicated for the deposition of the whole series of sedimentary strata, there is that known in connection with the granite itself and its associated so-called plutonic rocks, which carries the mind even farther toward the trackless past. Repeated borings into the earth, to from 500 to 2000 feet, reveal the fact, that there is a rise of temperature within, at the rate of about 1° Fah., for every 54 feet of perpendicular descent. (Kosmos, iv. p. 173.) Eight miles down, then, a glowing heat must exist. This indication falls in with several other important facts. First, the oblateness of the earth — its polar compression and equatorial protrusion — proving that, at some age, it must have been in a fluid condition, susceptible of receiving form under the operation of centrifugal force; second, its moderate aggregate density— ascertained by carefully observing its attractive power in comparison with that of mountain masses, etc.—only about five and a half times that of water, (*ibid.*, p. 32,) indicating some internal repulsive energy counteracting the immense condensation which, otherwise, gravity would seem to necessitate; and third, the circumstance that the scoriæ from furnaces, and similar products furnished by chemists, as the result of fusion, often exhibit the very minerals which compose the original rocks. Such facts, together with the peculiar crystalline structure of the granitic mass, enforce the conclusion, that that universally underlying support of all other rocks, is, itself, but the slowly cooled crust of a once molten world. Immense, indeed, under existing laws of heat, must have been the time employed in such reduction of temperature.

Thus, by a regular but general and simple series of inductions, are we carried irresistibly backward, from the order of things now existing, through vast periods of formative change in the earth, to that unknown date, too remote for the most adventurous surmise, when all was "without form and void."

Another class of facts, however, now comes into view, connected with this course of inquiry into the time-records of the rocks, and furnishing the most reliable *relative chronometry* for those ante-human ages, that embracing the entire series of discovered fossils. These relics of the past are witnesses which, after the most searching cross-questioning, furnish one, consistent, unequivocal testimony, to the occurrence of successive orders of beings, in periodic course, with marked diversities gradually introduced, one after another, through prolonged intervals and ages.

Descending from the surface through such comparatively recent debris-beds, as those of the London clay, the geologist finds animal forms gradually changing, from those of existing species, into new and strange varieties; and by the time he has reached the chalk, nearly the whole organized system with which he started has been left behind. To express this class of facts, in the super-cretaceous beds, now referred to, known as the *tertiary* system, from its order in the grand ages of life, classifying Greek designations adapted to certain general proportions of displaced forms, have been proposed, and adopted into scientific nomenclature. They are *pleiocene* more recent, *meiocene* less recent, and *eocene* the dawn of recent life; these divisions, however, being carefully distinguished from any deposit of the human period. For, as will be shown in the next discussion, they have been satisfactorily proved to contain no traces of simultaneous human existence. It is in the *pleiocene*, or upper division of the *tertiary* system, that, with instances of mammalian species belonging to the present time, we find so abundantly remains of the mastodon and elephant, rhinoceros and hippopotamus, ox, horse, and deer, which, though specifically different from, are generically akin to families of our own time. In the *meiocene* portion of the *tertiary* formation, among forms more distinctly separated from the mammalia coexisting with mankind, occurs the great dinotherium, or gigantic tapir of Cuvier, exceeding in size the largest fossil elephant. And in the lowest or *eocene* section of the *tertiary* deposits, with other creatures diverse from any found in the higher divisions, are discovered those strange, thick-skinned pioneers of the tapir, elephant, rhinoceros, and horse families, specimens of which may be seen in the best museums, labeled with such names as "Palaotherium," and "Anoplotherium."

Now, when the gradual and successive changes in the order of animal life, thus brought to view, are considered in connection with the prodigious extent of the system through which the progression is witnessed; and when the whole is compared with what we know of the laws of permanence in the species around us, we are, by our mental constitution, compelled to assign to the *tertiary* period a duration to which we dare affix no definite numbers. Who, then, shall measure the antecedent term of the great *secondary* period of life? Here, first, we see a powder, worn down from coralline structures, and deposited in paste, imbedding its own curious memorials of life and change, built up into those enormous heaps of *chalk*, which, when afterwards upheaved, and in due time looked upon by intelligent human eyes, supply to Albion her classic name. Next, we here behold the still earlier *oölite*, in masses even more extensive, bearing in its deep recesses the tombs of those amphibious monsters, whale-lizards, and serpent-lizards, and bird-lizards, from twenty to seventy feet in length, that tenanted indifferently marshy shore or mighty wave, and multiplied, and fulfilled their cycle of existence, and found protecting graves, during the period of this vast accumulation. And here, in the yet more ancient, though not most ancient, and therefore called *new red* sandstone, the great salt-bearing deposit of the world, we meet with those footprints of great birds, and of frogs rivaling our ox in size, which reveal some of the strange secrets of that ancient time.

And what shall we say of that great *paleozoic*, or *primary life-period*, to which belong the coal-measures, the old red sandstone, and the Silurian limestones? Of the first of these, the coal formation, it may here suffice simply to mention in proof of its prodigious extent, and of the term its preparation required, the incalculable benefits which, as mighty reservoirs of comfort and power, they are conferring, and are destined yet more abundantly to confer, upon mankind. Of the second, the old red-sandstone system, the most thoroughly informed observer and most competent judge, (Hugh Miller, in his "Old Red

Sandstone,") testifies: "There are localities in which the thickness of the old red sandstone fully equals the elevation of Mount Ætna above the sea, (over ten thousand feet,) and in which it contains three distinct groups of organic remains, the one rising in beautiful progression above the other." And of the last member of this old life division, the Silurian series, Murchison, its most reliable explorer, estimates the extent and age-tokens as existing on no smaller scale.

Anterior, however, as we have seen, to all this incipiency, progress, and endless change of life, must be reckoned an unknown but vastly extended lifeless age, a period of adjustment in the frame-work of the globe, indicated, according to Humboldt and others, by the evidences of internal heat yet existing, and by the phenomena of crystallization, which the lowest and infossiliferous rocks always exhibit.

When all these inductions are combined, we have a series of ages of which our measures of duration furnish no standard.

This series of ages is so well described by the profound and distinguished Dr. Harris, in his "Pre-Adamite Earth," that we feel justified in giving the passage in full, by way of recapitulating the view we have presented. He says, p. 70, etc.:—

"Knowing about the date of man's introduction on the earth, we proceed to examine the globe itself. And here we find that the mere shell of the earth takes us back through an unknown series of ages, in which creation followed creation at the distance of vast intervals between.

THE CHRONOLOGY OF CREATION. 169

"But though in the progress of our inquiries we soon find that we have cleared the bounds of historic time, and are moving far back among the periods of an unmeasured and immeasurable antiquity, the geologist can demonstrate that the crust of the earth has a *natural* history. That he cannot determine the *absolute chronology* of its successive strata, is quite immaterial. We only ask him to prove the order of their position from the newest deposit to the lowest step of the series; and this he can do. For, nature itself, by a force calculable only by the God of nature, lifting up in places the whole of the stupendous series in a slanting ladder-like direction to the surface, has revealed to him the order in which they were originally laid, and invites him to descend step by step to its awful foundations.

"Let us then descend with him, and traverse an ideal section of the earth's crust. Quitting the living surface of the green earth, and entering on our downward path, our first step may take us below the dust of Adam, and beyond the limits of recorded time. From the moment we leave the mere surface-soil and touch even the newest of the *tertiary* beds, all traces of human remains disappear. So that let our grave be as shallow as it may, in even the latest stratified bed, we have to make it in the dust of a departed world. Formation now follows formation, composed chiefly of sand and clay and lime, and presenting a thickness of more than a thousand feet each. As we descend through these, one of the most sublime fictions of mythology becomes sober truth, for at our every step an age flies past. We find ourselves on a road, where the lapse of duration is marked not by the succession of seasons and years, but by the slow excavation, by water, of deep valleys in rock-marble; by the return of a continent to the bosom of an ocean in which ages before it had been slowly formed; or by the departure of one world and the formation of another. And, accordingly, if our first step took us below the line which is consecrated by human dust, we have to take but a few steps more before we begin to find that the fossil remains of all those forms of animal life with which we were most familiar are diminishing, and that their places are gradually supplied by strange and yet stranger forms; till in the last fossiliferous formation of the division, traces of existing species become extremely rare, and extinct species everywhere predominate.

"The *secondary* rocks receive us as into a new fossiliferous world, or into a new series of worlds. Taking the chalk formation as the first member of this series, we find a stratification of a thousand feet thick. Who shall compute the tracts of time necessary for its slow sedimentary deposition? So vast was it, and so widely different were its physical conditions from those which followed, that scarcely a trace of animal species still living is to be found in it. Crowded as it is with conchological remains, for example, not more than a shell or two of all the seven thousand existing species are discoverable. Types of organic life before unknown arrest our attention, and prepare us for still more surprising forms. Descending to the system next in order, the oölite, with its many divisions, and its thickness of about half a mile, we recognize new proofs of the dateless antiquity of the earth. For, enormous as this bed is, it was obviously formed by deposition from sea and river water. And so gradual and tranquil was the operation that, in some places, the organic remains of the successive strata are arranged with a shelf-like regularity, reminding us of the well-ordered cabinet of the naturalist. Here, too, the last trace of animal species still living has vanished. Even this link is gone. We have reached a point when the earth was in the possession of the gigantic forms of Saurian reptiles, monsters more appalling than the poet's fancy ever feigned; and these are their catacombs. Descending through the later red sandstones and saliferous marls of two thousand feet in thickness, and which exhibit, in their variegated strata, a succession of numerous physical changes, our subterranean path brings us to the carboniferous system, or coal formations. These coal strata, many thousands of feet thick, consist entirely of the spoils of successive ancient vegetable worlds. But in the rank jungles and luxuriant wildernesses which are here accumulated and compressed, we recognize no plant of any existing species. Nor is there a single convincing indication that these primeval forests ever echoed to the voice of birds. But between these strata, beds of limestone of enormous thickness are interposed; each proclaiming the prolonged existence and final extinction of a creation. For these limestone beds are not so much the charnel houses of fossil organisms, as the remains of organisms themselves.

"The mountain masses of stone which now surround us, extending for miles in length and breadth, were once sentient existences; tastaceous and coralline; living at the bottom of ancient seas and lakes. How countless the ages necessary for their accumulation; when the formation of only a few inches of the strata required the life and death of many generations. Here the mind is not merely carried back through immeasurable periods, but while standing amid the petrified remains of this succession of primeval forests and extinct races of animals piled up into sepulchral mountains, we seem to be encompassed by the thickest shadow of the valley of death.

"In quitting these stupendous monuments of death, we leave behind us the last vestige of land plants, and pass down to the old red sandstone. Here, too, we have passed below the last trace of reptile life. The speaking footprints impressed on the carboniferous strata are absent here. The geological character of this vast formation again tells of ages innumerable. For, though many thousand feet in depth, it is obviously derived from the materials of more ancient rocks, fractured, decomposed, and slowly deposited in water. The gradual and quiet nature of the process, and therefore its immense duration, are evident from the numerous 'platforms of death' which mark its formation, each crowded with organic structures which lived and died where they are now seen, and which consequently must have perished by some destructive agency, too sudden to allow of their dispersion, and yet so subtle and quiet as to leave the place of their habitation undisturbed.

"Immeasurably far behind us as we have already left the fair face of the existing creation, while traveling into the night of ancient time, we yet feel, as we stand on the threshold of the next, or Silurian system, and look down toward 'the foundations of the earth,' that we are not half way on our course. Here, on surveying the fossil structures, we are first struck with the total change in the petrified inhabitants of the sea, as compared with what we found in the mountain limestone; implying the lapse of long periods of time during the formation of the intervening old red sandstone which we have just left. But still more are we impressed with the lapse of duration, while descending the long succession of strata, of which this *primary* fossiliferous formation is composed, when we think of their slow derivation from more ancient rocks; of their oft-repeated elevation and suppression; of the long periods of repose, during which hundreds of animal species ran through their cycle of generations and became extinct; and of the continuance of this stratifying process, until these thin beds had acquired, by union, the immense thickness of a mile and a half. Next below this, we reach the Cambrian slate system, of almost equal thickness, and formed by the same slow process. Here the gradual decrease of animal remains admonishes us that even the vast and dreary empire of death has its limits, and that we are now in its outskirts. But there is a solitude greater than that of the boundless desert, and a dreariness more impressive than that which reigns in a world entombed. On leaving these slate rocks, we find that the worlds of organic remains are past; and that we have reached a region older than death, because older than life itself. Here, at least if life ever existed, all trace of it is obliterated by the fusing power of the heat below. But we have not even yet reached a resting-place. Passing down through the great beds of mica schist, many thousands of feet in depth, to the great gneiss formation, we find that we have reached the limits of stratification itself. The granitic masses below, of a depth which man can never explore, are not only crystallized themselves, but the igneous power acting through them has partially crystallized the rocks above. Not only life, but the conditions of life, are here at an end.

"Now, is it possible for us to look from our ideal position backward and upward to the ten miles' height, supposing the strata to be piled regularly, from which we have descended, without feeling that we have reached a point of immeasurable remoteness in terrestrial antiquity? Can we think of the thin soil of man's few thousand years, in contrast with the succession of worlds we have passed through; of the slow formation of each of these worlds on worlds, by the disintegration of more ancient materials, and their subsidence in water; of the leaf-like thinness of a great portion of the strata; of the consequent flow of time necessary to form only a few perpendicular inches of all these miles; or of the long periods of alternate elevation and depression, action and repose, which mark their formation, without acknowledging that the days and years of geology are ages and cycles of ages?"

That the chronology of creation is thus to be estimated on a scale of vast proportions; that the grandeur of immense duration is offered to our contemplation in the past history of the material universe, as the grandeur of immense extent is exhibited in the compass of its mighty mechanism, is as clearly the conclusion of science as it is impressively the intimation of those noble utterances of ancient inspired poetry, to which reference has been made.

But with the truths thus indubitably indicated, how is the record of Genesis i. to be reconciled? What is the adequate understanding of that brief but beautiful introduction to the great volume of revelation, which shall harmonize it with the subsequent disclosures of that volume, and with the registry that is so deeply inscribed, as we have seen, all over the volume of nature? Two such interpretations have been proposed. The one—that which we have already mentioned as in our view satisfactorily established on exegetical grounds, in connection with the geological facts now adduced—the construction which reads "*ages*" as the true meaning of the recurring "*yoms*" of that initial chapter; a reading which we shall presently endeavor to show is alone authorized, even by the structure of the record itself. The other, a suggestion offered by Dr. Chalmers, and admitted for near half a century, as well by great Christian naturalists as by able theologians, which supposes an interval of ages passed over in silence between the first verse of Genesis and the second, and the existing condition of our world to have been effected in six natural days, described from the second verse onward.

Of this last view, Dr. Harris is among the ablest recent advocates. And it is on this account, and for the sake of showing its inadequacy in part from his own statement, as well as because of its intrinsic excellence, that we have given from him the foregoing extract. Within a few pages of the passage quoted, he uses this language: "From a careful consideration of the subject, my full conviction is, that the sublime affirmation, *'In the beginning God created the heaven and the earth,'* was placed by the hand of inspiration, at the opening of the Bible, as a distinct and independent sentence; that it was the divine intention to affirm by it, that the material universe was primarily organized by God out of elements not previously existing; and that this originating act was quite distinct from the acts involved in the six natural days of the Adamic creation."

That the first verse of the inspired record has the meaning here assigned, we make no question; but that it is to be separated by the vast unnoticed interval of multiplied ages from all that follows, supposed to belong to the mere Adamic creation, and that such creation only is meant to be described in the second and succeeding verses, and as accomplished in six natural days, we think disproved by considerations of irresistible force.

In the first place, we ask, is it in accordance with the wondrous structure of revelation, in regard to other and kindred topics, that so incalculable a sweep of ages and events should be thus passed over without one allusion? Admitting, as we do in full, that the Bible was not intended to teach natural science in any of its branches, we cannot but believe that it was intended to manifest, with increasing clearness, inimitable harmony in all the relations of truth. The great disclosures of astronomy are not detailed in the Scriptures. Yet when, by the light of her glorious discoveries in the heavens, Science sits down to a reperusal of the inspired volume, and reads there, repeated in forms so various and striking, the sublime utterances, (Psalm xix. 1,) "The heavens declare the glory of God," and (Job, xxvi. 7,) "He stretcheth out the north over the empty place, and hangeth the earth upon nothing," she cannot but find in them a significance most impressively harmonizing with the revelations she has traced in the outward world. It is one of the soul-subduing proofs of the divine origin of the Bible. And is it to be supposed she will find no such affecting relations between the story she has seen undeniably written on the age-monuments beneath us, and the time-intimations of that wonderful Book?

But, again, we ask, what is to be done with that great fact of *progression* in the creative order, which Dr. Harris has himself so distinctly recognized and so justly sketched in his account of the geological periods? He truly speaks of "the total change from the petrified inhabitants of the sea," belonging to the Silurian system, to those of the "platforms of death," in the old red sandstone; and from these to those "spoils of rank jungles and luxuriant wildernesses, accumulated and compressed in the coal-series."

Here, he affirms, moreover, is "no trace of bird or reptile life;" and yet, in the next higher formation, he admits, as existing in abundance, those feathered giants whose footprints yet abide on the later red sandstone; and in the oölite above, "those Saurian monsters, more appalling than poet's fancy ever feigned." And with these begin to appear "traces of animal species still existing." Still ascending, he finds in the lower tertiary system another fossiliferous world, containing additional, though as yet "rare traces of existing species." He is in the *eocene* range—the dawn of recent life has opened. Higher up, he meets with more frequent "remains of those animal forms with which we are familiar," but mingled with many that to us are strange. He is in the *meiocene* or less recent age. And proceeding on his upward way, he recognizes, just below "the line consecrated by human dust," types of many familiar animal species, and some identical with man's contemporaries. Is it credible that all this means nothing, in connection with the sacred narrative? That it is all ingulfed in one dark, sealed cavern of oblivion? And that a like general progress from lower to human life, so remarkably though so briefly set forth in the record, imagined to belong only to the Adamic creation, is a mere casual circumstance of no grand significancy? We cannot so believe.

That *three* great master life-divisions should be so distinctly marked in the grand geological scale as to establish, in the fundamental nomenclature of that science, the terms *primary*, *secondary*, and *tertiary*, to indicate the general advance toward our present system; and that the Mosaic history should exhibit also *three* life-stages, we cannot deem a merely casual coincidence. But when we find a correspondence of the most striking character between each of the great geological divisions and the parallel stages of the sacred narrative, and the relative position of the parts identical in the two series, our impression of a designed coincidence begins to assume the force of a decided conviction. In the primary life-division, says Hugh Miller, (The Two Records,) "we find corals, crustaceans, molluscs, fishes, and in its later formations a few reptiles, but none of these classes of organisms give its leading character to the paleozoic; they do not constitute its prominent feature, or render it more remarkable as a scene of life than any of the divisions which followed. That which chiefly distinguished the primary from the secondary and tertiary periods, was its gorgeous flora." It was emphatically the period of plants. Of "herbs yielding seed after their kind." In no other age did the world ever witness such a flora. Of this extraordinary age of plants every coal-piled grate or stove, and every gas-illumined city, is a cheerful remembrancer and speaking witness, and no less every glowing furnace and ponderous engine. It is patent to all that the first great division on the geological scale of organized being was, like that first described in the Mosaic record, peculiarly a period of herbs and trees, "yielding seed after their kind."

So again with the next great division on the geological scale, the secondary life-period. It had herbs and plants, but not as they had been. In its course there lived also corals, crustaceans, molluscs, and fishes, and a few dwarfed mammals had been introduced on the stage. But none of these marked this age. Those huge birds and Saurian monsters of which we have spoken, distinguished from all others the secondary life-period; egg-bearing animals, winged, and wingless. And in marvelous agreement with all this, the second life-creation of Genesis is, of "moving (or creeping) creatures, and fowl, and great whales," or, as the margin has it, "great sea monsters."

In like manner, we find in the tertiary period a characteristic class of creatures. Certain genera that had existed before had their term extended into this age; and others appeared in its course that were to outlast its close. But there was one order of beings peculiar to it, by which it was marked off from the ages going before, and from the human era to come after—its great mammalian giants, beasts of the field, such as in size and number the world has in no other age witnessed. And here, as in the previous instances, the narrative, so to speak, equally *joints into* the natural order. The third and last life-creation before man, is of "cattle and beasts of the earth after their kind." Surely coincidences like these cannot reasonably be considered merely casual correspondences between two things entirely unconnected, the grand order of all mundane creations engraved upon the rocks, and a sketch of one fractional part thereof which interpreters would call the Adamic creation given by inspiration. How much more satisfactory to a comprehensively considerate and sober judgment is that view which exhibits the record as wondrously fitting the whole creative series!

But there is another fact in the case, respecting which we have again to ask, what is to be done with it on the day hypothesis? In the successive geological periods, we find a certain overlapping of organized forms, a continuance, more or less extensive, of some species which belong properly to one age, among the forms which become common in the next cycle. Creatures beginning in the primary division may be traced into the secondary, and in exceptional cases into the tertiary, though the species peculiar to the latter gradually rise into great preponderance. But there is no instance of a creature that has become extinct in an earlier formation being reproduced in a later. Says Lyell, (Principles of Geology,) quoting Buffon, "races die out, because time fights against them, and *new species* are from time to time called into being," not the old restored. A race, clearly noticed as having once passed away, returns upon the stage no more. The grand flora of the coal measures, when once buried, appeared not again. The frightful monsters of the oölite fulfilled their cycle, and disappeared, to show their hideous forms no more forever. And the gigantic beasts of the tertiary age, mastodon and mammoth, massive cave-bear and formidable cave-hyena, have not, we may gratefully thank Heaven, risen up again to terrify us and consume the harvests of the earth, since their ancient burial. This, then, is a natural law, written all over the geological monuments. Races once destroyed return not again.

Now, however, by the side of this law, we meet the remarkable fact, that *numerous species which ranged along in the tertiary period, greatly anterior to our time, are found coexisting with ourselves.* Not only are the remains of trees, under which the mammoth roamed, and which are found with the bones of that animal, of precisely the same species with some that grow in our own forests, but such creatures as the badger, the fox, and the wild cat, to say nothing of numerous shell-fish, identical with those now existing, are proved by their relics to have lived during the pre-Adamite tertiary age. Either, then, as in previous cases, such races have lived on continuously, from the tertiary into the human period, or before the Adamic time they were destroyed, and at that time re-created. The latter supposition is, as we have seen, contrary to the uniformly observed law of divine procedure; and is therefore altogether improbable. The former must then be accepted as the fact. That is, while a large portion of the creatures that existed during the tertiary age became extinct before man appeared, others *lived on in unbroken series into the human age, and actually occupied the earth when man was called into being.* But if this was so, there was no such annihilating catastrophe, as the day hypothesis assumes, immediately preceding the human term. No utter overthrow, breaking-up, and oblivion-working ruin of all former creations, just before man was made. Then, the *tohu* and *bohu*, the "without form and void" of the second verse of the inspired history, cannot be justly, as on the hypothesis in question they are, construed as denoting the results of such a catastrophe. But instead, they must be read as really descriptive of the world's condition next after its primary creation. This reduces to a mere chimera, a vanishing dream, the notion of that mighty gulf between the first grand sentence of our Bible and all that follows. But when that dream is dispelled, the day hypothesis is gone. It has neither room nor resting-place. It must be abandoned.

These several considerations seem abundantly to discredit the *day* rendering of the Hebrew *Yom*. But in doing that, they do very much more. They clearly establish the great probability of that reading which considers the successive *Yoms, ages* of indefinite extent.

This probability must, however, be subjected to tests of another kind before it can be admitted into the rank of established verities. Scripture, by its own nature, and by its independent position, as a great system of revealed truth, must at last be its own interpreter. It must, indeed, because from the same Author, harmonize with all other truth certainly known. And a true interpretation may be thus suggested from without; but no sense that it will not fairly bear in its own structure can be forced upon it, no matter how otherwise probable. The probability may be delusive. The really forced construction cannot be true. Ultimately, then, the Bible must interpret itself. And our extended Chronology of Creation, probable as it is rendered by the foregoing considerations, must be brought to the test of a fair scriptural examination.

We take up, therefore, the Sacred History of Creation.

And the first thing that strikes us, relative to the point in question, is the peculiar *indefiniteness* of its tone and expressions. No definite *date* for "the beginning" is hinted; no exact *boundary* for "the heavens and the earth." The whole history of visible created being is introduced in one brief but grand statement, abundantly specific as to the world's actual creation by the Almighty, but altogether general as to the secondary points of space and time. The *whence* for the world is settled once and forever, but *the when* and *the where* are left fully open to human inquiry.

Next, we discover nowhere in the record any token of a transition from the grandly indefinite to the contracted and precise. There is no notice whatever of any commencement to the exact periods of twenty-four hours that have been imagined; while the idea of a leap, so sudden and unnoticed, from the noble comprehensiveness of the introduction to a scale of such diminutive proportions, is at once destructive of the consistency of the record, and unworthy of its grandeur. From this general spirit of the history, therefore, we gather that it makes no mention of precise, petty periods of twenty-four hours.

Pass we, then, to *particulars;* and here a fact which every reader has observed immediately claims attention. Until the fourth *Yom*, no mention whatever is made of the luminaries by which natural days and all our divisions of time are marked. From the first, indeed, as intimated in the opening verse, we believe those luminaries to have existed, and only to have been made peculiarly manifest in the fourth *Yom*, perhaps by the clearing up of the atmosphere. But total silence respecting their office during the earlier *Yoms* seems unmistakably to indicate that those periods, at least, were not intended to be described as *natural days*. This particular in the narrative long ago occasioned questionings concerning the *Yoms*. St. Augustine, on account of it, was constrained to ask, (see Professor Lewis's "Six Days of Creation," for this and other suggestions,) "Quis ergo animo penetret quo modo illi dies transierint, antequam inciperent tempora quæ quarto die dicuntur incipere?"

But the particular time designations employed are in themselves, and in the manner of their use, no less significant against a natural-day interpretation. The "*evening*," "*morning*," and "*day*" are not only, according to their etymology in the original, and according to scriptural and common usage, terms of very general signification, but they are, in this history, so employed as really to forbid any special sense. The Hebrew word *ereb*, "evening," undoubtedly the mother of the Greek ἔρεβος, is derived from a verb which signifies *to mingle*. So that a mingling or blending time would seem intended to be described under that term. In like manner, the Hebrew *boker*, "morning," is derived from a verb meaning *to cleave or separate*, indicating that by that term a distinguishing time was meant to be characterized. These terms, then, are precisely analogous to Spring and Fall. They indicate not specified duration, but modes of being. And, accordingly, the Scriptures, as we do, speak of the morning and evening of the year, or of life, or of the world. Nor are the relations of these two words in the account less remarkable than their etymological meanings. In every instance the evening is placed first; and there is nothing, in the remotest degree, to intimate its beginning or its end. Had creation and its record opened with the gleaming light, there had been marked an initial moment. And had any hint been given of some recurring phenomena, termini for the evenings and mornings were possibly imaginable. But there is nothing of the kind. It is here, as Hesiod later wrote, Μέλαινα νύξ ἐγένετο, "black night came into being;" and Ovid sung, *Lucis egens aer*, "the ether was void of light."

Similar, precisely, are the indications of the *Yom*. It is a general term descriptive of no particular duration, and applied in many senses; as "the *Yom* of the Lord," "the *Yom* of Jerusalem," "the *Yom* of justice, or mercy." And in the history before us, this word is actually used in *four* distinct senses, viz.: (1) To specify the light-time, in v. 5, as we speak of daylight or daytime. (2) To denote the phenomenal days, which, with seasons and years, the sun was to mark off, as stated in v. 14. Indeed in that single verse the word is used in both these senses. (3) To characterize, as in ch. ii. v. 4, the sum-total of the whole series of creative periods. And (4) To express those strange, unphenomenal intervals, of whatever extent and however divided, indicated in vss. 5, 8, 13, as not marked off by rising or setting sun. Certainly for such a word, and in a document where it is thus variously used, no one precise and exclusive sense can be claimed, without some more significant condition than its periodical repetition. It assuredly may, and for reasons already given and others to be adduced, we think it should here as in other places it must, be read *age*. As in Micah, iv. 6, "In that *Yom*, (*age*,) saith the Lord, will I gather the outcasts of Israel;" and Isaiah, xii. 1, "In that *Yom* (*age*) shall ye say, I will praise the Lord, for he is become my salvation," etc.

But the manner in which these several terms are here used is, in another respect, still more remarkable. The literal translation in the first instance is, "there was an evening, and there was a morning, one day." And the affirming statement is in every case repeated, though the form of the numeral is varied. It is, as if, after describing a term of repose and an interval of change, an extended darkness and a succeeding progress of illumination, or a season of mingled and a term of divided life, it had been demonstratively said, "this was the evening and this was the morning."

The peculiar "*one day*," of the first statement, receives some light from a singular instance in Zechariah, xiv. 6-9: "And it shall come to pass in that day, that the light shall not be clear nor dark; but it shall be *one day*, which shall be known to the Lord, not day nor night; but it shall come to pass, that at evening time it shall be light. And it shall be in that day, that living waters shall go out from Jerusalem; half of them toward the former sea, and half of them toward the hinder sea; in summer and in winter shall it be. And the Lord shall be king on the earth; in that day shall there be one Lord, and his name one." Nothing can be more obvious than that the "*one day*" here is something widely different from an ordinary interval of twenty-four hours. And the parallelism of expression would indicate that something also greatly differing from the minute section of time is meant for the beginning of *Yoms*. Josephus, master as he was of the Hebrew idiom, noticed the peculiar intimation contained in this extraordinary phraseology, (Antiq., book i. ch. 1.) He says: "This was the first day, but Moses called it *one day*, the reason of which I am able to give even now, but shall put off its expression until another time." The promised explanation, if ever given, has not come down to us; but this reference to the case is enough to show that the account before us was, by so competent a judge, regarded as one of very peculiar significancy.

There is yet another circumstance in the history confirming the *age* interpretation. No evening and morning are assigned the *seventh Yom*. They are in every case before invariably repeated; here, however, they are very singularly omitted. Why is this? Does it not mark something, in the course of this period, distinguishing it from the others? And what is such time-distinction, if not that the other terms were finished, but this unfinished? In each instance, certainly, when the "evening" and "morning" are assigned to the *Yom*, that term is represented as brought to an end, closed, completed. Would that invariable form have been departed from in the seventh period, had the *Yom* in this case been also completed? The very omission of the formula of completion seems strikingly to intimate that the seventh *Yom* is not closed, that it is yet in progress. If so, this is not a brief term of terrestrial rotation, but a prolonged age, the grand cycle of man's earthly existence; a period of mighty meaning in the history of creation; consecrated to purposes not before developed; devoted mainly to a being of high faculty and immortal essence; and appropriated to a wondrous scene of discipline and redemption whose issue is to be in the moral universe boundless good, and glory unutterable to the Everlasting Father.

Of the creative history there are two other associated traits of great importance, which together conduct to the same conclusion; its *quasi prophetic* character, and its peculiar *optical aspect*. It is a description of events in the distant past knowable only by revelation, just as prophecy is a description of events in the distant future knowable only by revelation; and, like many exhibitions of the prophets, it is the statement of an eye-witness. Both of these facts are very significant.

The remarkable visual distinctness imparted to the narrative would seem to indicate that the grand old processes of creation were revealed to Moses, as so many divine disclosures are said in the Bible to have been made, viz., through a series of *visions*, or pictorial representations. Of course, if this were so, if the vast serial drama of creation were made to, pass thus representatively before the eye of the Prophet-Historian, he would describe the events exhibited as one who had witnessed them in person, and infuse into his account the very vividness which really marks the record. But whether this distinguishing feature of the history were thus or otherwise produced, one thing at least is certain, this peculiar mode of description—by obvious appearances—adapts the narrative most marvelously to every stage of natural knowledge, and renders it for the most scientific as well as for the least inquisitive age "optically true in all its details." He, surely, needs something more than reason to influence his judgment, who can see in this adjustment between the simple story of creation and the indefinite progress of scientific discovery, no impressive evidence of divine truth.

So, again, with the history in the general character of a prophecy to be read backward. The principle, sanctioned alike by experience and by direct scriptural authority, that prophetic statement is to be rightly understood only when fulfillment has shed the full light of verification on the predicting page, seems as instructive toward our conclusion as it is justly applicable to the case. "History," well says the gifted author of the "Mosaic Vision of Creation," "is the surest interpreter of the revealed prophecies which referred to events *posterior* to the times of the prophet. In what shall we find the surest interpretation of the revealed prophecies that referred to events *anterior* to his time? In what light, or on what principle, shall we most correctly read the prophetic drama of creation? In the light, I reply, of scientific discovery; on the principle that the clear and certain must be accepted, when attainable, as the proper exponents of the doubtful and obscure. What fully developed history is to the prophecy which of old looked forward, fully developed science is to the prophecy which of old looked backward." Here, then, also, the only sure canon of prophetic interpretation conducts us to the same great truth of divinely adjusted harmony between the inimitable creative record and the hoary monumental rocks.

Thus does the creative history itself, in every part and in every aspect, deny the partial, and declare the grandly comprehensive sense. But the scriptural evidence in favor of this sense is very far from being confined to this history. It is scattered, indeed, all through the Bible. The inspired Hebrew poets abound in references to creation and its sacred record. And yet in vain shall we look among all these allusions for one hint of a circumstance so remarkable as the compression of the mighty manifestations of infinite power and goodness into a term of days less than the lifetime of an ephemeral insect. On the contrary, they labor, as we have seen, to convey, in connection with it, ideas of vast duration. In carrying us back to those ancient ages, they are conducting us as far as mortals can go, toward the interminable "from everlasting to everlasting."

And when those wonderful Hebrew and Greek words, *olam* and *eon*, whose simple meaning is merely *prolonged time*, are found so commonly applied in the Scriptures, as such words are applied nowhere else, to describe *creations* and *worlds*, another and a most striking testimony is rendered, by the peculiar structure of inspired language, to the grand chronology of creation. One instance of this may here suffice. In Hebrews, i. 2, the phrase, "He made the *worlds*," is, τοὺς αἰῶνας ἐποίησεν, "he made the *ages*." Now this usage with αἰών, as has been justly remarked, (Professor Lewis, p. 354,) "is not in the classical Greek. We find nothing like it in Homer, or Plato, or Æschylus. They never use this word for the world, much less the plural for a plurality of worlds in space or time. But no mode of speech is better settled in the New Testament, as it had previously been in the Old. The inference seems unavoidable, that plurality of worlds in time, or creations in successive ages, must have been an idea conveyed by inspiration, and early entertained by the Hebrew mind."

Now when all these proofs are taken together, direct and indirect, general and special, from structure of language, and order of statement, in grandeur of thought and harmony of meaning, from the Bible as interpreting itself, and from nature as interrogated by science, and from amazing coincidences between the utterances of revelation and the last disclosures of scientific research, candor can scarcely be supposed capable of demanding, on such subjects, a nearer approach to demonstration.

But to the whole, it is objected that the reason given, Exodus, xx. 11, for the human Sabbath, in connection with what is said, Genesis, ii. 3, requires the *Yoms*, including the seventh, to be understood, as just such days as the six on which men are required to work, and the seventh on which they are commanded to keep a sacred rest. In this, however, there is little weight. The word *Yom* may very well be used in two different senses in the fourth commandment, just as we have seen it is used in four senses in the creative history. The creature's may well be a *Sabbath-day*, the Creator's a *Sabbath-age*. And this, as before suggested, is indicated by a remarkable omission in the earliest mention of the seventh *Yom*.

So far, indeed, is the fourth commandment from furnishing any serious objection to the estimate presented, that the relation between this view and that divine ordinance becomes an additional illustration of the truth we have been exhibiting. A weight of meaning is hereby added to the commandment immeasurably transcending that of the common exposition. This estimate imparts to the present cycle a significance no less impressive than is the grandeur with which it invests the past and the future. It exhibits as the Divine Sabbath man's whole earthly term. It makes his entire period here a season divinely ordained for sacred purposes; of which, and of a still more sacred state of being in the future, the weekly hallowed rest enjoined him is a perpetual type. Thus regarded, how supremely important is the fourth commandment! How greatly instructive the reason given for its appointment! This thought it were unjust not to permit its sagacious and devout propounder to illustrate in his own felicitous way of persuasive genius.

"What I ask, (see 'Two Records,') viewed as a whole, is the prominent characteristic of geological history, or of that corresponding history of creation which forms the grandly-fashioned vestibule of the sacred volume? Of both alike the leading characteristic is progress. In both alike do we find an upward progress from dead matter to the humbler forms of vitality, and from thence to the higher. And after great cattle and beasts of the earth had, in due order, succeeded inanimate plants, sea monsters, and moving creatures that had life, the moral agent, man, enters upon the scene. Previous to his appearance on earth, each succeeding elevation in the long upward march had been a result of creation. The creative fiat went forth, and dead matter came into existence. The creative fiat went forth, and plants, with the lower animal forms, came into existence. The creative fiat went forth, and the oviparous animals, birds, and reptiles came into existence. The creative fiat went forth, and the mammiferous animals, cattle and beasts of the earth, came into existence. And, finally, last in the series, the creative fiat went forth, and responsible, immortal man, came into existence. But has the course of progress come, in consequence, to a close? No! God's work of elevating, raising, heightening, of making the high in due progression succeed the low, still goes on. But man's responsibility, his immortality, his God-implanted instincts respecting an eternal future, forbid that the work of elevation and progress should be, as in all other instances, a work of creation. To create would be to supersede. God's work of elevation now is the work of fitting and preparing peccable, imperfect man, for a perfect, impeccable, future state. God's seventh day's work is the work of redemption. And, read in this light, his reason vouchsafed to man for the institution of the Sabbath is found to yield a meaning of peculiar breadth and emphasis. God, it seems to say, rests on *his* Sabbath from his creative labors, in order that by his Sabbath day's work he may save and elevate you; rest ye also on your Sabbaths, that through your co-operation with him in this great work, ye may be elevated and saved. Made originally in the image of God, let God be your pattern and example. Engaged in your material and temporal employments, labor in the proportions in which he labored; but in order that you may enjoy an eternal future with him, rest also in the proportions in which he rests."

"One other remark, ere I conclude. In the history of the earth which we inhabit, molluscs, fishes, reptiles, mammals, had each in succession their periods of vast duration; and then the human period began, the period of a fellow-worker with God, created in God's own image. What is to be the next advance? Is there to be merely a repetition of the past? An introduction the second time of man made in the image of God? No! The geologist, in those tables of stone which form his records, finds no examples of dynasties, once passed away, again returning. There has been no repetition of the dynasty of the fish, of the reptile, of the mammal. The dynasty of the future is to have glorified man as its inhabitant; but it is to be the dynasty, "the *kingdom*," not of glorified man made in the image of God, but of God himself in the form of man. In the doctrine of the two conjoined natures, human and divine, and in the further doctrine that the terminal dynasty is to be peculiarly the dynasty of Him in whom the natures are united, we find that great progression beyond which progress cannot go. We find the point of elevation never to be exceeded, meetly coincident with the final period, never to be terminated; the infinite in height harmoniously associated with the eternal in duration. Creation and the Creator meet at one point and in one person. The long ascending line from dead matter to man has been a progress God-ward, not an asymptotical progress, but destined from the beginning to furnish a point of union; and occupying that point as true God and true man, as Creator and created, we recognize the adorable monarch of all the Future."

Thus does the great chronology of creation, whose grandeur is only equaled by the evidences of its truth, conduct the mind by stages, that suitably exercise its best powers, to a vantage position, where the lessons of wisdom appear like the light-adorned landscape from the mountain's summit. Standing there, and listening to the great harmonies of nature and revelation, we look backward along the track of ages, and learn more of the wonders of His being who is "from everlasting to everlasting." We look downward upon the crowded monuments of untold buried generations of lower creatures, and we are taught more of the exhaustless riches of His benignity, who "openeth his hand and filleth all things living with plenteousness." We survey the vast array, as, in one mighty procession, cycle follows cycle of ascending grades of being, and we discover more of order in that all-wise plan, which, by such majestic steps, marches on toward consummation in the appearance, trial, recovery, and final experience of a race endowed with attributes akin to divine. More of those attributes do we also behold, in the very opening of the pathway that has led us to this summit. Thus to have traced the great chain of life through many and profound burials, and even to have groped along the thread of creative order beyond the dawn of organized existence, through preparatory ages of convulsion and erosion, up to that state of mingled elements in our globe, next subsequent to the primal creative fiat, we perceive to be an achievement not less magnifying, in our view, the wondrous endowments of the human mind than does the kindred exploit of scaling the heavens, and circling with planets and suns in their mighty rounds through space.

But we see more than this. Divine goodness we here discover, through a vast series, arranging not only for the comfort of the highest animated creature, and for the capacities and exercise of a philosophic mind, but for the delight of an imaginative and the culture of a religious soul. Chaos and consolidation, convulsion and subsidence, the growth and the grave of many a race, have, with consummate skill, been made subservient alike to the convenience and the adornment of this human habitation. They have furnished a bounteous soil and a genial air, gushing fountains and perennial fires, a home of safety, a treasury of truth, and a world of beauty. Besides every supply for his wants to be drawn by man, with "the sweat of his brow," from the bosom of his "Alma Mater," in the folds of her vestments are stored, for his discovery and extraction, mines of wealth and charmed mirrors of truth. And those vestments, how rich they are in beauteous adornment! The robe of nature is traced all over with poetry from Paradise. Mountain peak and ocean tide, leaping cataract and flashing cloud, rolling hill and sloping plain, smiling vale and frowning crag, laughing stream and mournful shade, pleasant landscape and delightful scenes,—the grand, the picturesque, and the lovely, almost everywhere displayed, and awakening in human bosoms those sympathies which swell responsive to the touch of genius, and rise to rapture as

> "Bright-eyed Fancy
> Scatters from her silver urn
> Thoughts that breathe and words that burn."

But more than all this, from so grand an eminence of harmonized truth appear higher and wider views of that great purpose of creative plan, whose issue is "an elevation not to be exceeded, a period never to be terminated." The abolition of change, the destruction of death, and the exaltation of once fallen creatures into union with the ever-blessed Creator, through the wondrous mediation, and in the everlasting kingdom of that Divine man, who is alike "the Alpha and the Omega, the beginning and the end," the "Ancient of days," and the Lord of all coming ages.

DISCUSSION IV.

THE AGE OF MANKIND.

THE common belief, derived from the Bible, that about six thousand years have elapsed since our planet witnessed that great miracle which ushered human creatures into being, is regarded by certain philosophers as untenable in the light of modern science. They estimate the past human period as vastly more extended. Just in proportion, therefore, as their views seem to be sustained, the chronology of Scripture would appear to be discredited. And this admitted, confidence in the higher relations of revelation could not but be more or less impaired. We are entering, then, upon no superfluous task in undertaking to investigate the grounds of these two chronologies; in endeavoring to trace what science really does teach as to the age of mankind, and what the Scriptures, under the scrutiny of learned criticism, disclose on the same subject.

Part of the field we have to survey has often been more or less carefully explored. Recent researches have, however, shed upon it so much additional light, that the examination may be now more satisfactorily conducted. These researches, especially as conducted by two eminent German scholars, Bünsen and Lepsius, whom we have already had occasion to quote, will be suitably used in elucidating our subject. As the most thoroughly informed of all Egyptologists, these learned men have had access to all that the old Nile monuments have thus far made known respecting ancient ages. At the same time they are savans of almost universal erudition. And, in addition to these qualifications, they have brought to their work a spirit much more than usually characterized by a simple love of truth. These qualities the reader will, we are sure, observe in some of the extracts we shall give, when we reach that branch of the subject to which their investigations more specifically pertain.

At present our inquiry relates to the scientific evidence in the case. We propose to examine the grounds on which Professor Agassiz, Dr. Usher, Dr. Leidy, and recently Sir Charles Lyell, etc., rest their claim for the indefinite antiquity of our race; and not only to trace, with them, indications in the one field they have chosen, but to bring testimony from other departments of science. What is on the whole substantiated, or rendered most probable, in the entire scientific view, will then be evident to the reader.

This is the instance of evidence offered by Agassiz:—

"The fossil remains of the human body I possess from Florida, were discovered in a bluff upon the shores of Lake Monroe. The mass in which they were found is a conglomerate of rotten coral-reef limestone and shells, mostly ampularias of the same species now found in the St. John's River, which drains Lake Monroe. The question of their age is difficult to answer. The point to settle is the rate of increase of the peninsula of Florida in its southward progress. . . . If we assume, from evidence we now have of the additions forming upon the reefs and keys, the rate of growth to be one foot in a century, it would require 135,000 years to form the southern half of the peninsula. .... Assuming, further, that the northern half of the peninsula, already formed, continued for nine-tenths of that time a desert waste, before the fossiliferous conglomerate could be formed, there would still remain 10,000 years, during which it should be admitted that the main land was inhabited by man."

The very remarkable *assumptions* in this case cannot but strike the reader, as they have surprised ourselves. That a philosopher of such world-wide reputation should hazard his standing, by committing himself to mere guesses of this kind, is to us matter for wonder. Let us concede each guess but the last, still there will remain a question which the learned Helvetian must find it impossible to answer. Why assume $\frac{9}{10}$ rather than $\frac{99}{100}$ or $\frac{999}{1000}$ of 135,000 as the period during which Florida may have remained uninhabited by man? And shall this process of assumption pass for scientific investigation? Is it not a species of desecration, when the noble name of Science is claimed for such sheer fancies?—Science, with her calm, severe, penetrating eye, and her step careful and sure as the march of truth!

But we have more to say of the case itself. Professor Agassiz fairly admits that his conglomerate consists mostly of ampularias of *the same species now found* in the St. John's River. The instance is therefore precisely analogous to that of the well-known fossil skeletons of

Guadaloupe, the comparatively recent age of which Lyell years ago established:—

"The lens shows," he says, (Principles of Geology, vol. iii. p. 265,) "that some of the fragments of coral composing this stone, still retain the same red color which is seen in the reefs of living coral surrounding the island. The shells belong to species of the neighboring sea, intermixed with some terrestrial kinds which now live on the island. Yet the rock in which these skeletons are imbedded is harder than statuary marble. Similar formations are *in progress* in the whole of the West Indian Archipelago; and they have greatly extended the plain of Cayes, in St. Domingo, where fragments of vases and other human works have been found at a depth of twenty feet. In digging wells, also, near Catania, in Sicily, tools have been discovered in a rock somewhat similar."

The guess, then, of one-tenth, or one-hundredth of a previous guess of so many years, as a possible period during which Florida has been inhabited, and its fossiliferous conglomerate accumulating, is, we hazard nothing in saying, utterly unreliable. It rests on no scientific foundation. It is entitled to none of the credit due to veritable science. It may therefore be set aside as really showing nothing respecting the antiquity of our species.

The instance adduced by Dr. Usher is, in many respects, similar to this of Agassiz, though on a grander scale and given more in detail:—

"The plain on which the City of New Orleans is built rises only nine feet above the sea, and excavations are often made far below the level of the Gulf of Mexico. In these sections, several successive growths of cypress timber have been brought to light. In digging the foundations for the gas-works, the Irish spadesmen, finding they had to cut through timber instead of soil, gave up the work, and were replaced by a corps of Kentucky axemen, who hewed their way downward through four successive growths of timber, the lowest so old that it cut like cheese. Abrasions of the river banks show similar growths of sunken timber; while stately live oaks, flourishing on the bank directly above them, are living witnesses that the soil has not changed its level for ages. No less than ten distinct cypress forests have been traced at different levels below the present surface in parts of Louisiana, where the range between high and low water is much greater than it is at New Orleans. These groups of trees, the live oaks on the banks, and the successive cypress beds beneath, are arranged vertically above each other, and are seen to great advantage in many places in the vicinity of New Orleans."

"An ingenious calculation has been made of the last emergence of the site of that city, in which these cypress forests play an important part. The history of this event is thus divided into three eras: 1. The era of colossal grasses, trembling prairies, etc., as seen in the lagoons, lakes, and sea-coast. 2. The era of the cypress basins. 3. The era of the present live-oak platform. Existing types from the Balize to the Highlands show that these belts were successively developed from the water in the order named; the grass preceding the cypress, and the cypress being succeeded by the live-oak. Supposing an elevation of five inches in a century, which is about the rate recorded for the accumulation of detrital deposits in the valley of the Nile, during seventeen centuries, by the nilometer mentioned by Strabo, we shall have 1500 years for the era of aquatic plants until the appearance of the first cypress forest; or, in other words, for the elevation of the grass zone to the condition of a cypress basin."

"Cypress-trees of ten feet in diameter are not uncommon in the swamps of Louisiana; and one of that size was found in the lowest bed of the excavation at the gas-works in New Orleans. In timber of this kind from 95 to 120 rings of annual growth have been measured in an inch; and, according to the lower ratio, a tree of ten feet diameter will yield 5700 rings of annual growth; indicating that number of years as the age of the tree. Though many generations of such trees may have grown and perished in the present cypress region, yet to avoid all ground of cavil only two generations are assumed, giving 11,400 years."

"The maximum age of the oldest tree growing on the live-oak platform is estimated at 1500 years, and only one generation is counted. These data yield the following table:—

"*Geological Chronology of the Last Emergence of the Site of New Orleans.*

Era of the aquatic plants.............................	1,500 years.
Era of the cypress basin...............................	11,400 "
Era of the live-oak platform.......................	1,500 "
Total period of elevation......................	14,400 "

"Each of these sunken forests must have had a period of rest and gradual depression, estimated as equal to the 1500 years of the live-oak era, which of course occurred but once in the series. We shall then certainly be within bounds, if we assume the period of such elevation to have been equivalent to the one above arrived at; and, inasmuch as there were at least ten such changes, we reach the following result:—

Last emergence, as above...................................... 14,400 years.
Ten elevations and depressions, each equal to this...144,000 "

Total age of the delta..............................158,400 "

"In the excavation at the gas-works above referred to, burnt wood was found at the depth of sixteen feet; and, at the same depth, the workmen discovered the skeleton of a man. The cranium lay beneath the roots of a cypress tree, belonging to the fourth forest level below the surface, and was in good preservation. The other bones crumbled to pieces on being handled."

"If we take, then, the present era at....................14,400 years,
and add three subterranean groups..................43,200 "

we have a total human period at least of..........57,600 "

"From these data it appears that the human race existed in the delta of the Mississippi, more than 57,000 years ago."

In all this there may be, as its propounder alleges, ingenuity, but it is undoubtedly entitled to no credit as a specimen of scientific investigation. Nearly every element of the calculation is again vitiated by the most unwarrantable assumption.

The authority for *ten* successive beds of cypress forest, grown over one another, is vague and worthless. The idea of alternate elevations and depressions of such sunken forests, is an enormous assumption, involving the supposition of prodigious volcanic forces. These, if real, leave no room for regular guess-work, immensely fitful as they are.

That such buried trees actually grew where they are found imbedded, is also an assumption, by no means to be admitted.

"When timber," says Lyell, "is drifted down by a river, it is often arrested by lakes; and, becoming water-logged, it may sink and become imbedded in the lacustrine strata. ... In the course of the Mackenzie River we have an example of the vast accumulations of vegetable matter now in progress. ... As the trees retain their roots, which are often loaded with earth and stones, they readily sink, and, accumulating in the eddies, form shoals, which ultimately augment into islands. ... Vast quantities of drift timber are buried under the sand at the mouth of the river, and it has formed a barrier of islands and shoals."

Occurrences of this kind, repeated in the floods of no great number of centuries, abundantly explain the phenomena of the Mississippi delta. "For," adds Lyell, "the trunks of trees borne down by the Mississippi, many of them subside, and are imbedded in the new strata which form the delta."

There is, therefore, no support for the assumption of cypress forests growing one over another in interminable succession.

And the further demand that four gigantic growths of the kind be allowed in the trifling vertical range of sixteen feet, is nothing less than preposterous.

As to skeletons in such cases, they may be of comparatively recent deposit. "At the distance of fifty miles from the base of the delta of the Ganges," says the eminent geologist already quoted, "there is a circular space of about fifteen miles in diameter, where soundings of a thousand feet sometimes fail to reach the bottom. As, during the flood season, the quantity of mud and sand poured by the great river into the bay of Bengal is so great that the sea only recovers its transparency at the distance of sixty miles from the coast, this depression must be gradually shoaling. Now, if a human body sink down to the bottom in such a spot, it is by no means improbable that it may become buried under a depth of three or four thousand feet of sediment in the same number of years." And if by the gradual or sudden action of internal force, this deposit were upheaved, and subsequently by some casualty laid open to human inspection, how many millions of ages would it not mark on the unscientific chronological scale of the instances we are examining?

The ingenious estimate of 57,000 years for the New Orleans skeleton is probably about as accurate.

"In the delta of the Ganges," Lyell further states, "bones of men have been found, in digging a well, at the depth of ninety feet; but as that river frequently shifts its course, and fills up its ancient channels, we are not called upon to suppose that these bodies are of extremely high antiquity, or that they were buried when that part of the surrounding delta, where they occur, was first gained from the sea." The parallel between such cases and the New Orleans exhumations may be judged of from the following fact, stated by Flint, in his "Geography of the Mississippi Valley." "At every flood, the Mississippi River overspreads a vast country, principally on its western sides, from ten to fifty miles in breadth, through the last five hundred miles of its course; and most of the water which overflows below Red River goes to the Gulf of Mexico without returning to the river."

No estimate of fifty thousand or five thousand years, in such cases, can justly claim the slightest confidence. It is not sustained by probability, it is repudiated by science.

Nor is less to be said in regard to other so-termed instances of indefinitely old human relics. "The human bones," says Lyell, quoting with approbation the judgment of Desnoyers, "associated in certain caverns, etc., with the fossil rhinoceros, hyena, bear, and several other lost species, must belong, not to the antediluvian periods, but to a people in the same stage of civilization as those who constructed the tumuli and altars of the primitive inhabitants of Gaul, Britain, and Germany. Since the flint-hatchets, and arrow-heads, and the pointed bones, and coarse pottery of such caves, agree precisely in character with those found in the tumuli and under the dolmens, (altars of unhewn stone.) It is not, therefore, on such evidence that we ought readily to admit the high antiquity of the human race."

Dr. Leidy, more cautious and more candid than the philosophers we have reviewed, fairly admits that no such high antiquity is scientifically established. That "primitive races of men may have inhabited the intertropical regions," in a vastly remote age, he indeed supposes. And that evidence of the fact will yet be discovered, he is "strongly inclined to suspect." Still his candid avowal is, *"No satisfactory evidence has been adduced in favor of this early appearance of man."* "While engaged in palæontological researches," he states, "I sought for earlier records of the aboriginal races of man than have reached us through vague traditions, or through later authentic history, but without being able to discover any positive evidences of the exact geological period of the advent of man in the fauna of the earth. The numerous facts which have been brought to our notice, touching the discovery of human bones, and rude implements of art, in association with the remains of animals of the earlier pleiocene deposits, are not conclusive evidence of their contemporaneous existence."

This, from so accomplished a palæontologist, who is sufficiently disposed, as his declarations show, to find, if possible, a high antiquity for mankind, is well-nigh conclusive as to the negative relations of science in the case. He is, in fact, an authority of great weight against the instances of Agassiz and Dr. Usher, and all others like them, that have been urged. His admissions afford also no slight support to the considerations we have been pressing, on the basis of fact, according to witnesses of the most unquestionable character.

Other instances of ancient deposit, supposed to indicate a high antiquity for the human race, now, however, claim our attention; instances recently accepted by observers of largest experience in this department of research, and—though much discussed pro and con in the scientific world at the present time, no less than eighteen communications, on one or the other side of the questions involved, having appeared within the last six months in the London Athenæum alone—more or less relied upon, as sustaining the idea of a past term for mankind much more extended than that commonly assigned. These cases are significant in themselves, but become doubly important by reason of the weighty names which give them no inconsiderable authority. Among these, that of Sir Charles Lyell carries of course most influence, especially in connection with the fact that heretofore his caution on this particular subject has been not less remarkable than his scientific judgment has been generally careful, comprehensive, and in the main reliable. The instances referred to, we shall first exhibit and then scrutinize. They cannot, perhaps, be better presented than in a late statement of the distinguished votary of geological science last mentioned.

At the meeting of the British Association for the Advancement of Science, September, 1859, in the section geology, the president, Sir Charles Lyell, read the opening address, which, so far as relates to the question before us, we give entire:—

"No subject has lately excited more curiosity and general interest among geologists and the public than the question of the antiquity of the human race: whether or no we have sufficient evidence to prove the former coexistence of man with certain extinct mammalia, in caves or in the superficial deposits commonly called drift or diluvium. For the last quarter of a century, the occasional occurrence, in various parts of Europe, of the bones of man or the works of his hands, in cave-breccias and stalactites, associated with the remains of the extinct hyena, bear, elephant, and rhinoceros, have given rise to a suspicion that the date of man must be carried farther back than we had heretofore imagined. On the other hand, extreme reluctance was naturally felt on the part of scientific reasoners to admit the validity of such evidence, seeing that so many caves have been inhabited by a succession of tenants, and have been selected by man as a place not only of domicile but of sepulture, while some caves have also served as the channels through which the waters of flooded rivers have flowed; so that the remains of living beings which have peopled the district at more than one era may have subsequently been mingled in such caverns, and confounded together in one and the same deposit. The facts, however, recently brought to light during the systematic investigation, as reported on by Falconer, of the Brixham Cave, must, I think, have prepared you to admit that skepticism in reference to the cave-evidence in favor of the antiquity of man had previously been pushed to an extreme. To escape from what I now consider was a legitimate deduction from the facts already accumulated, we were obliged to resort to hypotheses requiring great changes in the relative levels and drainage of valleys, and, in short, the whole physical geography of the subsequent regions where the caves are situated—changes that alone imply a remote antiquity of the human fossil remains, and make it probable that man was old enough to have coexisted, at least, with the Siberian mammoth. But, in the course of the last fifteen years, another class of proofs has been advanced, in France, in confirmation of man's antiquity, into two of which I have personally examined in the course of the present summer, and to which I shall now briefly advert.

"First. So long ago as the year 1844, M. Aymard, an eminent palæontologist and antiquary, published an account of the discovery, in the volcanic district of central France, of portions of two human skeletons (the skulls, teeth, and bones) imbedded in a volcanic breccia, found in the Mountain of Denise, in the environs of Le Puy en Velay, a breccia anterior in date to one, at least, of the latest eruptions of that volcanic mountain. On the opposite side of the same hill the remains of a large number of mammalia, most of them of extinct species, have been detected in tufaceous strata, believed, and I think correctly, to be of the same age. The authenticity of the human fossils was from the first disputed by several geologists, but admitted by the majority of those who visited Le Puy, and saw with their own eyes the original specimen now in the museum of that town. Among others, M. Pictet, so well known to you by his excellent work on palæontology, declared, after his visit to the spot, his adhesion to the opinions previously expressed by Aymard. My friend, Mr. Scrope, in the second edition of his "Volcanoes of Central France," lately published, also adopted the same conclusion, although after accompanying me this year to Le Puy, he has seen reason to modify his views—the result of our joint examination. . . . But while I have thus failed to obtain satisfactory evidence in favor of the remote origin assigned to the human fossils of Le Puy, I am fully prepared to corroborate the conclusions which have been recently laid before the Royal Society by Mr. Prestwick, in regard to the age of the flint implements associated in undisturbed gravel, in the north of France, with the bones of elephants, at Abbeville and Amiens. These were first noticed at Abbeville, and their true geological position assigned to them by M. Boucher de Perthes, in 1849, in his "Antiquités Celtiques," while those of Amiens were afterwards described, in 1855, by the late Dr. Rigollot. For a clear statement of the facts, I may refer you to the abstract of Mr. Prestwick's memoir in the Proceedings of the Royal Society for 1859, and have only to add that I have myself obtained abundance of flint implements during a short visit to Amiens and Abbeville. Two of the worked flints of Amiens were discovered in the gravel pits of St. Acheul, one at the depth of ten, and the other of seventeen feet below the surface, at the time of my visit; and M. Georges Pouchet, of Rouen, author of a work on the Races of Man, who has since visited the spot, has extracted with his own hands one of these implements, as Messrs. Prestwick and Flower had done before him. The stratified gravel resting immediately on the chalk in which these rudely-fashioned implements are buried, belongs to the post-pliocene period, all the fresh-water and land shells which accompany them being of existing species. The great number of the fossil instruments which have been likened to hatchets, spear-heads, and wedges, is truly wonderful. More than a thousand of them have already been met with in the last ten years, in the valley of the Somme, in an area fifteen miles in length. I infer that a tribe of savages, to whom the use of iron was unknown, made a long sojourn in this region; and I am reminded of a large Indian mound, which I saw in St. Simond's Island, in Georgia—a mound ten acres in area, having an average height of five feet, chiefly composed of cast-away oyster-shells—throughout which arrow-heads, stone axes, and Indian pottery are dispersed. If the neighboring River Altamaha, or the sea which is at hand, should invade, sweep away, and stratify the contents of this mound, it might produce a very analogous accumulation of human implements, unmixed perhaps with human bones. Although the accompanying shells are of living species, I believe the antiquity of the Abbeville and Amiens flint implements to be great indeed, if compared to the times of history and tradition. I consider the gravel to be of fluviatile origin; but I could detect nothing in the structure of its several parts indicating cataclysmal action, nothing that might not be due to such river-floods as we have witnessed in Scotland during the last half century. It must have required a long period for the wearing down of the chalk which supplied the broken flints for the formation of so much gravel at various heights, sometimes 100 feet above the present level of the Somme, for the deposition of fine sediment, including entire shells, both terrestrial and aquatic, and also for the denudation which the entire mass of stratified drift has undergone, portions having been swept away, so that what remains of it often terminates abruptly in old river-cliffs, besides being covered by a newer unstratified drift. To explain these changes, I should infer considerable oscillations in the level of the land in that part of France—slow movements of upheaval and subsidence, deranging but not wholly displacing the course of the ancient rivers. Lastly, the disappearance of the elephant, rhinoceros, and other genera of quadrupeds now foreign to Europe, implies, in like manner, a vast lapse of ages, separating the era in which the fossil implements were framed and that of the invasion of Gaul by the Romans." (Athenæum for September 24th, 1859, p. 404.)

In this whole statement, it will be observed, there are three several classes of deposit adduced, in connection with the supposed age of mankind. That of the cavern accumulations, that of the volcanic region of Central France, and that of the diluvian or modified drift-beds of the Somme Valley, and of corresponding localities in England, and perhaps elsewhere. Each of these it is proper to examine with as much fullness yet succinctness as may comport with a fair elucidation of truth.

Before doing so, however, we direct attention to the general conclusion derived by the eminent philosopher from all the instances together. It is given in a double form: first, in connection with the cave deposits, which are said "to make it probable that man was old enough to have coexisted, at least, with the Siberian mammoth;" and, second, as an inference from the circumstances attending the Abbeville and Amiens flint instruments, which "imply," he considers, "a vast lapse of ages, separating the era in which those fossil implements were framed, and that of the invasion of Gaul by the Romans," or which, as previously expressed in another form, induce him to "believe the antiquity of those instruments to be great indeed if compared to the times of history and tradition."

On this general conclusion these remarks occur; first, everything like dogmatic decision is, with accustomed propriety, avoided by this distinguished observer. He thinks a certain result rendered *"probable," "implied,"* by given circumstances, and therefore he *"infers,"* and *"believes;"* but there is no positive dictum, no arrogant disregard of other and what may be more than counterbalancing opposite evidence. Every term employed involves more or less a consciousness of liability to error, something of lingering doubt in the mind, and leaves room for subsequent correction.

Next, the *indefinite* expressions applied to the antiquity supposed differ widely from the specifications of Millenia attempted in the instances already examined. The several phrases certainly denote, on the part of the learned investigator, an opinion which we are satisfied can be proved extreme if not wholly erroneous. Still, taken together, and regarded as modifying each other, we do not know that these expressions, even in the sense of their author, necessarily involve any greater extension of the past human period than, as will presently appear, the Scriptures themselves seem to authorize. Several decades of centuries might, perhaps, as we shall see, be admitted here, or in any other case, on adequate grounds, without violence to the sacred records, or to the great facts of human history. Such interval would undoubtedly, as an item in man's past existence, be, if not hyperbolically "a vast lapse of ages," yet soberly "a period great indeed if compared with the times of (authentic profane) history or tradition," and might readily leave man "old enough to have coexisted, at least, with the Siberian mammoth."

This moderate range, however, while apparently not commensurate with Lyell's inferences, would not, it may be confidently assumed, satisfy the exorbitant demands of a large class of Scripture opponents. It becomes, therefore, doubly proper to examine in detail the reasons given by so influential a writer for his opinion, and to exhibit the grounds of a different estimate. The reader will judge on which side lies the truth.

How far the latest cave-evidence alone would have influenced Lyell's mind it may not be possible to determine. His own words respecting it are characteristically cautious. Recent facts reported by Falconer, from the Brixham Cave, "have prepared" him and others "to admit that skepticism," in regard to such "evidence in favor of human antiquity, had been pushed to an extreme." He "*now*" considers man's being "old enough to have coexisted, at least, with the Siberian mammoth," a legitimate deduction "from cave instances" "already acccumulated," only to be escaped by supposing "changes in the level of regions where the caves are situated, which "alone imply a remote antiquity for the human fossil remains."

As to this last suggestion, of an extended age being implied in great and repeated changes of level; a suggestion also applied, it will be remembered, to the appearances of the Somme Valley, we shall of course make no issue, so far as the general truth is concerned. The entire range of geological phenomena unquestionably proves that, on the whole, vast elevations and depressions of land or sea have required for their development immense periods; that the superficial structure admitting, and the internal forces producing them, exist on a scale, and operate under conditions, which make time an important element toward the final result. (See particularly on the subject, Hitchcock's able paper in the Smithsonian Contributions to Knowledge, vol. ix.) But as to the invariable application of this general law to all cases of considerable change, supposing such established, so as to found thereon anything like a reliable conclusion in a question so much controverted, and so important as that respecting the age of mankind, we are by abundant and undeniable facts authorized confidently to raise the most unequivocal issue. The truth is, this seems to be, like his persistent opposition to the doctrine of internal heat, established by so many facts, and received by such philosophers as Humboldt as scarcely less certain than the conclusions of astronomy, one of the instances in which Lyell, with all his ability and attainments, exhibits participation in the weaknesses of humanity,—a case in which he pushes to an erroneous extreme his favorite theory of the sameness of terrestrial energies in different ages. He has witnessed and described the slow emergence of the shores of Northern Europe, at the rate of from one to three feet in a century, (Principles of Geology, vol. ii. p. 280,) and the fact is too readily generalized, too specifically applied. Even such a rate, however, might introduce, in no very long time, all the changes of level alleged as necessary to be supposed if the cave-evidence is to be harmonized with a moderate human period. This single consideration seems at once to neutralize a main element of the great geologist's difficulty.

But the case is very much stronger against his inferences. For, while the land is thus in our day rising in Northern Europe, it appears to be sinking on the shores of the Mediterranean. Breislack mentions (Mantell's Wonders of Geology, vol. i. p. 118,) that "numerous remains of buildings are to be seen in the Gulf of Baiæ; ten columns of granite, at the foot of Mount Nuovo, are nearly covered by the sea, as are the ruins of a palace built by Tiberius in the Island of Caprea. Thus while the level of the sea is becoming lower in the North from the elevation of the land, it is rising in the Mediterranean from the sinking of its coasts."

Nor is this all; but such changes may take place, and do take place, at times, much more rapidly, and over immense tracts of country, so as utterly to forbid, as derived from them alone, all sweeping generalizations respecting a mighty past for mankind. A region of country along the western coast of South America, equal in extent to half of France, experienced thus a considerable elevatory movement in 1822-3, and again in 1835: the result, including effects of previous but recent similar disturbances, being a total elevation of more than fifty feet. (Mantell, vol. i. p. 112.) Nor let it be said that these movements occur only in the vicinity of active volcanoes. In such relations they may of course be most commonly looked for, but not exclusively there. As all countries exhibit proofs of such action in the distant past of the world's chronology, so the present constitution of the earth's crust seems to be such, and such the condition of its internal forces, that no extensive region can be pronounced at any time exempt from liability to agitations of the kind. Indeed, comparatively modern instances are not unfamiliar. The instructive author last quoted says of them that they "occur in almost every part of the world, and there is perhaps no considerable extent of country which does not afford some proof that similar physical mutations have taken place in modern times." The case of the British coast, from Brighton to Rottingdean, he adduces and examines, with this result, (p. 115:) "Here then we have unquestionable evidence that the Sussex shores have been subjected to changes similar to those produced by earthquakes on the Chilian coast."

With these facts in view, it is plainly delusive to attempt to rest an estimate of prodigious antiquity for mankind on the mere circumstance of even considerable changes of level.

In reference, however, to these and other questions connected with the cave accumulations, it should be borne in mind that the main facts have been for a number of years familiar to leading scientific minds, without, in their estimation, necessitating any such conclusion as that now indicated by Lyell. Dr. Leidy, assuredly as unprejudiced in favor of our views as he is well-informed and able, was far from ignorant of the general cave-indications, when, in 1857, in language we have already had occasion to quote, he affirmed with a decision as honorable to his candor as to his intelligence, "the numerous facts which have been brought to our notice touching the discovery of human bones, and rude implements of art, in association with the remains of animals of the earlier pleiocene deposits, are not conclusive evidence of their contemporaneous existence." A conviction almost identical with this has, by Sir Charles Lyell himself, been avowed and defended up to the present time. It is even alluded to in his recent address Nor does he therein intimate what decisive peculiarity, what *experimentum crucis* in the case of the Brixham Cave, co-operated with the Abbeville and Amiens flint hatchets, etc., to shake his long-settled judgment. We are at liberty, therefore, in the absence of such special explanation of that instance, to suppose that though in some respects, perhaps, more striking than other receptacles of the kind, it furnished no conclusive additional proof, nothing decisive of its own authority, or of the cave-evidence in general, toward a real determination of human antiquity.

Of this general evidence the value may, therefore, be still reasonably estimated by each considerate mind, in view of the leading facts. They are well summed up by Mantell, (vol. i. p. 184.) "As mankind, in an uncivilized state, commonly inhabit caves, traces of their having occupied recesses which had previously been the retreat of wild animals, might be expected. But as bones of extinct species occurred with these relics of man, it was assumed that they were coeval with each other; more accurate observations have, however, rendered it probable that the human remains were introduced at a later period. We have historical proof that the early inhabitants of Europe often resided, or sought shelter in caves. Thus Florus records that Cæsar ordered the inhabitants of Aquitania to be inclosed and suffocated in the caverns to which they had fled for safety, (an atrocious cruelty imitated in Algeria within our time by the troops and commander of a so-called Christian nation!) Many tribes of the Celtic race occupied these subterranean retreats, not only as a refuge in time of war, but also for shelter from cold, and as magazines for their corn, and for the products of the chase, and as places of concealment for the animals they had domesticated. The bones of such of these people as perished, or were buried in the caverns, would become blended with the mud, gravel, and debris of the animals already entombed; and a stalagmite paste might in some places be formed by the infiltration of water, as at Bize, and cement the whole into a solid aggregate. In concretionary masses of stone of this kind, containing bones of the bear and other extinct species, human bones, fragments of pottery, terrestrial shells, and bones of animals of modern times, may therefore be associated. Some of the bones found in these accumulations exhibit marks of having been gnawed, probably by hyenas; they belong to the tiger, bear, wolf, fox, weasel, elephant, rhinoceros, hippopotamus, horse, ox, and deer, imbedded with which are also bones of a species of hare or rabbit, water-rat, and mouse, with fragments of the skeletons of ravens, pigeons, larks, and ducks . . . From these facts it is inferred that such caves had been inhabited by hyenas for a considerable period, and that many of the remains found there were species which had been carried in and devoured by these animals, and that in some instances the hyenas preyed upon each other. The gnawed portions of elephants' bones serve to show that occasionally the large mammalia served as food. It is probable that many of the smaller animals were drifted in by currents, or fell into the chasm through fissures now closed by stalactitical incrustations. . . . Such are the contents of numerous caves, and this explanation shows how they may have been accumulated."

The view thus presented seems satisfactorily sustained by the most recent instances. Of the bone-cave at Brixham, Devonshire, referred to by Lyell, Prof. Owen, in his "Palæontology," just issued, says (p. 136) that, "during its careful exploration by a committee of the Geological Society of

London, in 1858–9, a stone weapon or implement (of human construction) was met with beneath a fine antler of a reindeer, and a bone of the cave-bear, imbedded in the *superficial* stalagmite." And he adds, "Dr. Falconer, F. G. S., has communicated (proceedings of the Geological Society, June 22, 1859,) the results of his examination of ossiferous caves at Palermo; and, in respect to the 'Maceognone Cave,' he draws the following inferences: 'That it was filled up to the roof within the human period, so that a thick layer of bone-splinters, teeth, land-shells, coprolites of hyena, and human objects, was agglutinated to the roof by the infiltration of water holding lime in solution; that subsequently, and within the human period, such a great amount of change took place in the physical configuration of the district as to have caused the cave to be washed out and emptied of its contents, excepting the floor-breccia and the patches of material cemented to the roof, and since coated with additional stalagmite.'"

This whole class of indications, therefore, clearly exhibits nothing to prove the supposed enormous human period, but tends instructively to an opposite conclusion.

On the case of the few remains found in the volcanic district of central France, we need not dwell. Lyell's own statement suffices. That Mr. Scrope, after fuller examination, had ceased to rely upon their previously imagined age, and that he has himself *"failed to obtain satisfactory evidence in favor of the remote antiquity assigned them."* But this very avowal, so creditable to the philosopher's fairness of mind, in view of the bias his judgment was experiencing from other quarters, suggests the significant fact, that opinions of scientific men on minute particulars of this kind are, and from the nature of the case must be, exceedingly variant, and should therefore be received with caution and canvassed with freedom. While some geologists have disputed the relation of these remains to the issue claimed, M. Aymard, M. Pictet, Mr. Scrope, and others, have accepted them as decisive; yet the latter gentleman finds reason to modify his first impressions, and his illustrious friend discovers in all the circumstances at last "no satisfactory evidence!" A more striking illustration of the unreliableness of single instances, of inferences and dicta founded thereon, and of the mere authority of individual names, need not be desired.

The old flint instruments lately discovered in the Somme Valley, and kindred deposits found or supposed to exist in other localities similarly situated, in connection with a leaning he has acquired toward a late development-hypothesis, presently to be noticed, after all, plainly constitute the main ground of Lyell's new impressions as to the long ages of man's past existence. The other cases are to this, apparently, but as the feather that turns the balance already weighted, the drop that overflows the goblet just quivering to the full. Yet in the Amiens case, etc., Lyell's inferences seem certainly more than a little extreme. Not that we mean to question the general credit due to the opinion of such a man as to the character, in the main, of deposits he has personally inspected; but, that we must maintain he is very far from infallible, and that the arguments on which he here rests his conclusion are delusive. He seems to go considerably farther than Mr. Prestwick, a gentleman regarded as possessing superior qualifications for a reliable estimate. "After a careful study of the geological relations of this (Somme Valley) bed, he," says Prof. Owen in his recent work, (Palæontology,) "refers it to the post-pleiocene age; and to a period anterior to the surface assuming its present outline, so far as some of its minor features are concerned." This, it will be perceived, is much more general and moderate than Lyell's "vast lapse of ages," etc. Nor does it at all necessarily involve an enormous human period.

In presenting his reasons for inferring from the deposits of the Somme Valley an immensely long human term, Lyell lays great stress upon "the wearing down of the chalk which supplied the broken flints for the formation of so much gravel at various heights, sometimes 100 feet above the present level of the river, . . . and for the denudation which the entire mass of stratified drift has undergone, etc. To explain which changes (he) infers considerable oscillations of level," etc.

Now to these several particulars in themselves we have not one word of objection to offer. Yet we beg leave, most confidently, to demur to their application here in evidence of any reliable trace of a prolonged human age. And their being so applied by Sir Charles Lyell is, and to the reader must, we think, appear, when his attention is directed to the facts, one of the most extraordinary instances either of unguarded expression, suggesting a serious error, or of inconsistent judgment, ever adventured by a philosopher of world-wide renown. That there have been, in the remote past, mighty and long-continued agencies operating on these old cliffs of early drift, and upon the older chalk that supports them, who can doubt? Agencies of water—dashing, dissolving, denuding, crushing, rounding, and readjusting ancient structures—and agencies lifted or lowered, it may well have been, by the internal forces supposed. Nor does it in one iota affect the present question, how long all those agencies may have thus operated. But is it not marvelous that Lyell should, whether intentionally or not, drag them into the human period, or thrust it into them, as he has done?

In some of the gravel thus anciently and mightily scooped, as great flint nodules, out of vast chalk-barriers, and crushed into fragments, and then ground, and rolled, and polished by resistless power, he finds old stone-implements, wrought by human hands, still retaining such distinctive marks that not only can their original purposes be for the most part discerned, but even some difference between the culture of the tribe that produced them and that of the Celtic family in general, is inferred, by Lyell himself, as by M. De Perthes and others, from their peculiarities. And yet these implements belong to the age of the formation of that gravel! The venerable and potent energy that through ages of strenuous action irresistibly reduced it, all that while laid gently deferential and kindly careful hands upon them; shielded from assault alike their substance and their shape, and kept them unharmed in the quiet resting-places where they had dropped from the fainting grasp of their artificers! Sir Charles Lyell certainly does not believe this. Nobody can believe it. And strange as it is that so genuinely scientific a man, and one usually so careful, should have made so serious a mistake, nothing is more certain than that he has here thus erred; and that the clear exhibition of this goes very far toward reducing into moderate limits his extreme inferences respecting the age of mankind. Can anything be more indubitably evident than that, had these human instruments been in existence in that region during the extended period of agitating energy suggested, exposed to all the violent action alleged to have worn down the old diluvial cliffs, washed the flints out of chalk, crushed them, and rounded them into prodigious piles of pebbles, they too must have been indefinitely abraded, broken, rolled, and reduced undistinguishably into pebbles or paste? The fact that nothing of the kind has happened with them, that not one trace of any such long course of rough treatment is left upon their structure or dimensions, dispels in an instant the magnificent illusion of the renowned Englishman's hypothesis as to the age of those buried hatchets and of their fashioners, the venerable Celts.

Those instruments, beyond peradventure, had never seen the light when the ages of heaving and dashing were rolling on, supposed by the philosopher. The eyes beneath whose gaze they were shaped never surveyed, the hands that wrought them never buffeted those continued and mighty surges. We need no prophetic voice reaching through the past to tell us this, no authoritative utterance of some venerated sage of science to affirm it. The stones themselves give forth the declaration with a clearness of statement not to be misunderstood. It is patent in the very revelations adduced by Lyell from the gravel pits of the Somme Valley.

Nor is this the only inconsistency in these inferences of the great geologist. He supposes the age of the implements in question immensely remote, because, moreover, numbers of them are buried beneath so many feet of mud, sand, clay, etc., and it must take a great while, "in comparison with the ages of history and tradition," "for the deposition of so much fine sediment, including entire shells, both terrestrial and aquatic." Yet there is "nothing that might not be due to such river-floods as we have witnessed in Scotland during the last half century!"

But even this is not all. There is, if possible, a still stranger self contradiction in these inferences of the eminent Briton. He finds those mighty agencies, through so long a period, tearing and wearing in this valley, and those river-floods tenderly putting to rest little shells in slowly settled inclosures of sand—and, coexisting with all this, during the same measureless ages imagined, "a tribe of savages making a long sojourn in this (identical) region." Shaping and depositing their strange implements, with the successive ages, just as the floods do their layers of mud, and in those ascending beds, now thirty, now seventeen, and now ten feet below what has become the surface of our time! If Sir Charles Lyell does not mean this, his supposition on the point is inconsequential. If he does mean it, he seems to endow with very wonderful qualities a tribe of early savages, who could witness all those sublimities, brave all those vicissitudes, and emerging, generation after generation, through so many overwhelming floods that had been certain destruction to other mortals, could cling with undying fondness to the home of their fathers, and, spite of all recurring desolations, await there the time of their own tardy extinction!

There is an explanation of all the circumstances connected with those old flint instruments, we venture to suggest, which brings them readily within the moderate period commonly accredited as man's past term. They occur, it should be noticed, in a low river valley; a fact which of itself indicates that the accumulations are not original diluvium or drift of at least the early part of the long post-pleiocene age supposed by Lyell, but that they are all secondary rearrangements which the river has made of those old materials. Suppose the pebbles thus produced during the agitations of the earlier part of the drift-period, and somewhere near in the deposits of a later division of that cycle, collections of relics belonging to the larger mammalia: suppose, also, some old Celtic tribe of a subsequent age, yet of centuries before Cæsar, if you please, to have occupied for a considerable time what they deemed a secure part of this fertile district, heaping their debris for generations in some such way as that of the Indian mound in Georgia, referred to by Lyell: then suppose some of those unusual seasons to occur, of which repeated instances are known in modern history, or some such change in the river-bed as is now not unfrequently witnessed, and in consequence floods at various intervals to invade, here the human heap, and there the diluvial pile, how immediately would the several elements begin to be mingled, scattered, and readjusted, precisely as they are found to be in the deposits around those low-standing cities on the northeastern border of the British Channel!

Nor is this mere supposition. The broad facts of the case exhibited in the "Antiquités" of M. De Perthes would seem satisfactorily to indicate this as the actual process.

In the first place, he shows (vol. i. p. 165) that the valley-surface about and between the two cities, with trifling inequalities, possesses "an average or mean elevation of only some two metres (less than seven feet) above the present level of the river."

In the next place, he details a number of circumstances which prove, beyond a doubt, that the stream and its borders now stand at some appreciable elevation above the range they occupied no very great while ago. For instance, this section exhibits the ascertained condition of things near one of the gates of Abbeville. (Vol. i. p. 188.)

A mere glance at the cut suffices to show a change of a good many feet in the relative level of the river and its surroundings since the sepultures were deposited in the peat d, and especially since the wooden frame-work between f and h was constructed; and yet the comparatively recent age of those sepultures and that frame-work, as will presently be seen, is indubitable.

232   SCIENCE A WITNESS FOR THE BIBLE.

Plan of the deposits at Portelette, showing their arrangement, and the sepultures they contain.

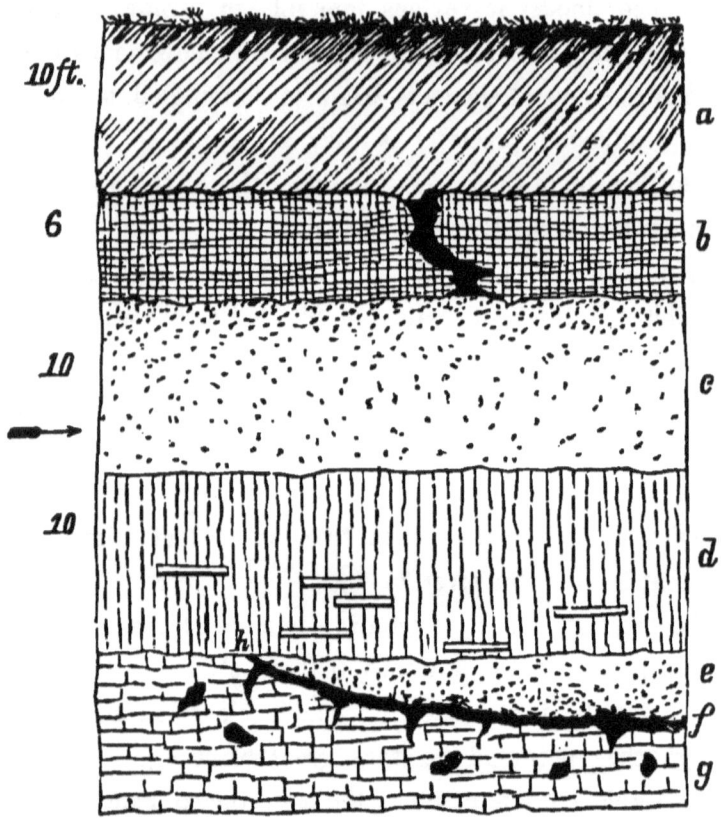

The arrow indicates the present level of the Somme. Depth about ten feet.
a. Alluvial and vegetable earth.
b. Calcareous tufa, porus and friable, containing hard and compact masses.
c. Very fine blue sand.
d. Peat, containing Celtic sepultures, designated by the marks.
e. Another bed of muddy sand.
f. Alluvial detritus, rounded silex, etc.
g. Foundation chalk-bed.
Between f and h, open-work platforms of rough oak planks or beams, trimmed apparently with stone instruments.

Certain circumstances, indicating how the river floods have been quieted in the vicinity of both these cities, so as to occasion immense deposits of less weighty matter, are brought to notice in an extract quoted (p. 223) from a Geological Memoir, by M. Ravin, on the basin of Amiens. "It is in the broadest and lowest localities of the Somme Valley where the waters were deepest and least agitated, in the sites at this day occupied by Abbeville and Amiens, that those old bones, etc., are accumulated in the greatest number. They have been deposited with the alluvium of that epoch, at the mouths of the larger tributaries which then emptied into such lakes; at the confluence of the Celle with the Somme, on the southwest of Amiens; and at that of the Scardon, toward Menchecourt at Abbeville.

The rate at which this process of filling up, this extensive change, has been going on in modern times, is evinced by tokens too significant to be misunderstood. One or two instances we present in M. De Perthes's own words, (vol. ii. p. 126.) "In 1844, when excavations were made between the Somme and one of the gates of Abbeville, the gate of Macardé, toward constructing there the foundations of a gasometer, and when a depth of six metres (about twenty feet) below the surface of the surrounding ground had been reached, in a bed of peat, remains of amphoræ, (well-known Roman jars,) and other vases of Roman or Gallo-Roman origin, were met with. Under this peat was a bed of sand, with ashes, charcoal, funeral pottery, and many shaped stones." These latter "indicate," thinks M. De Perthes, perhaps correctly, "a population anterior to the Romans, and probably to the Gauls." Nine or ten years later, in 1853, as excavations were going on in another locality, and had reached a point about seven metres (over twenty-three feet) beneath the soil of the town, and say eighteen inches below the level of the river, the same bed of peat was recognized; and here, (*ibid.*, 131,) "as at the gasometer, many remains of amphoræ were discovered. But what was not there found presented itself in this instance, a considerable quantity of that beautiful red Roman pottery of which each piece bears the name of the potter. *Cianvari, ma. Titini,* etc., etc. . . . The amphoræ were of different sizes; many must have been one metre in height, and two in circumference," (over a yard high and two feet in diameter.)

Now with such facts in view, the rationale which we have suggested, of the sand and gravel pits containing, variously associated, the mammalian remains and the old hatchets, etc., seems abundantly more satisfactory than the incongruous explanation proposed by Lyell. Especially when some additional circumstances are taken into account, connected with those ancient bones. "These," says M. Baillon, in a letter to M. De Perthes, (vol. i. p. 224,) "are first found at the depth of ten or twelve feet in the sands of Menchecourt, but they are found in much larger quantity at eighteen or twenty feet. Some of them were crushed before being buried. Others have the angles rounded, without doubt because they have been rolled by the waters, but they have not been buried as deeply as those which have remained entire. These last are disposed at the bottom of the sandpits." (Just as our explanation would suppose, for these would have been the latest of the former deposits in the drift beds, nearest the surface, least injured, soonest reached and washed out by river floods, and so deposited first and unbroken in the Amiens and Abbeville basins.) "They are entire, without fracture or friction, and it is probable that they were still articulated when thus covered over. I have found a hind limb of the rhinoceros, the bones of which were still in their ordinary relative situation. They must have been joined by their ligaments, and even surrounded with muscle at the epoch of their burial. The complete skeleton of the same animal lay scattered within a short distance." Why these should lie at the bottom of the series, on Sir Charles Lyell's theory, seems wholly inexplicable. They should rather have been broken into minutest fragments, and rolled into tiniest bone beads, if not reduced to impalpable powder, and borne off irrecoverably by the waters.

The general relation of the deposits in the sand pits may be seen in the annexed section, (M. De Perthes's "Antiq.," etc., vol. i. p. 234.)

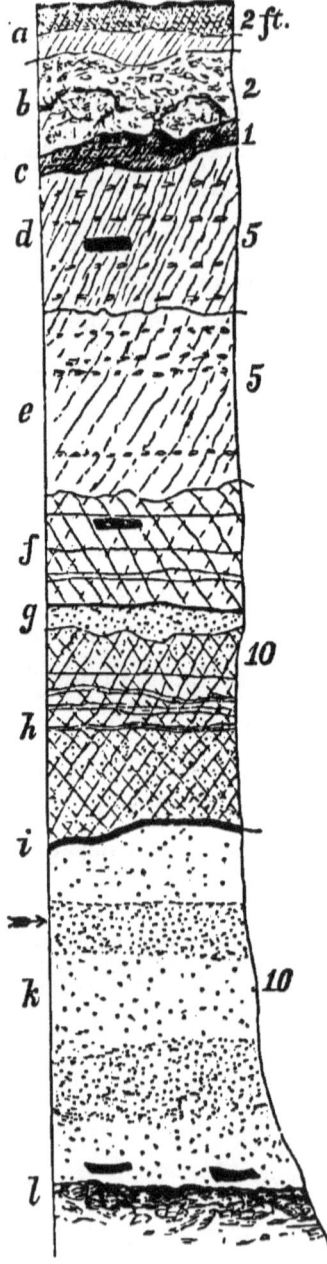

a. Vegetable earth, etc.
b. Upper bed of silicious pebbles, containing parcels of rolled chalk fragments, etc.
c. Brown ferruginous potter's clay.
d. Marly clay, interspersed with silicious fragments of white surface.
e. Marly sand, traversed by beds of pea-form chalk fragments, and silicious grit.
f. Yellowish clay streaked with ochry sand.
g. Bed of sharp yellow sand, rolled chalk fragments, and broken shells.
h. Potter's clay, veined gray and yellow, and both pure and sandy.
i. A thin ochry vein.
k. Alternate beds of gray and white sand, and collections of shells.
 It is chiefly in this sand that the shells and bones are found.
l. Lower bed of rolled silex.
━. Sites of discovered stone implements.
 The arrow marks the river level.

On the hypothesis of Lyell, how is it possible to account for the occurrence of these stone instruments at depths varying so widely as here exhibited?

Nor in this view does the idea of M. De Perthes seem tenable. His facts, carefully collected through years of diligent research, after the manner of Layard at Nineveh, and Lepsius in Egypt, are valuable, and entitled to attentive consideration. But his supposition that an antediluvian race shaped those ancient flints, a race here by the deluge destroyed and buried, in common with a world of gigantic mammifers, appears to be in conflict alike with the disposition of these beds and their strange contents, and with the general range of facts in all superficial geology. Neither does it, to our apprehension, square with the scriptural account of the miraculous Noachian flood.

The universal tradition of such a catastrophe, found wherever man now exists, insisted on by this diligent investigator, is no doubt a striking confirmation of the scriptural statement concerning the event in question. And some of the traces of water-action on the globe may possibly be referred to that occasion. But while it would seem from the account that no portion of the human family had then so distantly wandered, or, in knowledge, at least, quite so far degenerated, it would also appear that the Noachian waters arose too gently, remained too briefly, and subsided too quietly, to accomplish the abrasions, separations, and accumulations here, as well as elsewhere, witnessed. The olive leaf (Genesis, viii. 11) speaks instructively on this subject, as does the nutriment found by the creatures with Noah, when (v. 17) they went forth again upon the green earth. That the human race (save one family) then perished, together with a vast number of animals associated with them, is rendered unquestionable; and that the compass of the desolation must have been coextensive with human diffusion. But that beyond this the brute creation was destroyed, and all the world overwhelmed, is a construction of the narrative not necessitated by its hyperbolical forms of speech, and distinctly denied by many geological facts. That man previously dwelt, and was then overwhelmed, and the brute creation with him, in Western Europe, can scarcely be credited without proof much more substantial than has yet appeared. Still, this hypothesis appears on the whole considerably less improbable than that of Sir Charles Lyell. Especially in connection with certain other facts it may be well to recall. That immense mutations, attended by animal burials on an enormous scale, have occurred in that part of the world, at no very remote age, there are convincing proofs. To some of these reference has been made; others are found in the numberless remains lying in the alluvial silt of the Thames Valley, and along the east coast of England, which indicate that the British Islands were formerly inhabited by multitudes of elephants and other gigantic creatures, and render it (Mantell, Wonders of Geology, vol. i. p. 149,) "probable that the land of Britain was united to the continent many centuries before the Roman advent." The time of this separation may perhaps be associated with that also indicated in the Isle of Man. The Irish elk, there in skeleton in surprising numbers, tells of a great change in the relative extent of land and sea, since such herds of so bulky a race could not have subsisted in so limited a district. And the known modern age, presently to be shown, to which specimens of this creature may be traced, furnishes a criterion for determining that the mutations referred to occurred within a comparatively moderate period. Nor can it be easily, we presume, if at all, proved, that the date of those changes was more ancient than the era at which the Scriptures, as will be found, allow us to reckon the deluge. Although, therefore, so far as time alone is concerned, we might adopt this hypothesis, still, for reasons already intimated, we do not attribute to those agencies and to that epoch the appearances of the Somme Valley.

The considerations last adduced connect themselves with one of the elements in Lyell's time-argument yet to be more specifically noticed. His allegation that "the disappearance of the elephant, rhinoceros, and other genera of quadrupeds, now foreign to Europe," "implies a vast lapse of ages, separating the era in which the Amiens flint instruments were formed, and that of the invasion of Gaul by the Romans."

This assumes as settled by the circumstances, that these quadrupeds coexisted with the fashioners of the Abbeville flints. Whereas it may be affirmed, we think, with some confidence, that such coexistence is anything but proved by the case; that the probabilities rather preponderate the other way. So that this inference is, perhaps, like the others, illusory.

But suppose it otherwise; let it be admitted here, let it be proved, if possible, anywhere, that some of these extinct mammalia for a season coexisted with man; does it necessarily throw indefinitely backward the epoch of Adam's birth? Assuredly not! Why may not certain of these creatures have lingered on into the cycle succeeding that which was distinctly their own, and to an age that may readily be embraced within our received human chronology? That theirs was in the main an antecedent period is certain. That the meridian of their day had long passed ere yet the earth was given in charge to human beings. But that their evening was closed before man's morning dawned, even as registered in our sacred books, who shall affirm? If the idea be well founded, (Mantell,) that "the termination of a race, like the death of individuals, may be the natural and inevitable result of their organization," the disappearance of species and genera may well, under the divine laws, proceed, as does individual decay, gradually. So that the declining stage of one group might be protracted far into the youthful term of a higher race. Indeed there are not wanting indications that it may actually have been so with some of those very extinct mammalia, that instances of their continuance may have occurred up to a date within the accredited period of human existence.

The great Irish elk, for example, just now mentioned, though unknown upon earth these many centuries, was, there can scarcely be a doubt, in part contemporary with the early human population of the British Islands. "Besides the good state of preservation conspicuous in certain skeletons taken from marshes, as of Curragh, Ireland, a skull of one was discovered in Germany, associated with urns and stone hatchets; and in the County of Cork, a human body was exhumed from a wet and marshy soil, beneath a bed of peat eleven feet thick, the body in good preservation, and enveloped in a deer skin covered with hair, which appeared to be that of the gigantic elk. . . . Yet beds of gravel and sand containing recent species of marine shells, with bones of the Irish elk, have been observed in the vicinity of Dublin at an elevation of two hundred feet above the level of the sea. This extinct quadruped, though found in peat bogs and marshes of comparatively very recent date, must have been, therefore, an inhabitant of Ireland antecedently to some of the last changes in the relative position of land and water." (Mantell.) But remains of this creature, thus partially contemporary with Adam's descendants, are also in some places "found extensively associated with those of the extinct elephant, rhinoceros, hippopotamus, horse, ox, deer, bear, and hyena." (*Ibid.*) Moreover, "with the relics of such extinct animals are found those of many species which still inhabit England, as the badger, otter, weasel, and of others which are known to have been contemporary with the earliest British tribes, as the bear, boar, and wolf." (*Ibid.*) Nor is it at all certain (see Sir R. J. Murchison's "Geology of Russia") that all the specimens of the Siberian mammoth had passed away before the era usually allowed for man's advent. So too with the mastodon and other gigantic creatures whose remains have been found associated in comparatively recent deposits in North America: as at Bigbone Lick, in Kentucky; in the bogs of Louisiana; on the Hudson, in New York, etc.

"Even, then, if it be admitted, though yet requiring proof," as Hitchcock well says, (Smithsonian Contributions, vol. ix., art. 3, p. 64,) "that his remains (undisplaced) are found with those of such extinct animals, this by no means throws back man's origin to what is usually understood by the drift period; for many races of animals have disappeared since alluvial agencies have been at work."

This is corroborated by Prof. Owen's later and significant statement, (Palæontology.) "A future generation of geologists may have to record the final disappearance of the arctic buffalo, (*Ovibos Moschatus.*) Remains of *Ovibos* and *Rytena* show that they were contemporaries of *Elephas primigenius* and *Rhinoceros tichorrhinus.* But recent discoveries (as in the Somme Valley, and previously at Hoxne in Suffolk,) indicate that in the case of the last two extinct quadrupeds, a rude primitive human race may have finished the work of extermination begun by antecedent and more general causes."

From a careful review, therefore, of the whole case on which Lyell founds his argument for the extreme antiquity of mankind, we submit with deference, but with confidence, that his inferences are altogether unsustained; that the question as to the age of our race is left very much where it was before; and that the probabilities suggested by science still remain, that the human term has been about what the sacred books, interpreted with neither rigidness on the one hand nor violence on the other, exhibit. With this additional positive testimony,—the instances adduced corroborate all others in regard to the great truth originally set forth with exclusive and characteristic prominence in the Scriptures, that, in the language of Professor Owen, "man is the latest as he is the highest creature known to have been called into being on this planet."

Here, however, we meet another and kindred question brought to notice in Sir Charles Lyell's address of September, 1859, and one which bears, as upon almost all departments of thought and inquiry, so especially upon the controversy respecting the age of mankind,—the question whether men and other living beings around them are really *creatures* at all, in any appreciable or practical sense; whether they are not rather *developments*, which *nature* has somehow in the course of countless ages effected, by the slow operation of her laws changing some ancient low organic form, equally unknown in its character and origin, into, first, fish, then reptiles, then birds, then mammalian brutes, and finally into human beings!

To this latter hypothesis, discredited alike by the requirements of inductive philosophy, by the established laws of evidence, by the moral instincts, the individual aspirations, and the social interests of mankind, and by all the sacred realities of religion, Lyell—incredible as it would have appeared, in direct conflict with his own unretracted and unanswered arguments, under some strange influence—has permitted himself to lend at least the qualified support of his great scientific name. Alluding to the since published work of Darwin, on the "Origin of Species," which had then been only in manuscript submitted to his inspection, he, in the address referred to, used this language: "On this difficult and mysterious subject," (why so difficult and mysterious, we ask, except on the assumptions of atheistic materialism?) "a work will very shortly appear, by Mr. Charles Darwin, the result of twenty years of observation and experiments in zoology, botany, and geology, by which he has been led to the conclusion, that those powers of nature which give rise to the races and permanent varieties in animals and plants are the same as those which, in much longer periods, produce species, and, in a still longer series of ages, give rise to differences in generic rank. He appears to me to have succeeded, by his investigations and reasonings, in throwing a flood of light on many classes of phenomena connected with the affinities, geographical distribution, and geologic succession of organic beings, for which no other hypothesis has been able, or has even attempted to account."

In this brief and cautious statement, Darwin's theory, now before the public, is perhaps as adequately represented as was to be expected in so partial a notice. And yet from it the reader would gather not only a very imperfect, but a most erroneous idea of that theory. In the first place, to an attentive student of Darwin's volume, it is clear beyond all question that his system, instead of being a "conclusion to which he has been led by twenty years of observation and experiments," etc., was long ago with him a foregone conclusion, to the ingenious defense of which he has for years devoted the resources of an active, and, in one direction, well-furnished mind; an original belief, or abstract conception, like a hundred others in the history of opinion, assumed as true, and then acted on as a governing influence in the mind, toward reducing into a system accordant with itself facts and phenomena of every kind, how inconsistent soever with the assumption;—a case in principle not unlike Aristotle's labored ratiocination in defense of the old idea of the incorruptibility of the heavens. In the next place, the monstrous character of Darwin's "conclusion," "hypothesis," or whatever it may be called, would hardly, save by the most practiced minds, be imagined from Lyell's carefully-worded account and approval. This is the summing up of the theorist himself, (p. 419, nearly the last page of his book:) "I believe that animals have descended from at most only four or five progenitors, and plants from an equal or lesser number. Analogy would lead me one step farther, namely, to the belief that all animals and plants have descended from some one prototype. . . . . . I should infer that probably all the organic beings which have ever lived on this earth have descended from some one primordial form, into which life was first breathed"!!

The blackness of atheism here seems relieved by one little ray of light, let in through the figurative phrase ' life *breathed* into the one primordial form;" but examination shows that it is only a delusive phosphorescent glimmer mistaken for heaven's own beam. That "life breathed," is only a figure; not supposed to represent any real occurrence in the early time, but only serving to occupy attention and mislead thought. Else why its application to the "one primordial form," assumed as the progenitor of the lowest class of vegetable existences, no less than of the half-reasoning brutes and the heaven-aspiring intelligences by which our planet has been peopled?

Still, we do not mean to charge absolute atheism on Mr. Darwin or his theory. It is due to him to recognize the fact that he does once or twice refer to a Deity as very remotely concerned in the processes of the universe. And of the old scheme, which he issues in renovated form, it should be conceded that it does not necessarily involve the total negation of a Great First Cause, since it is undeniable, as has been urged, that "God might as certainly have *originated* the human species by a law of development, as he *maintains* it by a law of development."

But if not absolutely, the hypothesis is at least relatively and practically atheistic, and annihilative of some of the most important beliefs entertained by men. To this for a moment we direct attention, and then one or two considerations will be presented, going to show how obviously this volume, notwithstanding its high indorsement, is in the truest sense unscientific; how it virtually repudiates the sound inductive method of inquiry, and for ascertained fact substitutes imagined possibility, ingenious speculation, and an enormous use of the vast unknown.

That any theory, whatever its scientific pretensions, tends

to the destruction of those essential convictions which lie at the basis of individual character, social order, and domestic happiness, is a consideration that ought assuredly to discredit it, and must be regarded as adequate primary proof of its being utterly untrue. Let us see how it is with Darwin's development idea, indorsed by Lyell in connection with his impression that savage man appeared on earth "a vast series of ages" ago.

"If," as has been well argued, "during a period so vast as to be scarce expressed by figures, the creatures now human have been rising by almost infinitesimals—from compound microscopic cells, minute vital globules within globules, begot by electricity on dead gelatinous matter," as former developmentarians held, or "from some one primordial form," at the unknown lowest point of the organic scale, as Darwin, with Lyell's sanction, now holds—until they have at length become the men and women whom we see around us, we must hold either the monstrous belief that all the vitalities, whether those of monads or of mites, of fishes or of reptiles, of birds or of beasts, are individually and inherently immortal and undying, or that human souls are *not* so. The difference between the dying and undying—between the spirit of the brute that goeth downward, and the spirit of the man that goeth upward—is not a difference infinitesimally, or even atomically *small*. It possesses all the breadth of the eternity to come, and is an *infinitely great* difference. It cannot, if one may so express it, be shaded off by infinitesimals or atoms; for it is a difference which, as there can be no class of beings intermediate in their nature between the dying and the undying, admits not of gradation at all. What mind, regulated by the ordinary principles of human belief, can possibly hold that every one of the thousand vital points which swim in a drop of stagnant water, are inherently fitted to maintain their individuality throughout eternity? Or how can it be rationally held that a mere progressive step, in itself no greater or more important than that effected by the addition of a single brick to a house in the building state, or of a single atom to a body in the growing state, could ever have produced immortality? And yet, if the *spirit* of a monad or of a mollusk be not immortal, then must there either have been a point in the history of the species at which a dying brute—differing from its offspring merely by an inferiority of development, represented by a few atoms, perhaps by a single atom—produced an undying man, or man in his present state must be a mere animal, possessed of no immortal soul, and as irresponsible for his actions to the God before whose bar he is, in consequence, never to appear, as his presumed relatives and progenitors, the beasts that perish. Nor will it do to attempt escaping from the difficulty, by alleging that God, at some certain link in the chain, *might* have converted a mortal creature into an immortal existence, by breathing into it "a living soul;" seeing that a renunciation of any such direct interference on the part of Deity in the work of creation forms the prominent and characteristic feature of the scheme, nay, that it constitutes the very nucleus round which the scheme has originated. Thus, though the development theory be not atheistic, it is at least practically tantamount to atheism. For, if man be a dying creature, restricted in his existence to the present scene of things, what does it really matter to him, for any one moral purpose, whether there be a God or no? If, in reality, on the same religious level with the dog, wolf, and fox, that are by nature *atheists*—a nature most properly coupled with irresponsibility—to what one practical purpose should he know or believe in a God whom he, as certainly as they, is never to meet as his Judge? or why should he square his conduct by the requirements of the moral code, farther than a low and convenient expediency may choose to demand?"

Fatal as the hypothesis appears in this view, it is in other aspects fraught with mischiefs scarcely secondary, though of a kind calculated more signally, if possible, to expose its absurdity. The cattle on which he feeds, if not a man's brethren, are, on this theory, at least his first cousins, and the trees he fells at pleasure or the plants he consumes, his kindred, removed only one additional step. Against the latter he may without a thought whet the axe and the scythe, and the knife against the former without a pang! Why should the petty circumstance of kinship a trifle nearer give *men* impunity from similar treatment? What harm—what so great wrong, to knock one on the head? To cut him down? Nay, if pleasant to the palate of some dainty epicure, to convert his muscle into steak and surloin? The dignity, safety, or satisfaction of human existence were somewhat questionable, could Sir

Charles Lyell's authority, backing Mr. Darwin's ingenuity, make this doctrine the ruling belief of the world!

Respecting the scientific relations of a scheme involving moral issues so portentous, its history is more than a little significant. The hypothesis is very far from being, as seems intimated in Lyell's brief statement, a purely original and very fresh emanation from the mind of so competent a naturalist as Mr. Darwin. In some of its accompaniments, as presented by him, it is of course new, and his own; but in characteristic idea it is as old as some of the oldest speculative systems of the world. Epicurus, following, perhaps, earlier dreamers, (see Cudworth's Intellectual System, chap. ii. sec. 22, and Fenelon's Lives of Ancient Philosophers,) maintained that "the sun, gradually warming the fat and nitrous early earth, soon covered it with herbage and shrubs; there also began to rise on the surface of the ground a great number of small tumors like mushrooms, which, having in time come to maturity, the skin burst and there came forth little animals, which, by-and-by retiring from the place where they had been produced, began to respire;" and so in process of time our globe was peopled! Rather more than a hundred years ago the notion was reproduced by Maillet, in his Telliamed, a sort of scientific romance, characterized as "a popular work, as wild and amusing as a fairy tale," addressed to the lively French mind, then agitated by the demoralizing influences transmitted from the age of the Fourteenth to that of the Fifteenth Louis, and by the latter even exaggerated, as if in preparation for the convulsion of the next half century.

In preparing his readers for the theory of transmutation of species, Maillet insisted that the change from marine to terrestrial vegetation amounted to very little, and in proof made his Indian philosopher affirm that "the fishermen of Marseilles are in the habit of dragging up from the sea flowers colored like the rose and fruits flavored like the grape." Fifty years later, the celebrated Jean Baptiste Antoine Pierre Monet, Chevalier De Lamarck, under similar influences, but with larger though still very incomplete knowledge, issued to the same people, while yet in the whirl of their revolution, the notorious development hypothesis, which has since borne, and will probably, whatever varying phases it may assume, continue to bear his name. Not only was he necessarily ignorant of some of the governing facts in the history of organic beings which geological research has brought to light since his time, but, in common with Maillet and others, he speculated on the supposition, now abundantly disproved, of a primitive universal ocean. "That the philosopher who perfected the development dream occupied this position, is a fact," as Hugh Miller has convincingly urged, "sufficient in itself to show how certainly it is indeed but a dream," and nothing approaching a genuine evolution of inductive science. With another generation came the "Physio-Philosophy," etc. of the German Professor Oken, extending Lamarck's system. It was composed, the author alleges, (see preface to translation,) "in a kind of *inspiration*," and "modified," as he confesses, "in its arrangement of plants and animals," to suit the exigencies of the development scheme, "just as discoveries and anatomical investigations rendered some other position of the objects a matter of necessity." This was succeeded some years ago by the plausible and popular though anonymous "Vestiges of Creation," the false assumptions, unsustained pretensions, and, on the whole, shallow sophistry of which, in common with those of all the existing works of the class, were so unanswerably exposed by Hugh Miller in his "Footprints of the Creator."

The scientific claims of Mr. Darwin's developmentism would certainly seem to be rather poorly sustained by its antecedents. Nor is its relation to the general judgment of leading scientific mind, past and present, less significant. The author, though by adducing the "grave doubts" now "entertained" by Sir Charles Lyell, and otherwise, attempting to diminish the force of the fact, is obliged to admit (p. 271) that "all the most eminent palæontologists, namely, Cuvier, Owen, Agassiz, Barrande, Falconer, E. Forbes, etc., and all our greatest geologists, as Lyell, Murchison, Sedgwick, etc., have unanimously, often *vehemently* (?) maintained the immutability of species."

This, however, well-nigh conclusive as it is, may not be sufficient toward the truth we wish to exhibit as fairly as our limits allow. A glance, then, at the system in its latest phase becomes proper.

That Mr. Darwin's discussion is skillful and able, no intelligent reader will deny. Indeed the fact is patent, from the impression which even in manuscript it made on such a mind as Sir Charles Lyell's. Already known as an extensive inquirer and suggestive writer, the author has unquestionably brought to the advocacy of an old idea new and large resources of knowledge as a naturalist and of ingenuity as a theorist. Hence, of course, he has in several respects improved upon the doctrines of his predecessors. The machinery of the system he has considerably varied. And some of the difficulties, to which previous advocates had exposed the cause by claiming to know too much, he sagaciously avoids, partly by an adroit use of manifold information, and partly, where this fails, by a still more adroit resort to the boundless and yet ever-at-hand unknown.

The main-spring of the machinery constructed by this ingenious author is what he designates "natural selection." It is represented as composed of two elements, viz., variability in living organisms, and a general struggle for existence. Thus, (pp. 63–77:) "As more individuals are produced than can possibly survive, there must in every case be a struggle for existence, either one individual with another of the same species, or with the individuals of distinct species, or with the physical conditions of life. . . . . How will this act in regard to variation? . . . Can it be thought improbable that variations, useful in some way to each being in the · great and complex battle of life, should sometimes occur in the course of thousands of generations? If such do occur, can we doubt, remembering that many more individuals are born than can possibly survive, that individuals having any advantage, however slight, over others would have the best chance of surviving and of procreating their kind? On the other hand, we may be sure that any variation in the least degree injurious would be rigidly destroyed.

This preservation of favorable variations and the rejection of injurious variations, I call natural selection."

Such is the principle of the apparatus. How does it work? By the one exclusive law of protection to the individual. Every consideration of ends more remote, of relation to other purposes, of connection with a great providential plan, of the bearing of what are known as final causes, is by the nature of the case shut out, and accordingly by the propounder of the system wholly rejected. Each living thing is what it is, or very slowly changes from what it was to something else, solely under a chance variation, which is perpetuated exclusively by its becoming available for the continuance of individual life in the ceaseless strife of being. If, then, other ruling purposes in the relations of any organism can be satisfactorily shown, the theory is not only discredited, but well-nigh disproved. This is distinctly admitted. Reference is made (p. 177) to those who consider extreme and deceptive the idea that "every detail of structure has been produced for the good of its possessor;" "who believe that very many structures have been created for beauty in the eyes of man, (or for his benefit,) or for mere variety," or for some other general end. And the author adds, "this doctrine, if true, would be fatal to my theory." Now we press home the question, is it not true? At any rate, a thousand times more satisfactorily sure than the antagonist scheme? Can considerate men, in their right minds, be made to believe that the nutritious qualities of our harvest grains are mere accidental results of a struggle for life through uncounted ages on the part of cereal plants, having no reference to the supply of bread for human kind? That the delicious fruits clustering in vineyard and orchard are only similar chance products, simply happening to be pleasant to the taste, constituted, however, not at all with reference to that, but exclusively on account of their helping to perpetuate the tree? That the exquisite grace of the rose and fragrance of the violet are, in like manner, nothing but casualties, continued solely through the circumstance that they, in some inconceivable way, aid against a thousand foes the plants that bear them? May it not be quite as rationally held, that coal and iron, with all their wonderful adaptations to human comfort and culture, are but hap-hazard productions, packed away and preserved alone because of some hidden influence limited to those substances? Or that the gorgeous coloring of morning and evening vapors and the matchless beauty of the rainbow exist partly by chance and partly for the good of the clouds?

The positive supports of such a system are a few truths generalized greatly beyond knowledge or probability. As, for instance, the fact that the universe is regulated by law—that considerable variations, often by mankind turned to account, occur in species—that naturalists are sometimes puzzled to determine between specific differences and those which belong only to varieties—that districts peculiarly insulated have occasionally been found with a peculiar flora and fauna—and that there is a singular parallelism between the phenomena of embriology and the general order of advance in animated nature. Considerations of this character have of course from the first constituted the staple of developmentarians. And though abundantly shown to furnish no adequate ground for their hypothesis, they are still presented as its foundation. Without pausing to consider them, we direct attention to the negative aspect of the scheme,—the difficulties which are acknowledged to lie in its way.

Respecting these, Mr. Darwin even admits, (p. 154,) "some of them are so grave, that to this day I can never reflect on them without being staggered." "But," he adds, as the utmost to be yet ventured, "to the best of my judgment, the greater number are only apparent, and those that are real, are not, I think, fatal to my theory." Let it be considered only as thus stated by paternal partiality, simply that opposing facts are just "not fatal" to the doctrine, it is at least clear, that, after all thus far said in its behalf, any claim for the theory, as approximating a conclusion of science, is wholly inadmissible.

Two of these difficulties we adduce by way of illustration, viz.: First, the readily occurring reflection that transitional instances might be expected to abound among organic forms, if the doctrine be true; and, second, the fact that numerous species—some of them so elevated in structure, that Hugh Miller was able, with a few of their relics, to slay the philosophies of Lamarck, Oken, and the "Vestiges," as Samson did a thousand Philistines with an ass's jaw—are traced in the lowest fossil-bearing strata of the geological scale. Are these objections removed?

Not at all. But the hypothesis is carried round them through the trackless region of the infinite unknown. Transitional form? Oysters converted into sturgeon! turnips into toads! butterflies into nightingales! snakes into greyhounds! oxen into elephants! and ourang-outangs into men! Why, it takes millions of ages to do all this; and since rational beings, though partially developed an immense while ago, have existed for a period compared with the whole life-term but as yesterday, it is of course impossible that we should really know anything about these changes. One would, however, suppose Mr. Darwin's accidental variations and "natural selection" might have scope for some appreciable influence in species spread over millions of acres of space as readily as in those descending through millions of years of time. Yet the beetles and bulls of the remotest quarter of the earth are to-day not one whit more like eagles and lions, or any other species, than were those which the Egyptians embalmed forty or fifty centuries ago. But if this is to be reckoned nothing, how with the geological ages? Are there any cases of transmutation registered in the rocks? Not one has been found. Why not, if the truth be as Mr. Darwin supposes? Because the record, he answers, is too imperfect. This is the case in few words, (p. 246:) "Geology assuredly does not reveal any such finely graduated organic chain; and this is, perhaps, the most obvious and gravest objection which can be urged against my theory. The explanation lies, I believe, in the extreme imperfection of the geological record."

Here, then, the whole inquiry loses itself in unrelieved darkness, through which there is no groping, save boldly by guess.

Nor is it otherwise with "the allied and even graver difficulty," (p. 268,) "the sudden appearance in the lowest known fossiliferous rocks of numerous species." The supposition is ventured, that the dawn of life was inconceivably earlier, and that "during vast ages preceding the Silurian, the world swarmed with living creatures." But to the question, why we do not find records of those immense primordial periods? the confession is returned, "I can give no satisfactory answer. . . . The case at present must remain inexplicable. . . . To show that it may hereafter receive some explanation, I will give the following hypothesis." And the possible or conceivable is again explored.

Such is the scheme. Theory built upon supposition, inference supported by hypothesis,—till a structure is devised that shall obliterate moral responsibility, destroy all the more elevated sentiments of humanity, and convert the world into a great menagerie, subject only to laws of life. Dr. Johnson's severe but just censure of speculation thus conducted may well be here brought to mind. "He who will determine against that which he knows, because there may be something which he knows not—he that can set hypothetical possibility against acknowledged certainty—is not to be admitted among reasonable beings."

Palæontology, however, and geology are not the only

sciences which afford information on the question before us. There is also a registry derived from the heavens, which may aid us toward some approximate solution of our problem. Astronomy furnishes, at least indirectly, one standard by which, generally, if not definitely, to measure the probable age of mankind.

Laplace tells us, in his "Système du Monde," that "the Chinese are, of all people, those whose annals offer the most ancient observations which we can employ in astronomy. The first eclipses which they mention can serve only for chronology, on account of the vague manner in which they are described. But those eclipses show that at the epoch of the Emperor Tao, some two thousand years before our era, astronomy was thus cultivated in China as the basis of religious ceremonies. The first useful Chinese observations belong to about eleven hundred years before our era."

"The earliest Chaldean observations transmitted are eclipses of the moon, observed at Babylon, 719-20 before our era."

"We have very few authentic documents relating to the astronomy of the Egyptians. . . . The astronomers of Alexandria were forced to recur to Chaldean observations, though some time previously Thales, Pythagoras, etc. had been attracted to Egypt by the reputation of its priests for astronomical and other knowledge."

"The Indian tables suppose an astronomy considerably advanced, but everything leads us to suppose they are not of such high antiquity. The impossibilty of the general conjunction which they require, proves that they have been constructed in modern times."

With these declarations of a philosopher of the past age, whose position in his department remains without approach to any claim of rivalry, may be associated a statement recently attributed to a gentleman of our country who has won for himself a distinguished name among existing practical astronomers. The papers have just announced, as lately affirmed by Professor Mitchell, in one of his lectures: "He had not long since met, in the City of St. Louis, a man of great scientific attainments, who, for forty years had been engaged in Egypt in deciphering the hieroglyphics of the ancients. This gentleman had stated to him that he had lately unraveled the inscriptions upon the coffin of a mummy now in the London museum, and that in them, by the aid of previous observations, he had discovered the key to all the astronomical knowledge of the Egyptians. The zodiac, with the exact position of the planets, was delineated on this coffin, and the date to which they pointed was the autumnal equinox in the year 1722 before Christ, or nearly thirty-six hundred years ago. Professor Mitchell employed his assistants to ascertain the exact positions of the heavenly bodies belonging to our solar system on the equinox of that year, (1722 B.C.;) and to his astonishment, on comparing the result with the statement of his scientific friend, already referred to, it was found that on the 7th October, 1722 B.C., the moon and planets had occupied the exact points in the heavens marked upon the coffin in the London museum."

This, if reliable, both confirms Laplace's allusion to early astronomical attainments in Egypt, defective as they were in a later age, and shows a striking correspondence between the times of the earliest known observations there and in China.

If to these statements be added the significant fact, that, since the unknown age when our signs of the zodiac, and the constellations with which they then corresponded, received the names they bear, the retrograde motion of the equinoctial points upon the ecliptic, which is at the rate of about an entire circuit in twenty-five thousand years, has caused a recession of the signs from their constellations of only about thirty degrees, answering to a period of a little over two thousand years, the evidence is conclusive that astronomical records are of very limited antiquity.

The bearing of this conclusion upon our immediate inquiry is obvious. It is not to be believed that the magnificent spectacle of the heavens, so peculiarly resplendent over the plains of Chaldea, Egypt, and India, could long have remained without special notice by human creatures. The ever-varying and impressive phenomena exhibited in those serene skies must have attracted the attention of rational beings within a moderate age after their establishment in countries so situated. Nor is it much more likely that observation, once begun, could have proceeded for any protracted period, without some effort, however rude, toward registering the result for subsequent use. Such efforts, again, could scarcely fail, in a moderate series of generations, to exhibit defects in the methods employed, and suggest improvements, which should issue in a system capable of being transmitted to after-ages. The age, therefore, at which astronomical records begin to be thus transmitted is no insignificant index of the age at which the people, handing them down, became established. And the general agreement of that record-age, among the widely separated nations mentioned by Laplace, seems not a little to favor this conclusion. It is, undoubtedly, a fact of some important meaning, that the early astronomical notices, handed down in China and Babylon should be dated within about four centuries of each other; and that those transmitted in the venerable chronicles of India should be found, when adequately sifted, to correspond, perhaps, as nearly with such as have been preserved among the mysterious monuments of the Nile.

Not to make this era of astronomical records an approximate measure for the whole past term of human existence, to suppose that men could have looked upon the skies for hundreds of centuries, without having curiosity quickened into observation, and observation preserved in records, would imply a degree of intelligence in primitive man scarcely above that of the very brutes. Indeed, a process of development is involved in the supposition, which agrees only with the exploded speculations of Lamarck, and the "Vestiges of Creation;" or with the scarcely less anti-inductive as well as morally destructive theory of Mr. Darwin.

That all reliable tradition accords with the positive indications thus gathered from two leading departments of science, is an additional circumstance entitled to its own weight. The Bible excepted, there is not, as every reader knows, a written history in the world reaching back three thousand years. Nor does the creative genius of Homer, from his distant position, venture to deal with events beyond that term. The oldest inscription ascertained by Layard, Hincks, and Rawlinson, at Nineveh, ascends only to 1250 before Christ; and Manetho himself, with all his extravagances, does not pretend to claim for the Egyptian empire an origin earlier than about 3570 years before Alexander. Still considerably less than six thousand years before our time.

The moderate human period thus concurrently indicated by geology, astronomy, and history, derives additional confirmation from the known course of development of the leading nations, within the historical period, in numbers, intelligence, and social culture. No unprejudiced mind, clearly discerning that general progress during one or two thousand years, can readily be persuaded that the ancestors of these branches of the human family could have lain in darkness, feebleness, and stagnation, for uncounted antecedent ages.

Nor, in this view, apart from any question of Scripture chronology, and even supposing his free interpretation of its earlier data admissible, does Bünsen's inference, (vol. iv. p. 12, etc.) from what he considers indications contained in the development of language, seem at all satisfactory, that "about ten millenia before our era are demanded for the Noachian period, and for the beginning of our race another ten thousand years."

The conclusion reached in these several ways is, however, but a general one. A few decades of centuries are indicated as summing the generations since man appeared upon earth; but specifically how many, is not even suggested. There is no token in the skies or the earth, none in legendary or monumental lore, that points decisively to the birthday of our race. No guidance but that of Scripture can conduct us to the dawn of time, as related to ourselves. Turn we now, therefore, to the sacred books, to learn what they teach as to the entire age of our species.

To those who have given no special attention to the early chronology of the Bible, it may seem an easy task to obtain from them a solution of our problem. But further examination will soon satisfy them that there are perplexities in the case, they had not supposed: real difficulties, which have long exercised the genius and learning of Christendom, and which can scarcely yet, if they ever may, be satisfactorily solved.

It is in reference to some of these difficulties that we introduce the researches of Bünsen and Lepsius. Not that their views or conclusions seem to us altogether unobjectionable, but because their works on the subject are the most recent and able known to us; because they bring criticism to bear upon the questions at issue, in its scientific rather than its theological aspects; because they furnish from the old registries of Egypt some tests, for the time-measures of the Bible, not heretofore accessible; and because they have conducted their investigations in a spirit of reverence as well as of freedom. "With reverence and freedom must science be pursued," says Lepsius, in dedicating to Bünsen his "Chronology of the Egyptians." "Reverence for everything that is venerable, sacred, noble, great, and approved; freedom, wherever truth and a conviction of it are to be obtained and expressed. Where the latter is wanting, there fear and hypocrisy will exist; where the former, insolence and presumption will luxuriate in science as in life."

In justice to the subject as well as to them, we must permit these eminent men to present somewhat in detail their own views.

"There is, probably," says Bünsen, (Egypt's Place in Universal History, vol. ii. p. 160,) "no subject upon which, during these two thousand years, so much talent and learning have been expended, by the most intellectual nations of the earth, Greeks and Byzantines, Romans, Germans, and their kindred races, as upon the solution of the several chronological questions connected with Egyptian and Jewish history." And this he explains by a most important remark, which may suggest instructive reflections concerning the providential purpose of the existing form of Scripture history. Human culture has been incalculably promoted by the investigation of great issues involved in the structure of biblical narrative. And to stimulate intellectual enterprise in such directions was, doubtless, part of the purpose for which difficulties were permitted to enter as incidental elements of the sacred record. "We must not forget," continues Bünsen, "that to the progress of enlightened culture at every period of Christianity, and its effectual resistance to the opposing influence of barbarism, a far deeper and more comprehensive range of critical research is indispensable than was required at any period of the ancient world. This necessity arises not only from the more advanced state of universal history, but more especially from the fact, that the research of every Christian period must come to a previous understanding with a tradition, which, in itself essentially historical, is also of standard importance in universal history. We must therefore endeavor, by comparing sacred with profane history, on the one hand, and with the laws of reason on the other, to find a common basis for reconciling its principles of truth with the world and with science. It was this consideration which first opened to Clemens of Alexandria, Origen, and Augustine, the philosophy of history, with more enlarged views of general chronology."

Then, in order to justify himself, under the acknowledged difficulties with which the items of Scripture chronology are invested,—by certain disagreeing numbers in the Hebrew, Samaritan, and Septuagint texts, by the many various readings of ancient manuscripts in regard to numerals, and by the apparent conflict between such enumerations as those of 1 Kings, vi. 1, which makes the fourth year of Solomon only four hundred and eighty years after the Exodus, and Acts, xiii. 20, which assigns four hundred and fifty years to the Judges alone up to Samuel,—for thoroughly examining the subject, "in a spirit of reverence as well as of liberty," the learned critic thus proceeds:—

"Whoever adopts as a principle that chronology is a matter of revelation, is precluded from giving effect to any doubt that may cross his path, as involving a virtual abandonment of his faith in revelation. He must be prepared not only to deny the existence of contradictory statements, but to fill up chasms; however irreconcilable the former may appear, by the aid of philology and history, however unfathomable the latter. He who, on the other hand, neither believes in a historical tradition as to the immortal existence of man, nor admits a historical and chronological element in revelation, will either contemptuously dismiss the inquiry, or, by prematurely rejecting its more difficult elements, fail to discover those threads of the research which lie beneath the unsightly and timeworn surface, and which yet may prove the thread of Ariadne."

"The ground taken up in this work is one of exclusively historical research, but entered upon with a deep feeling of the respect due to the general chronological statements of Scripture, which have been considered, during so many centuries, as forming the groundwork of religious faith, and are even at the present moment intimately connected with the Christian faith. It will, therefore, still remain our safest method, starting from the assumption that the centre of revelation is of a historical character, to admit as established the truth of all facts in the civil history of the Jews, however remotely they may be connected with revealed religious truths, until the contrary has been demonstrated. But historical science neither can, nor will, in any such case, permit the exclusion or obstruction of critical research."

Pursuing, therefore, such research, Bünsen finds that from the dedication of Solomon's temple, "all the Scripture data accord in the most satisfactory manner with the traditions and contemporary monuments of Egypt." But, "beyond the building of the temple the continuous narrative of Scripture ceases, and consequently here also ceases the up to this point reasonable harmony in the chronological system of the critics. And we have two great periods to pass through, in which the Jewish and Egyptian chronology must be compared; and the pivots of these two periods are nothing less than the pivots of the history of Egypt, and perhaps of the world." These two periods are from Solomon to Moses, and from Moses to Abraham. With regard to them he examines minutely Judges, Genesis, and other sacred books, arriving at last at this conclusion: "No systematic chronological tradition was in existence for the times prior to Solomon, and that the general sums total met with in 1 Kings, vi. 1, etc., must be considered as matters of adjustment and not of tradition."

By applying similar processes to still more remote times in the biblical narrative, the erudite Chevalier adjusts them to the extended periods indicated by Manetho and the Egyptian monuments.

Upon certain of these points we presently shall have

something to say. First, however, the other accomplished Prussian must be permitted to speak for himself.

In full agreement with Bünsen, he is, after careful examination, satisfied that Manetho and the Egyptian monuments are to be credited for the existence of an Egyptian monarchy, as far back as 3893 years B.C. Notwithstanding that the estimate of Archbishop Usher, founded chiefly on an arrangement of the Masoretic Hebrew numbers, allows only 2348 years B.C. for the time of the deluge, and the calculation of Dr. Jackson, based on an adjustment of the figures of the Septuagint, admits but 3160 years, and a recent computation by Dr. Seyffarth, (Summary of Recent Discoveries in Biblical Chronology, etc., 1859,—S. E. Quarterly Review, April, 1860,) based upon a different adjustment of the Septuagint, and upon certain alleged astronomical data, assigns at furthest not more than 3447 years B.C., as the date of that event. This obvious conflict between the Egyptian age, which he finds substantiated, and the three disagreeing post-diluvian ages professedly derived from inspired authority, Lepsius endeavors to search out and explain, in his own spirit of mingled "reverence and freedom." And of his effort to this end he thus speaks, ("Chronology of the Egyptians:" Dedication.)

"The section of my volume which endeavors to establish the relation of the Egyptian to the old Hebrew chronology will meet with most opposition. Considering the intimate connection that necessarily subsists between the philological and dogmatical methods of examining the sacred records,

23*

it is perfectly natural that whenever a step in advance, or an error, strives to obtain a place on the philological side, theological interest, so much more universally distributed, takes a part either for or against it. Whoever would dispute its right to do this, must deny to theology in general its character as a science. The Christianity which derives its origin and its sustenance from the Bible is essentially and intrinsically wholly independent of all learned confirmation. Still, it is the duty of theology, whose task it is to fathom Christianity in a rational manner, and prove its results, to decide scientifically what are the essential points in the Holy Scriptures on which it founds its system of Christian belief. Should its true supports not be recognized, but imaginary ones placed in their stead, it will not injure Christianity, but the theological system, or that portion of it which was built on unstable ground. That truth which is discerned by the sound progress of any science whatever cannot be hostile to Christian truth, but must promote it; for all truths, from the very beginning, have formed a compact league against everything that is false and erroneous. Theology, however, possesses no other means than every other science to distinguish scientifically, in any department, between truth and error, namely, only a reasonable and circumspect criticism. Whatever is brought forward, according to this method, can only be corrected or entirely refuted by a still better and more circumspect criticism. It seems to me also that the practical, religious meaning which the Old Testament possesses for every Christian reader is very independent of the dates of periods, the exact knowledge of which could only have been imparted by means of a purposeless inspiration to the authors and elaborators of those writings, many of whom lived several centuries later."

Noting, then, the conflict between the 430 years of Exodus, xii. 40, as the time of Israel's sojourn in Egypt, (the 70 interpolate, "and Canaan,") and the 430 of Galatians, iii. 17, as the interval between the Abrahamic Covenant and the Law, and the discrepancy, already mentioned, between the 450 years of Acts, xiii. 20, and the 480 of 1 Kings, vi. 1, and the disagreement again of these with the sum of the individual numbers in Judges, and observing that the 430 is just double the period (215) from Abraham to Jacob, and the 480 equivalent to 12 generations of 40 years each, Lepsius supposes that there may be in these instances "a play of numbers involving some higher providential meaning," or that "this external garb of numbers is to be regarded as unessential for the religious."

"On the other hand," he adds, "I have clung to the Levitical registers of generations as a far more certain guide; and thus, in place of a chronological fabric which had been already long considered untenable, I immediately obtained a true historical foundation, and a chronology bordering, at least, on a perfectly reliable one, as far back as Abraham, and this not only coincided with all the other historical relations in the writings of the Old Testament, but also with the already established Manethonic-Egyptian computation of time. . . . And this is no slight satisfaction to me, as affording one more guarantee of the genuineness of the Egyptian chronology."

. . . "I do not believe that a sound critical examination can consider so many and such universal agreements and confirmations to be accidental, or the result of an artificial correction . . . We therefore believe, that by a new path, namely, the Manethonic chronology, we have found the key to the relative portions of time in the Old Testament so far as these are connected with Egypt; and in an inverse manner we may now consider the agreement that subsists between the chronology of the Hebrew history—both the true chronology, represented in the genealogies, and the false one, which was afterwards erroneously adopted—and the Egyptian numbers, to be indeed strongly confirmatory of the authenticity of these last, as they appear according to our restoration of them."

"It is very evident that our carrying back the Old Testament chronology to its natural relations, as far back as Abraham, must be not merely of chronological, but of truly historical importance in the highest meaning of the term. . . . It cannot be denied that the agreement we have pointed out between the true chronological thread, as it is represented to us by the genealogies, and the Egyptian history, as well as the confirmation of so many notices respecting Egypt, from the time of Moses and Joseph, establishes a far greater *historical* character for the Hebrew accounts, as far back as Abraham, than would have ever been allowed them by a strict criticism, had we been obliged to ascribe to the old authorities themselves the numbers which were inserted at a later age."

The reader will, no doubt, share with us the gratification of finding this accomplished man a witness so unimpeachable at the last for the historical truthfulness of the Mosaic books, and not only rendering his rare acquisitions tributary to the general support of ancient Scripture, but, whatever corrections he feels called on to make in certain conflicting numerals, actually deriving from the Hebrew genealogies the very best tests of his own monumental restorations.

Nor is the remark here out of place, how surely all thorough research is found in the end to corroborate the Bible on the whole. Difficulties may indeed be exhibited in a clearer light, and errors made more manifest, which have, in some way, during the progress of ages, found place in the documentary vehicles of revelation, but the reality of the truth itself, and the general accuracy of its accompanying narrative, never fail to be in the end more and more signally established. Strikingly is this exemplified in the case before us. Lepsius, as a later and more advanced explorer of the monuments and their associated questions than Bünsen, has not only verified the Scripture history up to the time of Solomon, but has satisfactorily traced its chronology up to Abraham. He has discovered, it is true, that certain numbers, heretofore relied upon as pertaining to the inspired history, must have some other than a chronological meaning, or must be regarded as incidental errors, through imperfection in the channels by which revelation is transmitted from age to age; but after thus eliminating the error, he finds the narrative not only trustworthy, but standard truth. Such researches, free, full, and withal reverential, are of incalculable value. They interfere sometimes, indeed, with favorite yet erroneous ideas, by furnishing means for a truer comprehension of the elements of Scripture; but they never contradict its actual utterances. So far otherwise, they always expand and harmonize them. Just, then, as the structure of the sacred narrative respecting the physical world, though adapted not to scientific but to ordinary intelligence, according to the common appearances of things, has been ascertained fairly and marvelously to admit, and to be, on the whole, illustrated and confirmed by the grand discoveries of astronomy, geology, etc., a fact of itself well-nigh conclusive respecting the superhuman character of such narrative, since no other ancient cosmology can, and none other merely human could, face modern science without absolute and irreconcilable contradictions, even so do the fullest results of Egyptian research and the latest developments of universal history fall in with, illustrate, and more convincingly display the general fidelity of even minute Scripture history.

Gladly, however, as we pause to notice another triumphant vindication of the sacred oracles, in the coincidences brought to light by Lepsius, we must now proceed with our inquiry into the Scripture record of ancient times. And to do so satisfactorily we have to look a little into the diverse periods assigned by the Hebrew, Samaritan, and Septuagint texts, to the pre-Abrahamic Patriarchs, before the births of their eldest sons; periods which constitute the only Scripture basis for any chronological estimate of the era of the deluge, or of the creation of man.

On the questions connected with these, which have for two thousand years called forth, on opposite sides, all the resources of genius and learning, any dogmatism is impertinent folly. We can only say that after due care bestowed upon the inquiries of Usher, Jackson, Hales, and others, and patient investigation for ourselves, we are satisfied to adopt the Hebrew numbers, as least likely to have been systematically changed, though Dr. Seyffarth and others assign this very reason for preferring the Septuagint. Nor are we disturbed, as there is no good reason why we should be, by the fact that such variations occur in unessential elements of the documents of revelation, as if the credit to which those documents are entitled, because of their inspired character, were thereby impaired. That a very special guardianship of Divine Providence has been, is, and ever will be, extended over the inspired books, to preserve them from all ruinous, or even serious corruption, we have abundant reason to believe; but that such guardianship is conducted through human vigilance, we also know, and that as to visible modes of preservation and transmission, the sacred records have been left subject to some, at least, of the vicissitudes incident to human infirmity. No other mode, indeed, of conveying a revelation to all parts of the world and all generations of men could, so far as we know, be adopted, without interfering with the conditions of a moral probation. ⁻Such limited contingency, however, on the one hand, and such presiding care on the other, are at once consistent with the undisturbed relations of human responsibility, and with the absolute integrity of all that is essential in revealed truth.

This consideration is particularly applicable to the whole system of numbers found in the Bible. While they constitute no essential part of revealed truth, but stand only as adjuncts incidentally associated with it, they are, of all forms of idea or expression, least likely to remain unvaried in frequent quotations and transcriptions. And especially was this the case when figures had not come into use, and the ordinary alphabetical signs had to be employed as numerals. No one can glance at a Hebrew or Greek alphabet, without remarking how minute a change would substitute one letter for another, and how very liable ancient transcribers must have been to omit or introduce some dash or point, thereby occasioning an unobserved numerical disagreement, which might afterwards have a serious aspect. By so simple and obvious a reflection much of the perplexity is removed, which otherwise attaches to the diversities between the old texts, and to the apparent discrepancies in the same text.

But this is not all that may be justly said respecting such instances of seemingly erroneous numerations as those dwelt upon by our critics. And we think it well to add a suggestion or two concerning these, before examining the period anterior to Abraham.

The distinct mention of 480 years, 1 Kings, vi. 1, (supposing no mistake,) to Solomon's temple, "after the children of Israel were come out of the land of Egypt," we cannot regard with Lepsius as merely intended in some symbolical sense. Nor can we see, as Bünsen seems to do, though he rather admits the 480 years to be historical, that there is any necessary conflict between that period and the 430 years of St. Paul. (Acts, xiii. 20.) The Apostle evidently embraces the whole period from Moses to David in a general and not exact enumeration, describing it as "*about the space*" of so many years; whereas the beginning of the time specified 1 Kings, vi. 1, may have been reckoned from some date unknown to us, considered as marking the establishment of the Israelites in Palestine, that being only the completion of their removal from Egypt. Again, in regard to the 400 years affliction, Genesis, xv. 13; the 430 years sojourn in Egypt, Exodus, xii. 40; the 400 years evil, Acts, vii. 6; and the 430 years, from the Abrahamic Covenant to the Law, Gal. iii. 17, the discrepancies may very well be only apparent. The prophecy in Genesis is manifestly only in general terms, and it is strictly quoted in Acts; while the statement in Exodus may, according to the form given it by the 70, be understood as embracing the whole time from Abraham. And as St. Paul's argument in Galatians depends not at all on any particular number, he may speak only hypothetically of some computation then commonly received from the Septuagint. Nor are the statements respecting that period invalidated by the circumstance, remarkable as it is, that the interval between Abraham's arrival in Canaan and Jacob's going down into Egypt is found, by adding the several ages which compose it, to be exactly half of the 430 years of Exodus xii. and Gal. iii. The coincidence must, no doubt, quicken the eye of criticism, but the correspondence is not therefore unreal.

But whatever else may be said of these cases, they do certainly seem to render this much clear, that the Scriptures, as they have reached us, do not furnish a positive systematic chronology for the periods between Solomon and Moses, and Moses and Abraham, though they do, as certainly, afford approximate data the most reliable for a general estimate of that entire interval. Central history is given, with a margin for adjustment in details.

And this, there is reason to infer, is still more remarkably the case with the brief scriptural sketch of the pre-Abrahamic ages. Circumstances connected with the transmitted genealogies of those ages, the analogies of other genealogical registers given in the Bible, and the general Eastern custom in such matters, afford at least room for the supposition, that all the individuals who existed in the series are not mentioned in the record. If this principle of interpretation be admitted, the era of the deluge may readily be removed backward to suit the old Egyptian chronology, believed by Bünsen and Lepsius to be substantiated, or to meet any other fairly established claim of history. Indeed, on this supposition the epoch of man's creation has no specific determination in the Scriptures. If so, our ordinary estimates, "*Anno mundi,*" are not absolute measures, from the starting-point on the track of time, but merely convenient relative indexes, like highway mile-posts, marked from no known beginning. We may count them as we travel, and note how we progress, but they tell us not how far back lies the unknown origin of the route.

Respecting the opening for such interpretation, we observe that the 70 introduce a Cainan between Arphaxad and Sala in Genesis, x. 24, though on what authority we do not know, as no mention of him is made in our Hebrew copies of Genesis, x., and the 70 do not repeat his name in their register, 1 Chronicles, i. 17. Yet St. Luke includes him in the family succession from Noah to Abraham, recorded in the third chapter of his gospel. This record must of course be admitted as of highest authority, under the safest view of New Testament inspiration. One name was, it must then be admitted, passed over in the Hebrew registers of Abraham's ancestors, and in the Septuagint lists, except in a single instance. That other names may not have been similarly omitted can hardly be made out; for, although the Evangelist found reason to restore this individual to his place between Sala and Arphaxad, it by no means follows that he must necessarily have been instructed to restore every other name that might have been omitted in the original patriarchal family tables. The reality of succession, which, apparently, he chiefly intended to convey, is the same, whether reckoned from father to son, or from grandfather to grandson, or great-grandson. This we see exemplified in the line of priests, 1 Kings, iv. 2, and 1 Chronicles, vi. 8, 9. In the one case "Azariah, *the son of* Zadock the priest," is designated; in the other, the form of record is, "Zadock begat Ahimaaz, and Ahimaaz begat Azariah," making Azariah not strictly the son, but the *grandson* of Zadock. Similar instances occur in other places. In fact, as Layard states in his last volume, chap. xxvi., "The term '*son of*' appears to have been used throughout the East in those days, (the early Nineveh period,) as it still is, to denote connection generally." Consecutive names, therefore, are not necessarily given in the genealogical tables. Indeed, some singular examples of apparent omissions in such tables force themselves upon attention. For example, 1 Chronicles, vi. 1–4, gives only *six* generations from Levi to his descendant Phineas; whereas in chapter vii. of the same book, verses 23–27, *eleven* generations are given from Joseph, who was contemporary with Levi, to his descendant Joshua, who was contemporary with Phineas.

Gaps, then, may exist in the patriarchial lists—nay, it would even seem to be rendered probable by such considerations, that they do exist. If so, those lists give no full view of the series or its time, though they undoubtedly furnish a general historical succession, as elevation beyond elevation may unerringly mark for the traveler his distant way, while no glimpse is gotten of interlying valleys.

There seems, therefore, no conclusive objection to the idea suggested by Michaelis and adopted by the sagacious Prichard, that generations have been omitted in the earlier genealogies. On the contrary, this supposition appears, as we have seen, to be sustained by the greater probability.

At any rate, it is sufficiently likely, to cast the gravest doubt over the customary computation of the Adamic era.

Scripture itself, therefore, we conclude, does not specify the number of centuries that have rolled over mankind. Not even the venerable sacred history tells, with voice unmistakable, how far we now are from the dawn of human time. No record, then, has handed down all the reckoning from the first, and it has not pleased Him whose glance embraces all time to supply the ancient omissions. Hence we know not, we probably never shall know on earth, at what age, before our day, this planet received

> . . "A creature, who, not prone
> And brute as other creatures, but endued
> With sanctity of reason, might (erect
> His stature, and upright with front serene,)
> Govern the rest, self-knowing, . . .
> And worship God supreme, who made him chief
> Of all His works." . . .

We cannot even find with certainty the date of the later day, when

> "The voice that taught the deep his bounds to know,
> 'Thus far, oh sea! nor farther shalt thou go,
> Sent forth the floods, commissioned to devour,
> With boundless license and resistless power."

But though we think this conclusion fairly indicated by a careful examination of the whole case, and are prepared to recognize, as allowable, a considerably more extended chronology than that in common use, we do not feel called upon to admit that the Egyptian periods are so made out as to require or even sanction a departure from the estab-

24*

lished conventional reckoning. Bünsen and Lepsius are indeed very confident concerning those periods, and they have had opportunities of investigation which we do not pretend to have approximated. Yet we have carefully examined their researches, as well as those of Rossellini and Wilkinson, and we cannot but see reason for still withholding a confident assent to their system. Dr. Seyffarth gives also, we find, significant reasons for allowing to the Egyptian empire only 2781 years B.C. We acknowledge that Lepsius makes out a strong case, especially from the agreement of his restorations with the extended Levitical registers, and that as we accept this as a collateral testimony in favor of the Bible history, so it bears forcibly in favor of his Pharaohnic ages, so far as the parallel goes. That, however, is not very far. And for the rest, we cannot but have misgivings. The very elaborate arguments on the subject imply that the matter is far from being clear. And it is obvious that, in the nature of the case, grave doubts attach to the authorities on which, in part at least, our learned friends rely. Manetho, the so-described Egyptian priest, who is reported to have written in Greek, under one of the Ptolemies, accounts of the ancient annals preserved in hieroglyphics on the monuments of the temples, etc., is known only in fragments of his works handed down by one or two authors of the succeeding centuries, and chiefly conveyed to our time through Syncellus, a Byzantine monk of about A.D. 800. And these fragments of Manetho furnish the general guidance to Egyptologists, in their endeavors to construct a connected chain, from the scattered links of information found within a few years on the monuments. But, in the first place, if Manetho were a genuine Egyptian author, a point seriously mooted by Hengstenberg and others, he may not be correctly reported; indeed, his advocates acknowledge that in some cases he is not. In the next place, he may not have accurately given the ancient records; and Bünsen contends that there was a pseudo-Manetho, who perpetrated enormous fictions. And, in the third place, it is no slight tax on belief, that the makers of the monuments were altogether truthful in their representations. Over and above which considerations, is the further doubt unavoidably attaching to the interpretation of records still so imperfectly comprehended as the Egyptian.

It may be, indeed, that the doubts raised by these considerations would disappear, or greatly diminish, were our acquaintance with the facts as full as that of Professor Lepsius. But with the light we have, it is impossible for us to receive, as established, the very high antiquity claimed for the old Egyptian empire. At the same time, we have great respect for the researches and conclusions of such men as Lepsius, and are very far from being indisposed to accept his results when satisfactorily established. Nay, we are free to admit that the ancient term thus claimed for the Egyptian polity seems to be rendered less improbable by the evidence of a like remote past in the old Chinese records and calendar. (See Williams's "Middle Kingdom," vol. ii. p. 146.) There is, in our view, no necessary conflict between the remotest chronology that may be made out from Egypt, or any other quarter, and the Scriptures, as they may be fairly interpreted.

Time and advancing knowledge will doubtless make some things clear that are now obscure on these subjects; and such elucidation we are content to await, with full confidence in the everlasting verities of the blessed Bible, and in the wonderful adaptedness of the inspired oracles to whatever real discoveries may be made in any department of human inquiry.

But although there be some indefiniteness in the old time-records of the sacred books, they undoubtedly furnish the only reliable data for approximating the past term of our species. They may not supply the means by which we can ascend, in regular course, the current of time, and measure its entire length, but they place us on an eminence whence one, and another, and another extended reach of the mighty stream can be distinctly seen, and whence, notwithstanding some meanderings which may be hidden from view, a satisfactory general estimate may be formed of its whole extent. The six thousand in use as the standard expression for this measure may be within the fact by a good many centuries, and yet it may be wholly unnecessary to change the received mode of reckoning based on the estimate that the human family is about six thousand years old.

If, however, the inspired history does not specify our exact age, it shows the birthday of mankind as an event not only very recent, relatively, in the history of our planet, but most conspicuous amid the wonders of which it has been the scene. It takes us to a point not distant from our passing day, where we look upon that miracle of creation, the first man. It bids us view the vast solitude of nature all untenanted by a single creature that can think, or speak, or love. The heavens are lit with glory, but there is no eye to gaze delighted on their splendor. The ocean rolls in power, but there is no ear to measure its majestic music. The fields groan with yellow grain and the trees with golden fruits, but there is no hand to gather in their treasures. The flowers bloom and beautify the world, but there is no appreciative sense that catches their fragrance or that rejoices in their loveliness. The inspired word then bids us look again: Eden is occupied by knowing, conversing, adoring creatures. The fiat has gone forth, "Let us make man in our image;" the clay has taken form and proportion unparalleled on earth; the Lord has breathed thereinto the breath of life, and living souls, amid priceless privileges, have entered upon their charge and destiny.

As we look upon that miracle, the mighty issues it involves come crowding on the sight. Sin, sorrow, death, in ever-extending course, through all the ages. Forbearance, mercy, grace, in long and wondrous exercise. Iniquity at length subdued. A Saviour recognized in all lands. The Father's kingdom come, and his will done on earth as in heaven. Then—the great consummation!

In the presence of that ancient miracle, catching glimpses of this new creation, faith may well kindle into glowing utterance:—

> "Oh scenes surpassing fable, and yet true!
> Scenes of accomplished bliss, which who can see,
> Though but in distant prospect, and not feel
> His soul refreshed with foretaste of the joy?"

And however far in the future may be the realization of this, or however unsustained, in reference to the past, the old idea of a Sabbatical age, we may still anticipate the day when, if not numerically, yet essentially, the sketch of the sweet bard of Olney shall be more than realized:—

> "The time of rest, the promised Sabbath, comes.
> Six thousand years of sorrow have well-nigh
> Fulfilled their tardy and disastrous course
> Over a sinful world; and what remains
> Of this tempestuous state of human things
> Is merely as the working of a sea
> Before a calm, that rocks itself to rest."

DISCUSSION V.

THE MONUMENTS OF LOST RACES.

THAT extensive communities of men have, at various periods, disappeared from the regions which they previously occupied, and given place to or become merged in others of different characteristics, is a fact exhibited in nearly every quarter of the globe, and every age of history. We have almost seen with our own eyes the waning of Indian council-fires, the extinction of once powerful aboriginal tribes, and the rise of the mightiest of civilized nations, where, but as yesterday, the red man reared his rude wigwam and fashioned his simple armor. Our ancestors of the imperial island had, at no very distant age, experienced changes which, if less marked, were, on the whole, scarcely less significant. The stern, inflexible Celt, whom the genius of Cæsar and the disciplined energy of Rome failed at last to subdue, yielded, in time, to the enterprising, dauntless, progressive Teuton; and the more than semi-barbarous Britain of Caractacus and Boadicea, became the enlightened England of Alfred, of Wickliffe, and of Bacon.

But change, the reader need scarce be reminded, has not always been improvement. On the contrary, in instances not a few has civilization gone backward. Revolution has resulted in disaster; and darkness has supervened where the culture of ages had diffused no despicable light. Thus was it when the iron empire of Romulus and Augustus, enfeebled by long corrosions of vice, crumbled beneath the assaults of undisciplined barbarians. And thus was it when successive convulsions overwhelmed Babylon and Thebes, Jerusalem and Athens, Antioch and Byzantium, and resigned their ancient glories to be trampled in the dust by the lawless Arab and the sensual Turk.

To describe these great alternations in society, not only truthfully but with vividness, to trace them satisfactorily to their causes, and so to exhibit the lessons they teach, as at once to convince the judgment and move the heart, is the appropriate office of history. And it is as they thus exemplify the influences which determine man's weal or woe, that the records of the past become no less instructive than they are fascinating.

Our historical delineations are, however, very far from embracing all the mighty vicissitudes which are otherwise evidenced as having been experienced by mankind. The Sacred Scriptures themselves, clear, comprehensive, satisfactory as they are in regard to certain great leading facts pertaining to humanity, deal mainly with but a single, and that a comparatively obscure, people. Only in a way fragmentary and incidental, do they touch upon the concerns of a few other nations, as they came in contact with the race chosen to be the medium of heaven's communications with our world. But restricted as are these notices, they are all we have throughout a long series of primitive ages. Profane history everywhere presents the phenomenon of its own birth when the world's population was already venerable with uncounted years. It everywhere found tokens of antecedent changes, and monuments of races whose career was shrouded in the mists of fable, while their origin was lost in the depths of mystery. This phenomenon, it is true, we can explain. It was the natural result of a single practical deficiency among the nations, during an indefinite period. Their failure to contrive the elements of a written language, or to recover them where they had been lost. During the period, whatever its extent, through which this great want prevailed, occurrences could be transmitted only by oral tradition. But, as footprints on the sand are obliterated by wind or wave, so is truth lost that is committed only to tradition; or it is thoroughly corrupted by admixture with fictions of every kind, as the crystal stream becomes defiled by confluence with impure, turbid waters. Thus to explain, however, the mystery which envelops the pre-historical ages and non-historical races is not by any means to supply their lost annals, nor find the links which connect them with the known system of human development. And yet something of this kind may be done. There are means by which thoughtful research may restore, and has restored, more than a little of lost history. There are appliances through which the resolute spirit of truth-seeking inquiry may, as it were, summon back to reliable utterance many a mouldered generation, and gather from lips long silent the story of their times. These means are the monuments which buried races of men have left behind them, in almost every quarter of the globe. These appliances are extensive critical examinations of those monuments, after the sure method of inductive science. It is to a brief investigation of this kind that attention is now invited.

The importance of the subject appears from one or two plain considerations. In the first place, these monumental relics of ancient races have been appealed to by the adversaries of revelation as furnishing evidence in conflict with the teachings of our holy books. But more ample examination is here, as in other departments of inquiry, showing that the sum total of testimony is greatly in favor of the disclosures originally presented in the Bible. This evidence it is certainly desirable to have presented in some clear and condensed form. And in the next place, the attentive contemplation of such memorials of the past is, on many accounts, calculated to promote the high purposes of rational culture. It enlarges the sphere of thought and sympathy. It carries the mind back into ages where it cannot but experience the double influence of the strange and the ancient. It quickens interest in the common destiny of the great brotherhood of mankind. And it stirs generous emotions by placing the spectator in the very midst of the struggles, the sufferings, and the achievements of his long-forgotten brethren. It was under the experience of emotions of this kind, excited by the view of an old ruin in the British Islands, that Dr. Johnson recorded that utterance of wisdom, which is as strikingly beautiful as it is emphatically just: "Whatever withdraws us from the power of our senses; whatever makes the past, the distant, or the future, predominate over the present, advances us in the dignity of thinking beings. Far from me and from my friends be such frigid philosophy, as may conduct us unmoved over any ground which has been dignified by wisdom, bravery, or virtue. That man is little to be envied, whose patriotism would not gain force upon the plain of Marathon, or whose piety would not grow warmer among the ruins of Iona."

Assured, then, that the theme is worthy of attention, we proceed to its development.

Our plan is simple. We shall first survey, with as rapid a glance as may consist with profit, specimens of the monuments which decayed races have left in different parts of the world; endeavoring so to group them, that a bird's-eye view may be gotten of their characteristics and relations. We shall then suggest the inferences they seem clearly to warrant, and urge the conclusions they fairly establish.

We begin with relics in our own country. These are, undoubtedly, as we shall see, memorials of races akin, in general character, to the red men who occupied the continent, at the time of its discovery, from Cape Horn to the Arctic Circle. In glancing at these monuments, it is proper to notice the prejudice which certain writers interested in discrediting the great principle of human brotherhood, have endeavored to attach to the red race. They have been represented as creatures so low in the scale of rational endowment, as to be entitled to the epithet "cinnamon-colored vermin," etc. This is, assuredly, an unamiable misrepresentation. The Indian is, indeed, under every variety, confessedly an example of the degrading effects of ignorance and want, and of the fixedness, also, with which hereditary traits are stamped upon communities, by influences habitually operating through long ages. But he is very far from being the cipher or the wretch, relationship with whom should be indignantly scorned. He has often exhibited qualities of both mind and character immensely above the average European standard. De Witt Clinton, in his discourse before the New York Historical Society, in 1811, did not overstate the case, when he said of the Iroquois: "No part of America contains a people which display the energies of the human character in a more conspicuous manner, whether in light or shade, in the exhibition of great virtues or talents, or of great defects." The remark might certainly be extended to other tribes. Who is not familiar with the high endowments of the celebrated Pocahontas— her feminine tenderness—her devoted fidelity? Who is surprised that distinguished families claim it as an honor that they inherit the blood of this Indian heroine? Who imagines that the proudest pedigree of the world has anything to boast over the descendants of this noble character?

The American aboriginal monuments are of various kinds, and appear in every extensive region of the continent. They may be regarded as radiating from Mexico and Central America, to the lowest point of the Old Empire of the Incas, on the south; and on the north, throughout the whole extent of what is now the magnificent domain of the United States.

Rather more than a hundred years ago, a party of Spanish travelers, crossing the Mexican province of Chiapas, unexpectedly discovered, in an extensive forest, the ruins of immense stone buildings, which covered an area of many miles. The place had been previously unheard of. Its name, with its people, had disappeared. From an Indian village, however, not far distant, a name was borrowed; and the forgotten ruins have since been known as the City of Palenqué.

The extent and magnificence of these remains conclusively prove that here must have stood, in some ancient time, a great city—the capital of a people, numerous, powerful, and possessing more than a few appliances of art. When the busy hum of life filled these halls; at what date their dispossessed occupants, fleeing from ruthless invaders, looked for the last time upon the homes of their fathers, or, awaiting attack, perished around their hearths and altars, no record remains to tell. The old stones themselves must be interrogated for the story.

It seems clear that the people who left behind them these traces preceded the Aztecs, or Mexicans of Cortes' time. This is evidenced not only by the vast accumulation of earthy mould at the base of the ruins, and by the prodigious forest growth among them, but by the fact that when the great Spanish conqueror passed within a few leagues of this spot, nearly three and a half centuries ago, he heard not a whisper of any such city, as then astir with an active population. It was, no doubt, at that day, as now, a heap of mouldering ruins. These ruins, and others like them in several parts of Central America, have been repeatedly explored; and the result is a historical restoration, to some reliable extent, of the lost race which preceded that of Montezuma's empire. That it was a kindred race, is evident from the characteristic features of the buildings.

The principal structure remaining among the ruins of Palenqué stood on a great pyramidal mound of nearly three hundred feet square, and forty feet high, faced with stone. Upon this foundation rose the building, covering a space of about two hundred feet square. The walls, of massive stone laid in mortar, were carefully adjusted to the points of the compass; and the entire front was stuccoed and painted. On this stucco were represented human figures, some of them colossal, in various and significant attitudes, with hieroglyphics near, which, no doubt, originally explained their meaning. These figures, in facial outline, resemble the Choctaw and Flathead Indians of our own country. On the interior walls remain similar representations, of which some are very striking; and generally, though disproportioned, they indicate considerable conceptive power and mechanical skill in the artist. The extensive floor of the building is of cement, as hard as that seen in the remains of the best Roman baths and cisterns.

In this region there exist also other monuments of a most remarkable character: vast truncated pyramids, faced, generally, with stone; huge sculptured, monolithic altars; and obelisks, also of a single block, from five to seven feet on the side, and twelve to thirty high, elaborately carved, sometimes into colossal human figures, and sometimes ornamented with hieroglyphics and strange devices. Among these ornamental carvings, Mr. Stephens was struck by representations of the elephant's trunk; and in one place he discovered, near the base of an obelisk idol, a colossal stone head of a crocodile. Neither of these creatures, it will be remembered, belonged, at the age of the discovery, to the American continent.

Around all these works, that so strangely tell the tale of other days and an ancient race, the deepest silence now reigns. For generations giant forests have shed over them the gloom of a shaded solitude; and, until a recent day, man had lost the knowledge of their existence.

But although the voices which once echoed among them be hushed, and the hands which wrought them have long since crumbled into dust, there are witnesses yet surviving to explain the meaning of these works. The very structures looked upon by Cortes and his veterans, in the heart of the Mexican capital, were of the same type. The pyramidal mound, the stuccoed and painted palace, the sculptured idol and altar, and the hieroglyphic tablet, were all there. The difference in detail indicates, indeed, another hand, and a succeeding age. But the correspondence proves kindred ideas and a common descent.

There is, however, stronger evidence even than this. On the way between Vera Cruz and the capital, not far from the modern City of Puebla, the traveler yet sees some venerable piles, which mark the spot where stood the mighty City of Cholula, the most imposing, perhaps, of the several great capitals on the Mexican plateau, which were crowded with inhabitants at the time of the Spanish conquest. This populous and comparatively refined city, said by Cortes to have contained twenty thousand houses within its walls, and as many more in its environs, was admitted by the Aztecs to be of high antiquity, and to have been founded by the race which possessed the land before themselves. The inhabitants of this town excelled in such arts as working in metals, manufacturing cotton and agave cloths, and producing a delicate kind of pottery, said to have rivaled in beauty that of Florence. But this capital, so conspicuous for its refinement, and its great antiquity, was even more venerable as the centre of the old religion of the country. There stood the vast temple dedicated to the "God of the air," (the reader who will take the trouble to turn to Ephesians, ii. 2, will note a singular significance in this designation,) with all its colossal paraphernalia of symbolic sculpture and costly ornament — the mightiest mass, by far, ever erected by human hands on this continent, and scarcely surpassed in dimensions by any other work of man upon the globe. Of this structure, the base was an enormous truncated pyramid, whose sides faced the cardinal points. These sides were much over a thousand feet in length, and the height of the mound was nearly two hundred feet. On the summit rose the walls of the sumptuous temple, to whose shrine, venerated throughout the land, pilgrims continually resorted from the farthest recesses of the valley. The undying fires which here shed a dreadful glare upon hecatombs of human victims, in the time of the conquest, and flung their radiance far and wide over the devoted region, may light us to the reading of those other monuments of the primitive race at Palenqué, Uxmal, and Copan. And thus read, those ruins reveal much that may be relied upon of that ancient people. Room, indeed, is scarcely left for doubt, that they belonged to the Toltec family, the almost historical race, which is known to have preceded the Aztecs, in taking possession of the Mexican plateau. An old Mexican annalist, relied upon by Prescott, relates, from interpretations derived from their monuments, and from tradition, that this early race, the Toltecs, had come from the north into the pleasant valley before the seventh century of our era; that after several centuries they were pressed upon by successive warlike tribes, which came, as they had done, from the northwest; that under this pressure they left many of their ancient homes, and migrated to other lands, yielding the country to the occupancy of the invaders; and that the Aztecs, as the last and most powerful of these, succeeded, about the middle of the fifteenth century, in establishing that extensive empire which the Spaniards, within the next hundred years, found so remarkably consolidated under the sceptre of Montezuma.

In the southern section of the continent exist memorials of the past, not less striking than are those at which we have glanced. They are also, in some respects, like them.

And the correspondence is sufficient to indicate a common element in their origin: yet they so differ as to suggest a separation of centuries in their development, even under the moulding influence of that dominant family which gave character to the great works of the Peruvian empire. The traveler, especially in the central portions of the southern table-land, still meets with ancient monuments, remains of temples, palaces, fortresses, terraced mountains, great military roads, and other public works, which, how unscientific soever may be their execution, astonish him by their number, the massive character of their materials, and the grandeur of the design. Upon most of these, however, it is not necessary for us here to dwell, because the Inca dynasty, under whose presiding genius they were mainly contrived, and the obedient multitudes by whom they were constructed, were yet in possession of the country when Pizarro hurled from their lofty seat the children of the sun, and crushed the credulous race over whom they ruled. To only one of the oldest and most impressive of these relics would we direct attention. It is found on the shores of Lake Titicaca, was a venerable pile in the time of the conquest, and is thus described by M. D'Orbigny, (L'Homme Americain, t. i. p. 323:) "These monuments consist of a mound raised nearly a hundred feet, surrounded with pillars; of temples from six to twelve hundred feet in length, opening precisely toward the east, and adorned with colossal angular columns; of porticoes of a single stone, covered with reliefs of skillful execution, though of rude design, displaying symbolical representations of the sun, and the condor, his messenger; of basaltic statues loaded with bas-reliefs, in which the design of the carved heads is half Egyptian; and lastly, of the interior of a palace formed of enormous blocks of rock completely hewn, whose dimensions are often twenty-one feet in length, twelve in breadth, and six in thickness. In the temples and palaces the portals are not inclined, as among those of the Incas, but perpendicular; and their vast dimensions, and the imposing masses of which they are composed, surpass in beauty and grandeur all that were afterwards built by the sovereigns of Cuzco."

In connection with vast remains of this kind there are two significant facts to be borne in mind, namely, that sun-worship had here absorbed nearly all other elements of religion, and that the mummied dead were generally buried in a sitting posture, whether in rock-hewn sepulchral chambers or in galleries beneath vast mounds of earth or stone.

Turning northward from the Mexican valley, we trace the monumental history of the old races throughout the wide extent of the United States, amid elements again changed in character, according to the different features of the country, yet still exhibiting significant correspondences with those of the centre and south. Evidences of ancient culture considerably beyond anything found among the forest tribes by the early European settlers present themselves to notice all along the Mississippi valley. Among these are very imposing remains of large defensive, industrial, sacred, and sepulchral works. Of such structures, their most competent early observer, Virginia's celebrated commander against the western Indians in revolutionary times, General George Rogers Clarke, thus speaks: "These works are numerous in every part of the Western country, ... but are larger as you descend toward the Mississippi. Many of them would require fifty thousand men for their occupancy. Some of them have been fortified towns, others encampments entrenched; but the greater part have been common garrison forts, many of them with towers of considerable height, to defend the walls with arrows and other missile weapons.... That the people had commerce is evident, because the mouth of every river has been fortified. ... That they were a numerous people is also evident, not only from their many works, but also from their habitations being raised in low lands. ... Covered ways to water are common, and causeways across marshes frequent. The Indians," adds General Clarke, "give an account of these works. They say they were the work of their forefathers, that they were as numerous as the trees in the wilderness, that they affronted the Great Spirit, and he made them kill one another."

These statements are much more than sustained by recent explorations. Especially do the carefully prepared descriptions of such ancient works by Mr. Squier and others, accompanied by splendid illustrations, in the first and some subsequent volumes of the "Smithsonian Contributions to Knowledge," exhibit the astonishing significance of structures like these, so long ago noticed.

"They consist," say these authorities, (vol. i. pp. 3–7, etc.) "of constructions of earth or stone, in immense numbers, and often of prodigious dimensions. The lines of embankment are from five to thirty feet in height, and inclose areas of from two to four and even six hundred acres."

Some industrial remains of these ancient races correspond with their great military works. In the copper district of the Northwest, they have left traces of mining operations on a large scale. (Schoolcraft, i. 96.) Many of their excavations, following the course of the veins with singular accuracy for long distances, are from ten to fifteen feet wide, and from twenty to twenty-five feet deep. In the bottom of one of these cuts, covered by fifteen feet of accumulated earthy rubbish, in which were growing trees of probably five hundred years of age, was found, not long since, an enormous mass of pure copper, of about six tons weight, with every particle of rock hammered clean from it, supported by underlying timbers, and surrounded by traces of the use of fire. Near it were picked up several implements of copper, showing that those old miners possessed the arts of welding and hardening copper—arts now unknown. Still, they were ignorant of the use of iron, and worked with comparative awkwardness. Either they failed at last to break or lift out this immense boulder, or the exigencies of war, of pestilence, or of famine, compelled them to desist from their labors.

That the numerous population, implied by these works, and those before mentioned, must have been maintained, to a great extent, by agriculture, would of course be at once inferred. But the fact is singularly evidenced by a very peculiar kind of industrial remains, in some of the most fertile regions of the West. There are curious appearances, known as antique garden-beds, (*ibid.*, 54,) or traces of ancient field-husbandry, which seem to denote a remote period of fixed agriculture. Some of these fields are said to embrace hundreds of acres, and the area in which they occur covers more than hundreds of square miles. Trees of the largest kind are standing amid certain of these old trenched grounds, but in general the preservation of their remarkable outlines is due to the prairie grass, which forms a compact sod over them as firm and lasting as if they were impressed in rock.

In connection with these traces of the ancient population, something also remains of their system of worship and modes of sepulture. Of architecture in wood or stone they seem to have known, indeed, but little. At least they have left no such tombs or temples as those of the old Toltecs. Still, they did construct, both for worship and for burial, large mounds of earth, which are now covered by the sod or the forest, and which, if not mutilated by axe and spade, may yet stand as long as the old fortress of Cuzco or the pyramids of Cholula.

"These mounds," say the Smithsonian Contributions, (vol. i. pp. 5-140,) "are of all dimensions, from those of a few feet in height and a few yards in diameter to those which, like the celebrated structure at the mouth of Grave Creek, in Virginia, rise to the height of seventy feet, and measure at the base one thousand feet in circumference. Indeed, the truncated pyramid at Chahokia, Illinois, has an altitude of ninety feet, and is at the base upwards of two thousand feet in circumference.... To say that they are innumerable, in the ordinary sense of the term, would be no exaggeration. They may be literally numbered by thousands and tens of thousands. They prevail from the great lakes of the north, through the valley of the Mississippi, and the seats of semi-civilization in Mexico, Central America, and Peru, even to the waters of the La Plata on the south. We find them also on the shores of the Pacific Ocean, near the mouth of the Columbia River, and on the Colorado of California. In form they are simple cones or pyramids, frequently truncated, and sometimes terraced.... .. They are the principal depositories of ancient art; they cover the bones of the distinguished dead of remote ages; and hide from the profane gaze of invading races the altars of the ancient people." The traces of fire always accompanying these latter reveal a predominant element in the religion of the tribes that constructed them, while the examined tombs exhibit tokens scarcely less suggestive. "Burial by fire," (vol. i. p. 161,) "seems to have been frequently practiced by the mound builders; urn burial also appears to have prevailed; ... and, as elsewhere, in the bottom of the great Grave Creek Mound, ten skeletons were discovered, all in a sitting posture."

Fire burial was, we know, common among the Mexicans. Clavigero states, (vol. ii. p. 108,) that "many ordered their ashes to be buried near some temple or altar." While in cases of inhumation the sitting posture was generally adopted.

Practices very similar to these have notoriously prevailed

among the North American Indians, from the earliest date of European acquaintance with them. Among some tribes, however, other customs respecting the dead exist well-nigh as remarkable; for instance, the gathering of such remains as have been exposed on scaffolds and in the forks of trees, and depositing them, with various ceremonies, in the huts of relatives, etc., (Smithsonian Contributions, vol. i. p. 172;) the provisions, etc., deposited with the inhumed, and the periodical offering of libations and viands at the graves of ancestors, "a duty," says Dr. Schoolcraft, (i. 38,) "obligatory on every Indian in good standing with his tribe."

That the precursors of the modern red men had, moreover, methods of recording events, not indeed in alphabetical or even hieroglyphical writing, but by means of rude symbolical pictures, is certain. The fact that all the more intelligent Indians now existing use such pictography, would place this beyond dispute. But it is exhibited in various specimens, which successive explorers have brought to light. The best known of these will suffice as an illustration. On a rock near the mouth of the Taunton River, which flows between Massachusetts and Rhode Island, there is a very old inscription, part of which seems to be of this symbolic Indian character, while another part is Scandinavian. The inscription having been copied by Schoolcraft, (i. pp. 114–118,) and referred to the scholars of Copenhagen, one of them, Mr. Magnusen, read from it a brief record of the landing and defeat of a body of Northmen at this point in 1001. From portions of it, however, a venerable Indian of high intelligence, and well versed in the pictographic systems of his race, rendered for the archæologist a consistent statement of some other events; the two interpretations not interfering the one with the other.

The monuments of old races in Central, Southern, and Northern America, at which we have thus glanced, seem unmistakably to indicate an original relationship in the ancestral stocks of the several families. The diversities are such as naturally to result from extensive geological, climatic, and other like influences, while the correspondences cannot, without violence to reason, be attributed to chance. The grade of civilization, the mound and temple system, the fire and sun worship, the tumulus over the dead, and peculiar processes of sepulture, etc., and the pictorial methods of record, belong to them all.

Besides these there are two other classes of remains remarkably agreeing in the whole region—the red man himself, and his system of speech. In all the old representations, as now however variant, however affected by soft airs and sunny slopes that invite to stationary life, or by the vast plains and mighty forests which beckon to hunter-wanderings, the Indian is the Indian still; and whether he speak amid the rumbling of southern volcanoes, or among the breezes that ripple northern lakes, on the summit of the Andes, or the shores of the Chesapeake, one hereditary plan of utterance directs his tongue. The late distinguished Mr. Gallatin, who, during many years, devoted the energies of his fine intellect to this among other subjects, says, in perhaps the last public document ever penned by his hand, (see *ante* "Human Family," p. 83:) "The grammar or structure of the several languages of the aborigines of America, seems to leave no doubt of the general unity of the race."

Passing now from our western coast to the islands of the great Pacific, we look a moment at some of their ancient monuments. Like those of our own country, they consist of old defensive works, temple mounds, and memorials of the dead.

Of the old fortresses in the Sandwich Islands, "several are," says Ellis, (Polynesian Researches, vol. iv. p. 81, etc.) "very extensive. That at Maeva in Huahine, near Mouna Tabui, is probably the most imposing. It is a square of about half a mile on each side, and incloses many acres of ground well stocked with bread-fruit, containing several springs, and having within its precincts the principal temple of their tutelar deity. The walls are of solid stonework, twelve feet in height. On the top of the walls, which are even and well paved, and in some places ten or twelve feet thick, the warriors kept watch and slept."

One of the sacred structures is thus described: "It was an irregular parallelogram, over seven hundred feet long and four hundred broad. The walls were twelve feet high and fifteen thick. Holes were still visible in the top of the wall where large images had formerly stood. Within this inclosure were three large *heiaus*, (temple mounds,) two of which were considerably demolished, while the other was nearly entire. It was a compact pile of stones laid up in a solid mass, one-hundred and twenty-six feet by sixty-five, and ten feet high. Many fragments of rock, or pieces of lava, of two or more tons each, were seen in several parts of the wall, raised at least six feet from the ground. The erection of such a place, under the circumstances, and with the means employed, must have been a Herculean task, and could not have been completed but by the aid of many hands. We could not learn how long it had been standing."

"Their rites of sepulture," adds Mr. Ellis, (vol. iv. p. 262,) "corresponded exactly with those practiced by some of the tribes on the opposite coast of North America. Sometimes piles of stone were erected over the body; sometimes burning was practiced, and parts of the skeleton were deposited in temples for adoration, or distributed among relatives, who guarded them with religious care; and sometimes graves were made, and the bodies deposited, generally in a sitting posture, in their houses."

The Society Islands are marked by remains in most respects similar. Of the pyramidal temples it is said, (*ibid.*, i. p. 262:) "These piles are often immense. That which formed one side of the square of the large temple of Atehuru, was two hundred and seventy feet long and ninety-four wide at the base, and fifty feet high; being at the summit one hundred and eighty long and six wide. The outer stones of the pyramid, composed of coral and basalt, were laid with great care, and hewn or squared with immense labor."

Here prevailed (*ibid.*) an imperfect process of embalming, and here, too, bodies when interred were not laid out, but placed in a sitting posture.

Proceeding onward toward the eastern border of the Old World, we find other objects of interest. In the Island of Java (Crawford's Indian Archipelago, vol. ii. p. 196,) are remains of many ancient temples. "One group, known as the ruins of Prambanai, and spoken of by the natives as 'the thousand temples,' occupies a rectangular area six hundred feet long and five hundred and fifty broad, and consists of four rows of small pyramidal structures, inclosing a court, in which is placed a large pyramidal edifice."

Farther north, the Lew Chew Islands, as recently explored by officers of our government, offer one or two objects that claim our attention. The present inhabitants, like those of Japan, belong mainly, it appears, to the Chinese variety of the Mongolian stock. And yet the explorers met with several remarkable traces of an older race connected with Hindostan: neglected rock-tombs like those of Syria and Egypt, and emblems most significant of Brahmin mythology. (See U. S. Expdn. to Japan, Com. Perry, p. 173.) They also noticed instances of the peculiar Egyptian arch, and massive remains in that remarkable style of architecture known in Europe as the old Cyclopean. The custom of burying the dead in a sitting posture was here also observed. "Great reverence," says the narrative, (p. 319,) "is paid to the dead in Lew Chew. They are put in coffins in a sitting posture, and are interred in well-built stone vaults, or tombs constructed in the sides of the hills." And two other circumstances are mentioned, which will be seen to connect this singular practice with some of the most characteristic features of the Chinese social system. "Periodical visits are paid by surviving friends and relatives to the burial places, where they deposit offerings upon the tombs. And on the burial of the rich dead, articles of food are offered, and, after being allowed to remain for a short time, are distributed among the poor."

The religious edifices and pyramidal shrines of the Japanese are described by Kœmpfer as "sweetly seated" in the midst of large square inclosures, approached by spacious avenues, and embracing within their walls springs, groves, and pleasant walks. "The empire," remarks this author, (Kœmpfer's Japan, vol. ii. p. 416,) "is full of these temples."

Of this ancient, and in many respects interesting people, the antiquities, customs, and general monumental history, including their physical peculiarities and the relations of their language, more abundant information than has heretofore been accessible will, it may be hoped, soon be obtained through the free intercourse towards which an opening has been made in their present embassy to the United States. As a specimen of what may be thus expected, the reader is requested to turn to the interesting note of Lieut. J. M. Brooke, U.S.N., which throws more than a little light on several questions involved in our discussions.

Entering, however, the Asiatic continent, and looking over the crowded Empire of China, we find no memorials indeed of "lost races," but numerous tokens of buried generations whose social development must have been of high antiquity; so that some of the phenomena here properly fall within the range of our subject.

The great defensive wall bounding the empire on its

northern frontier presents itself among these as the most conspicuous—if not, as has been said, (Williams's "Middle Kingdom," vol. i. p. 25,)—"the only artificial structure which would arrest attention on a hasty survey of the globe." It is indeed a work of herculean labor. A mound of from twenty to thirty feet high, with about an equal average thickness, over twelve hundred miles long, generally faced with masonry or covered with tiles, defended by massive towers at suitable intervals, and dating back more than two thousand years, certainly testifies, beyond mistake, to the vastness of population and grade of civilization here existing centuries before our era.

The other prodigious national achievement in China, its immense canal, is of too recent an age to fall strictly within our purview, venerable as are its six hundred years in comparison with the age of similar commercial channels among Western nations. Still, it is connected at least in idea with the northern rampart, and with the old highways of the country; since it is related of the renowned ancient emperor who built the wall, (Middle Kingdom, i. 212,) that "he made progresses through his dominions with great splendor, built public edifices, and opened roads and canals to facilitate intercourse and trade between the provinces."

Few if any remains of large substantial buildings have been here, from whatever causes, left by the old races; but there are in the aspect of the country features that exhibit not less surely the peculiarities of ancient custom. "A lofty solitary pagoda, an extensive temple shaded by trees in the opening of a vale or on a hill-side, etc., are some of the peculiar lineaments of Chinese scenery."

(i–35.) In some places also, relics of the past do appear, which seem to link this strange people with other hoary nations. For instance, at Nanking, once the most celebrated city of the empire, (i. 82,) "there still exist some remarkable monuments, in the form of sepulchral statues. These statues are near an ancient cemetery, called the 'Tombs of the Kings,' and formed an avenue leading up to the sepulchres; they consisted of gigantic figures like warriors, cased in a kind of armor, standing on either side of the road.... Situated at some distance from the statues are a number of rude colossal figures of horses, elephants, and other animals, placed without any distinct arrangement, whose purpose may have been to ornament particular tombs, but which have been scattered by other hands. There is a peculiar antique Egyptian cast about them all."

These remains point to some of the most universally distinguishing traits of this aged people; the ideas concerning the dead, which they strangely mingle with a prevalent atheism, and the worship they address to their ancestors. Sentiments involved in this form of idolatry supply, undoubtedly, the actuating principle in the entire system of popular superstition. "The doctrines of Confucius (ii. 258) and the ceremonies of the state religion exhibit the speculative intellectual dogmas of the Chinese; the tenets of Lautsz, and the sorcery and invocation of his followers, may be regarded as the marvelous and subtle part of the popular creed; while the idle, shaven priest of Budha impersonates its sensual and scheming features; but the heart of the nation reposes more upon the rites offered at the family shrine to the two 'living divinities' who preside in the hall of ancestors, than all the rest. This sort of family worship has been popular in other countries, but in no part of the world has it reached the consequence it has received in Eastern Asia." And great as are the follies and vices with which it is associated, this course of sentiment seems to have been connected also, from a very early age, with protective if not virtuous influences. Certain at least is it, that human corruption, fearful as it is here as everywhere, has not developed two of the most fatal forms of wickedness witnessed in so many other regions—human sacrifices and the actual deification of vice. Nor is the fact less than impressive, in view of the promise attached to the fifth commandment, that even a pagan people, in many respects vile to loathsomeness, yet marked among the nations by filial reverence, although in a greatly corrupted guise, should, beyond all comparison, have had its "days long in the land" originally given to its ancestors.

Certain facts here presented in the processes of sepulture are remarkable in connection with customs elsewhere prevalent, *e.g.* "On the day of burial (ii. 264-6) a sacrifice of cooked provisions is laid out and the coffin placed near it. . . . And at the grave everything he can possibly want in the land of shadows is burned for the use of the deceased. The sacrifice is then carried back, and the family feast on it, or distribute it among the poor." The strange sitting posture of the corpse, associated with arrangements like these in Lew Chew, and with proceedings in part akin to them among the aborigines of America, if ever here prevalent, has not been perpetuated as a custom. And yet it is to some extent employed, particularly in association with certain phases of Budhism. Of the Lamas in Thibet it is said (i. 196) that, "as soon as the breath has departed, the body is *seated* in the attitude in which Budha is represented, and in this posture of contemplation the corpse is burned."

Two other memorials of the old generations here existing we briefly mention, viz., their venerable annals and the uncouth, cumbrous character in which they are recorded. That the former reach back reliably to 2852 B.C., seems to be conceded (ii. 199;) while the latter is probably the oldest form of writing now in common use on earth. It is known also to have been derived in part, like the old hieroglyphic and other systems, from rude primitive attempts at pictorial delineation. "Most of the original forms (i. 461) are preserved in the treatises of native philologists, where the changes they have gradually undergone are shown."

India, the sunny, irrigated, fertile home of hoary multitudes, venerable culture, and wild mythology, as of exuberant nature in her every kingdom, next claims attention. The primitive race here, if not "lost" in a material sense, has undoubtedly, since the Mussulman conquest, so decayed, as to present a phenomenon adapted to our subject. The old tombs and temples are those of a people to be seen in India no more. Such venerable remains, including innumerable gigantic and gorgeous pagodas, piled upon huge pyramids whose sides face the cardinal points, the traveler beholds everywhere, from Cape Comorin to the Himalaya, and from the Ganges to the Indus. Some of the older of these monuments are among the most noticeable of all the works left by early races. One or two of them will suffice for our illustration.

About thirty-five miles south of Madras are extensive ruins, known as "the Seven Pagodas," also bearing the name "Mahabalipoor." This name signifies "the city of the great Bali," and the sculptures refer chiefly to the exploits of that deified hero, celebrated in the Sanscrit epic narratives known as the Mahabarat. "While the structures in the west of India are dedicated almost exclusively to Seva, the destroyer, this is sacred to Vishnu, the preserver, of whom in the principal temple there appears a colossal image, sleeping on an enormous hooded snake." (Murray's excellent Sketch of India, in Harper's Family Library, vol. ii. p. 225.) "This has been a place of considerable importance" (says Bishop Heber, Journal, vol. ii. p. 213,) "as a metropolis of the ancient kings of the race of Pandion; and its rocks, which in themselves are picturesque, are carved into porticoes, temples, bas-reliefs, etc., many of which are of great spirit and beauty. The ruins cover a great space. . . . Here the surf, according to the Hindoos, rolls and roars over the city of the Great Bali! One very old temple of Vishnu certainly stands immediately on the brink, and amid the dash of the spray; and there are really some remains of architecture, among which a tall pillar is conspicuous, which rise from amid the waves, and give proof that in this particular spot, as at Madras, the sea has encroached on the land, though in most other parts of the Coromandel coast it seems rather receding than advancing. There are also many rocks rising through the white breakers, and peculiar desolation marks the surrounding scenery." Standing amid these old monuments, we might therefore truthfully apply, in part at least, Southey's poetic sketch :—

> "Well might the sad beholder ween from thence
> What works of wonder the devouring wave
> Had swallowed there, when monuments so brave
> Bore record of their old magnificence.
> And on the sandy shore, beside the verge
> Of ocean, here and there a rock-hewn fane
> Resisted in its strength the surf and surge
> That on their deep foundations beat in vain.
> In solitude the ancient temples stood,
> Once resonant with instrument, and song,
> And solemn dance of festive multitudes;
> Now as the weary ages pass along,
> Hearing no voice, save of the ocean flood,
> Which roars forever on the restless shores;
> Or visiting their solitary caves,
> The lonely sound of winds that moan around,
> Accordant to the melancholy waves."

From this desolate spot we proceed to another, in some respects much more impressive.

Penetrating a hundred or two miles into the interior, from Bombay, on the northwest coast of the Peninsula, toward the ancient City of Deoghir and the modern Dowlatabad, we reach the granite mountains in which are excavated the wondrous temples of Elora. These we find among the most stupendous works ever executed by man. A single temple of one hundred feet high, sixty wide, and one hundred and fifty deep, cut out of solid granite, is an achievement of industry truly astonishing. But when we behold similar works crowded together through an extent of two leagues, the mind cannot but pause in amazement, to realize the incredible labor. Here, too, are thousands of figures of ancient Hindoo sculpture, whose age, like that of the structures they adorn, is lost in the darkness that preceded the dawn of history. The chief temple still bears the name of a more than mortal architect, whom Brahma is said to have assisted. Its vault is supported by several rows of columns. Numerous colossal monoliths, representing Indian gods, stand in conspicuous places; and on each side of the colonnades are hewn sphinxes, quite in Egyptian style. In view of which, the statement may well be credited, as years ago published, that Indian soldiers of the English army in Egypt, at the close of the last century, exclaimed, while gazing with astonishment at some of the old images of the Nile Valley, that "Hindoos must have inhabited Egypt." "The first view," says Mr. Erskine, "of this desolate religious city is grand and striking, but melancholy. The number and magnificence of the subterraneous temples, the extent and loneliness of the same, the endless diversity of sculpture in others, the variety of curious foliage, of minute tracery, highly-wrought pillars, rich mythological designs, sacred shrines, and colossal statues, astonish and distract the mind. The empire whose pride they must have been has passed away, and left not a legible memorial behind."

Sepulture, in this vast peninsula, was, it is well known, extensively substituted by the destructive agency of fire. The funeral pile is one of the characteristic features of Hindoo custom. And yet there are tokens which seem to indicate the probable origin, here, of the old idea of a sitting posture for the dead. Mention has been already made of the peculiar attitude in which the Lamas of Thibet were placed as soon as they had expired, in correspondence with the posture of repose in which Budha is represented. But the latter, it appears, is only a secondary exhibiton of older representations, with which Budha and his system are believed to be connected. In the first volume of Sir William Jones's Asiatic Researches may be seen delineated, in characteristic sketches, the elder forms of Brahma, Vishnu, etc., in this very strange position, supposed adapted to contemplation. And it is far from improbable that from these representations, and the ideas associated with them, was derived the custom, so diffused, as we have seen, of placing human bodies in the tomb sitting instead of recumbent.

Of the old races in India, there are monuments more remarkable than all the wonders of the chiseled granite. Those venerable documents of theology, of law, and of poetry, which oriental scholars within the last century brought to light. Significant, indeed, are these, as records of ancient thought, as memorials of the early intellectual struggles of a heathen race singularly ideal and imaginative. A people, of whom, as they were in the days of Alexander and before, as in some measure they have been ever since, it has been strikingly, perhaps justly said: "There never was a nation believing so firmly in another world, and so little concerned about this; whose past was the problem of creation, whose future the problem of existence; while the present, which ought to be the solution of

27*

both, seems never to have attracted their attention or called forth their energies."

It is, however, the old language itself which constitutes the most instructive memento of the original proprietors of that southern clime; a language now proved to be the elder sister of Saxon, Gothic, Latin, and even venerable Greek; so that widely separated in essential qualities as their tribes have become under diverse influences, in the course of ages, Europe and India must be acknowledged to have originally received a kindred population; and the inhabitants of these distant regions are justly designated under one term, as the great Indo-European family. The testimony of the learned Professor Max Müller, on this subject, (*ante*, "Human Family,") will be recollected: "Many words still live in India and England that have witnessed the first separation of the northern and southern Arians, (as originally from Aram,) and these are witnesses not to be shaken by any cross-examination. The terms for God, for house, for father, mother, son, daughter, for dog and cow, for heart and tears, for axe and tree, identical in all the Indo-European idioms, are like the watchwords of soldiers. We challenge the seeming stranger; and whether he answer with the lips of a Greek, a German, or an Indian, we recognize him as one of ourselves. Though the historian may shake his head, though the physiologist may doubt, and the poet scorn the idea, all must yield before the facts furnished by language. There was a time when the ancestors of the Celts, the Germans, the Sclavonians, the Greeks and Italians, the Persians and

Hindoos, were living together beneath the same roof, separate from the ancestors of the Shemitic and Turanian races."

From India proceeding to the interior of Asia, we need not linger long about the material remains of ancient Persia. Altogether to overlook this region, source as it was of mighty influences in former ages, may not, indeed, be allowable, in connection with our subject. Here was the centre of that great system of sun and fire worship, which seemed to permeate the ancient world. Here were cradled energies which, in many a fierce contest, strove for empire with Babylon, with Egypt, and with Greece. And here, on one spot at least, the site of that gorgeous Persepolis, which was a wonder of the world when the Macedonian conqueror applied the torch of vengeance, the traveler may still behold, in singular perfection of art, and bearing many a strange old inscription, spite of all the ravages of fire and of time, piles of masonry scarcely rivaled on the earth. But to follow even Niebuhr in his explorations of these, were needless for our purpose, because we are in the main acquainted with the ancient Persians and their neighbors through the old historical races, and through their own sacred books now given to Europe. And we thus know them to have been intermediate, no less in character than in position, between India and Babylon.

If from Central Asia we follow the known track of early migration toward its farthest limits in Western Europe, monuments of other races, which antedate history, present themselves again to view. In some places old rock-inscriptions are discernible, in a rude symbolic pictography, which tends more or less toward some development of a hieroglyphic system, and which, by its peculiar complexity of outline, in certain instances, suggests association with the originals of the interminably involved Chinese character. Altars, too, are found, on which the early wanderers kindled their sacrificial fires. Conspicuous among these are the old Druid temples of Stonehenge in England, and Carnac in Brittany, which, with others that remain, both in Britain and Gaul, are supposed, from their significant form, to have been dedicated to the united worship of the sun and the serpent.

Nor are the tumuli less remarkable which, in Scythia, Germany, Scandinavia, and the British Isles, forgotten generations heaped upon their ancient dead. The Scythians, whose tumuli are scattered in great abundance over the plains of Russia, Southern Siberia, and Tartary, "labored," says Herodotus, "to raise as high a monument of earth for their dead as possible," (Melpomene, lxxi.) The richness of these Scythian barrows is remarkable; and, according to Strahlenberg, (Siberia, p. 366,) the local governors of Siberia used formerly to authorize caravans or expeditions to visit and ransack the tombs, reserving to themselves a tenth of the treasures. In the second volume of the British Archæologia is an account of the opening of one of the larger tumuli in Southern Siberia. Within the mound were found three vaults, constructed of unhewn stones, and of rude workmanship. The central and largest vault contained the remains of the individual over whom the tumulus had been erected, also his sword, spear, bow, quiver, arrows, etc. In the vault at his feet were the skeleton and trappings of a horse; in that at his head was a female skeleton, supposed to be that of his wife. The male skeleton reclined (something like the sitting posture) against the head of the vault, on a sheet of pure gold, extending from head to foot; and another of like dimensions was spread over it. It had been wrapped in a rich mantle, studded with rubies and emeralds. The female was enveloped in like manner: a golden chain of many links, set with rubies, went round her neck, and there were bracelets of gold upon her arms. The four sheets of gold weighed forty pounds. (Smithn. Cont., ii. art. ix. p. 117.) In the Scandinavian monumental history, the earlier and later periods have been designated as an "age of fire," and an "age of hills." Odin is said to have introduced the practice of burning, and also that of the wife sacrificing herself with her deceased lord. (Mallet's Northn. Antiq., chap. xii.) The Germans, says Tacitus, added to the funeral pile the arms of the deceased and his horse. And Cæsar relates that the inhabitants of Belgium and Gaul buried or burned with the dead whatever was valued by them in their lifetime. The burial mounds of the ancient Britons evince similar practices. They are very numerous, and some of them of great size. At New Grange, in the County of Meath, Ireland, there is a structure of this kind seventy feet high, whose base covers two acres; and within it, as left from old times, there is a gallery sixty feet long, conducting to a great cavernous chamber, containing originally, as do the mounds generally, many interesting relics, ashes and urns, spears, shields, and mirrors.

But we must hasten to the central monuments of the Old World. Races that were more than ancient ere yet Athens had received a name, have left along the Italian shores, as well as in Greece, imperishable memorials of so vast a character as to have given rise to fables of Cyclopean giants. If, however, the ruins of Mycenæ, and other like cities of the olden time, furnished the earliest Greeks of history material only for wild conjecture, well may they have attributed to demigods such vastly greater achievements as the wonderful tunnels of the forgotten race. That which was made for the purpose of draining Lake Copais, in Argolis, is affirmed (see Niebuhr's Lectures) to have been cut to the sea, through the solid rock underlying the pro-Eubean hills, a distance of four miles. And similar works, executed in Italy, to reduce the swollen Lake of Alba, and some others, are of scarcely inferior dimensions or more recent age.

The Cyclopean buildings, left by these pre-Hellenic and ante-Roman races, seem to present a remarkable connecting link between the earlier civilization of southeastern Europe and that of the Euphrates and Nile valleys. "They have," says Niebuhr, "a great resemblance in style to those of ancient Egypt, especially to the peculiar colossal nature of Egyptian architecture. We, moreover, find in them pointed arches instead of vaults, just as in Egyptian buildings. . . . The sepultures in what is called the lion-gate at Mycenæ, which is noticed even by Pausanias, (in Hadrian's time,) have quite a foreign character. Notwithstanding all the ravages of barbarians, that gate is still standing undisturbed, and its ruins are perhaps now as completely preserved as they were at the time when Pausanias described them."

But if Italy and Greece received thus from Egypt a strange influence, at so early a day, to mould their architecture, vastly more important toward their own and the world's elevation was the influence they received, be it at a later day, from Asia, in the gift of letters—a gift without which history had remained lost in fable, and religion must have continued debased by superstition.

We linger, then, a moment around the graves of those old races that lie silent in the once teeming plains of southwestern Asia, before giving attention to the more wonderful remnants of antiquity, the most wonderful of the world, which lift their hoary heads over the mysterious land of the Pharaohs.

The ancient capital of Assur, and Nimrod, and Ninus, on the Tigris, "that exceeding great city of three days' journey," to which Jonah was sent with warning message, and whose requiem Nahum sung, lost for centuries almost from the map of the world, rises before us, as if to life again. And from the ruins we hear the story of her greatness and her desolation. The Median, the Greek, the Roman, the Persian, the Turk, the Arab, have been there, but only to trample Nineveh in the dust. It was Nineveh no more: a vast sweep of shapeless mounds,—nothing besides. Opening, however, at last before intelligent search, those mounds reveal, as at magical touch, the realities of the old ages. The huge figures that stood as stone sentinels before palace-halls, colossal winged lions and bulls with human heads, come forth as if living creatures from their lurking-places. The herald-office of Sargon and Sennacherib produces its registers on slabs of alabaster; and the archives of their state department are read from libraries of engraved tile. The race is gone, yet restored. We see the Eastern despot, and the abject people. He wields authority, unchecked, over property and life: they rather adore him as a god than obey him as a man. The restoration, in whole and in part, fits precisely the delineation found in our old Scriptures.

Before the monumental piles on the Euphrates, which mark the grave of Nebuchadnezzar's later empire, we pause only to listen to Mr. Layard's statement: "On all sides fragments of glass, marble, pottery, and inscribed brick, are mingled with that peculiar nitrous and blanched soil which, had from the remains of ancient habitations, checks or destroys vegetation, and renders the site of Babylon a naked and hideous waste. Owls start from the scanty thickets, and the foul jackal skulks through the furrows." We cannot but remember, as this is testified, how, when she was in the pride of her power, the prophets had written: "Babylon, the glory of kingdoms, the beauty of the Chaldee's excellency, shall be as when God overthrew Sodom and Gomorrah. Wild beasts of the desert shall lie there, and their houses shall be full of doleful creatures, and owls shall dwell there."

We now approach that marvelous monumental valley of Northern Africa whose genial climate, fertilizing streams, and impregnable natural defenses of inclosing rock and surrounding desert, rendered it the earliest home of quiet labor and progressive art; and whose serene atmosphere, embalming, as it were, the works of its inhabitants, from the very primitive time, has preserved them for the amazed contemplation of every age of mankind. We follow the track trodden by old Abraham, when, wending his obedient way from Mesopotamia, he sought a Syrian home—the path we still pursue, along which traveled himself and descendants, across the sands of Southern Palestine, when they went to obtain supplies from the granaries of Egypt. The venerable city of the priests of On, which rose before the patriarch's eyes, as, with his little caravan, he entered the wondrous valley, no longer lifts above the desert dust its massive battlements. An obelisk is there, the oldest of the world, bearing characters in which scholars read the epitaph of ages; and innumerable relics lie around its base, in the mounds heaped by desert winds. Nothing more remains. The minarets of modern Cairo, not far distant, glitter in the sun, but not on these does the eye rest. Over them, beyond the mighty Nile, against the western horizon, the great pyramids of Cheops and Cephrines lift their giant forms above the Lybian hills; and on these majestic memorials of more, perhaps, than forty, or even fifty centuries, the beholder cannot but gaze in mute astonishment. He sees them as they stood when Joseph and Mary, with the infant Saviour, found refuge here from Herod; as the boy Moses saw them from Pharaoh's palace; as Abraham and Sarah viewed them in their early sojourn; and the mind pauses amazed, solemnized.

Egypt being thus before us, we cast a rapid glance over its unique features, and then for a moment contemplate its mightiest works. We see the sacred Nile rolling its vast flood from the far south toward the middle sea of the ancient world. On its borders we behold a narrow level strip of alluvial soil, constituting a peculiar valley, not exceeding, above or south of the delta, an average breadth of four miles. On either side of this valley rise the strange verdureless hills, whose undulating outline slopes off into the Arabian or Red Sea wilderness on the east, on the west into the vast desert of Lybia. These hills, towering sometimes into lofty heights of naked rock, here advance their sombre forms to the river's edge, as if to lave them in the ancient stream; there, as it were, doing homage to the liquid divinity, they recede again with graceful sweep. Over their crest full often pours the desert dust, driven by winds that seem impatient to bury the old monuments from the desecrating hands which have mutilated them for ages. This valley is the ever-replenished garden which, during the early centuries, furnished food and homes for countless millions. Those hills supplied the material for enduring structures, and contain the chambers wherein the old generations laid their venerated dead.

Around these sepulchres we see no longer the children of those ancient dead. The race, over whom reigned Menes and Sesostris, exists no more. Here and there appears, indeed, a small community of oppressed and inferior creatures, though nominally Christians known as Copts, who claim descent from the early possessors of the land, and retain something of their language; but the

Egyptian is in Egypt no longer. More than two thousand years have rolled away since he became subject to other races; and for more than half that time he has really ceased to be known. The Persian hurled his gods from their throne. The Greek in part restored them, but only as subsidary to his own. He protected the people, it is true, and their ancient works, but it was with a spirit necessarily foreign. The genius which made Alexandria the centre of Greek letters, and gave the Septuagint to the world, could not, if it would, have left undisturbed the stationary system of the old castes and their avocations. But it was when the Roman came that the glory of Egypt departed. Of her ancient literature, gathered into that great library of the Ptolemies which Livy characterized as *elegantiæ regum curaque egregium opus*, and which contained, it is said, not less than 700,000 volumes, more than half was unintentionally destroyed by Julius Cæsar. (Plutarch.) And the remainder, replenished by the splendid Pergamian contribution of Antony, and by subsequent additions, was again devastated in the celebrated destruction of the Serapium by Theophilus—the Archbishop—under sanction of the Emperor Theodosius, A.D. 389, (Gibbon, xxviii.) When the Saracen followed, A.D. 638, with a culture scarcely less destructive than his own cimeter to all that opposed, the annihilation of this invaluable treasury of old learning was completed, (Gibbon, li., and Bishop Newton, xii.,) and rapidly failed the ancient population. And when the Mameluke succeeded, the work of Egypt's ruin was done. In contemplating here, therefore, the remains of antiquity, we are literally looking upon the monuments of a lost race.

The famed pyramid of Cheops first demands attention. Bearing in mind its gigantic proportions and nice adjustment, a base of nearly eight hundred feet on the side, ranged with the cardinal points, and covering some thirteen acres, and a perpendicular height of a little less than five hundred feet, we suppose ourselves to visit this in company with Lepsius, the most accomplished of explorers, and let him describe the scene: "A number of Bedouins gather around us, and wait for the moment when we shall ascend the pyramid, in order to raise us, with their strong brawny arms, up the steps, which are between three and four feet high. Scarcely is the signal given, when immediately each of us is surrounded by several Bedouins, who drag us up the rough, steep path to the summit, as in a whirlwind. A few minutes and our flag is unfurled on the summit of the oldest and highest of known human works. The panoramic view of the landscape spread at our feet now rivets our attention. On the one side the Nile valley, intersected by long serpentine dams, here and there dotted with villages and cultivated fields, over to the Moquottam hills, opposite, on whose most northerly point the citadel of Cairo rises above the town stretched out at their base. On the other side, the Lybian desert, a vast sea of sandy plains, and barren, rocky hills, boundless, colorless, noiseless, enlivened by no creature, no plants, no trace of the presence of man, not even by tombs; and between these scenes on the right and left, the ruined Necropolis, whose general position and simple outline lie spread out clearly and distinctly as on a map. What a spectacle! and what recollections does it call forth! When Abraham came to Egypt for the first time, he saw these very pyramids, which had been already built several centuries. In the plain before us lay ancient Memphis, the residence of the kings, on whose tombs we are standing; there dwelt Joseph, and ruled the land under one of the wisest and most powerful Pharaohs of the newly restored monarchy. Farther away, to the left of the Moquottam hills, where the fruitful low ground extends on the eastern arm of the Nile, beyond Heliopolis, (On,) distinguished by its obelisk, begins the blest region of Goshen, out of which Moses led his people to the Syrian desert. It would not, indeed, be difficult, from our position, to recognize that ancient fig-tree on the road to Heliopolis, at Matarieh, under whose shade, according to the tradition of the country, Mary rested with the Holy Infant. How many thousand pilgrims of all nations have since visited these wonders of the world, down to ourselves, who, the youngest in time, are yet but the predecessors of many other thousands who will succeed us, ascend these pyramids, and contemplate them with astonishment?

The accomplished savan has disappeared, we suppose, while we have been gazing on this scene. We therefore descend the enormous slope, and find ourselves safely at its base. Dr. Lepsius, however, imagine, rejoins us, and describes an exploration: "I descended to the elevated entrance of the pyramid, and providing myself and attendants with lights, we entered, like miners, the steeply-sloping shaft, and reached the gallery, and so-called king's chamber. We admired the infinitely fine seams of the enormous blocks, and examined the quality of the stones of the passages and chambers. In the spacious hall, whose floor, walls, and ceilings are entirely built of granite, and therefore return a metalic-sounding echo, we sang a national hymn, which sounded so powerfully and solemnly that our guides afterwards told the remaining Bedouins that we had selected the innermost part of the pyramid to perform divine service and utter a loud prayer."

Let us listen a little longer to one so competent to instruct on these subjects. As we look around upon the tombs over which the mighty pile, as it were, keeps watch, he tells us: "Almost all of these were built during, or shortly after, the erection of the great pyramids. The painting within them, on a very fine coating of lime, is often beautiful beyond conception, and is sometimes preserved as fresh and as perfect as if it had been done yesterday. The representations on the walls chiefly contain scenes from the life of the deceased, and appear especially intended to place before the eyes of the spectator his wealth in cattle, fish, game, boats, domestics, etc. We thus become familiar with all the details of his private life. The numerous inscriptions describe or designate these scenes, or they exhibit the often widely-branching family of the deceased, and all his titles and offices, so that I could almost compose a court and state calendar of King Cheops, or Cephren. The most splendid tombs, or rock-sepulchres, belonged principally to the princes, their relatives, or the highest official persons under the kings, beside whose pyramids they are laid; and not unfrequently I have found the tombs of father, son, and grandson, even great-grandson, so that whole pedigrees of these distinguished families, who, above 5000 years ago, formed the nobility of the land, are brought to light. The most beautiful of the tombs, which, with many others, I myself discovered beneath the sand, that here buries all things, belongs to a prince of the family of King Cheops."

The unhesitating confidence with which our renowned instructor thus declares the meaning of these old, and, to us, totally unintelligible inscriptions, has of course been observed. And we may not be offending, perhaps, against the intelligence of our readers, if we presume that, to some of them at least, it will not be uninstructive to have here presented an outline of the process by which the long-lost art of reading the hieroglyphics has been, to a great extent, recovered.

While some French troops, in Egypt, in the year 1799, were engaged upon excavations for the Fort St. Julien, near Rosetta, they dug up a mutilated slab of black basalt, marked with various characters. This was the since celebrated Rosetta stone. It contained an inscription in three forms, one of which was Greek, and proved to be a decree in favor of Ptolemy Epiphanes, concluding with these words: "This decree shall be engraved on hard stone, in sacred, common, and Greek characters." The stone fell into the hands of the English, after the French troops in Egypt had capitulated, and was deposited in the British

Museum. Copies of the inscriptions were, at an early day thereafter, distributed to learned men in Europe and America. And through the combined efforts and suggestions of several of these, Champollion at length succeeded in detecting the alphabetical nature of the symbols. In 1824 he published a system of reading them. And this has been since so extended by Rossellini, Lepsius, and other distinguished men, that the results have become indeed surprising.

In magic boat we now fancy ourselves borne rapidly up the mighty Nile to ancient Thebes. Three hundred miles are measured, and where stood the renowned city of a hundred gates we step ashore. The prospect we again survey with borrowed eyes: "Nowhere in all Egypt do such rugged hills embrace so beautiful a plain, and nowhere is there a spot so well suited for the capital of a great nation. The mountains are here, and the river flows between them, and Memnon sits calmly on his throne, and looks calmly over the river with stony eyes, unused to tears, and nothing appears to lament the dead glory. Neither sun nor moon shines less brilliantly, less joyously, that kings and princes, matrons and virgins, wise and foolish, weak and strong, are all alike dead in the past, dead in the valley, dead in the rock-hewn sepulchres; the palaces ruins, the temples ruins, the homes gone, the hearth-fires ashes long ago, the hearts of the men of Thebes dust, insensible, still, silent dust. You can scarce believe it the site of a ruined capital, once the wonder of the world for magnificence. There is nothing to indicate it, except immediately around Luxor and Karnak. Solitary on the eastern side stands Karnak; a majestic solitude indeed, among heaps of earth that may cover the floors of ancient habitations. Luxor, about two miles south, or higher up the river, has only near its own vast ruins, and the bereaved obelisk, whose mate was taken years ago to Paris. Karnak is a greater wonder than the pyramids. The heaping of stone together in such a mass was indeed a kingly idea of Cheops; but here was the same royal thought, the same masses of rock, hewn into graceful forms and shapes that indicated taste and design, and grouped in a temple that surpassed even the pyramids in extent. Approaching the great front from the river, we have before us the two propylon towers, whose vast size and height surpass all others in Egypt. Long before reaching the gateway between them, we are passing through an avenue of sphinxes, which are in fact rams of colossal size, facing the worshiper on each side as he approaches the temple. Passing through the pylon, or gateway, we enter a court of nearly 300 feet each way, with a corridor on each side, and the remains of a double row of columns through the centre. On the opposite side of this court stand two other lofty and grand propylon towers, passing between which we enter the great hall of columns. This hall is over 300 feet in breadth by nearly 200 in depth. In it there are still standing a hundred columns, while others lie prostrate. Of these columns, the central row, including base and capital, are 90 feet high, with a diameter of 12 feet. The others are 60 feet high and 9 feet in diameter; and for the most part, be it observed, they are of single blocks of stone. On the southern side of this great hall it was that Champollion discovered the since celebrated cartouche of Sheshonk, or Shishak, and the remarkable delineation representing his sack of Jerusalem, recorded in 1 Kings, xiv. 25, and 2 Chronicles, xii. Other courts of like character, save here and there a mighty obelisk, lie beyond, and still others, before reaching the sanctuary in which the gods sat of old to receive homage and sacrifice; and beyond it, the buildings stretch even farther to the east than this prolonged approach on the west. All these vast courts, and areas, obelisks, towers, and halls, are or were surrounded by columns, sphinxes, and statues, and every column and stone is covered with carving, and brilliantly painted. Not only was the temple colossal in its proportions, covering a space of more than half a square mile, but it was gorgeous beyond all description in its furniture and adornments."

Such are specimens of the monuments of this ancient race—only specimens; for the land is full of others, some of which are well-nigh more wonderful. And what a story do they tell of crowded population, protracted toil, grand design, mechanical skill, and developed art! Yet what, also, of strange delusion, misapplied energy, cruel oppression, and incredible suffering!

Our imperfect survey of the old races is now done. We have sought them not indeed in every inhabited region of the globe. For so extended an exploration, we have neither the adequate information, nor, as yet, the means of obtaining it; nor, if we had, would our limits authorize so full a discussion. We have, however, viewed the monumental records of ancient tribes in all the great divisions of the earth. We have traced them in our own country; along the great Polynesian Paradise, across the Pacific to the Eastern Asiatic islands; through China, India, and Persia; then along the ancient Scythian track to Western Europe; drawing inward thence, we have viewed them near the centres of early history, in Italy and Greece, Assyria and Egypt. It now only remains to gather up the results—to derive from these hoary monuments just conclusions. In doing this, with the facts mainly before us, we may be very brief.

The first inference we suggest, as clearly indicated by the concurrent testimony of these venerable witnesses, is, that they fortify other evidence proving the essential unity of the human family. The great principle is, indeed, as we have formerly shown, established in many ways. The masters of physiology and comparative anatomy have traced it in the special laws of animal function. The psychologist has found it in instinctive sentiment, and in intellectual, moral, and spiritual faculty. The ethnologist has beheld it in the ascertained facts of tribal origin, circumstantial variation, and transmitted peculiarities, among the dispersed people of the earth. And the learned philologist has proved it from the undeniable sameness of elements, grammatical and verbal, which he has discovered in all the examined languages of mankind. And the important truth we here see engraved on the imperishable tombs of the early races. The correspondent facts are too numerous and significant to admit of being supposed mere casual coincidences. Idea and custom, so singularly concurrent, point unmistakably to a common source. The elevated mound, often square and adjusted in one direction, often symbolically circular, and sometimes, by a compromise between these, constructed in the octagonal form, is almost everywhere. The sacrificial fire well-nigh universal. The mystical worship of nature, especially of the sun, of the heavens, and the earth, degenerating into gross forms of idolatry, sometimes cruel, sometimes groveling, is all around the globe. The same general sentiments toward the dead exist in every quarter, and kindred practices regarding them. In all we see the same out-working mind, variant, indeed, in energy and action, yet still the same, not only in general character, but in dominant idea and significant peculiarity. Especially does one great aspiration after immortality go up from the graves that surround the temples of the Toltec and the Druid, from Cuzco, Nanking, Elora, Nineveh, and Karnak.

Nor is the conclusion at all weakened, by whatever reasonable allowance may be made for the principle urged with anti-Christian purpose by certain writers, Mr. Squier, for instance, (see his paper, Smithn. Contribn., vol. ii. art. ix. p. 99,) that, to a certain extent, "these resemblances are the inevitable results of similar conditions. .... That human development must be, if not in precisely the same channels, in the same direction, and must pass through the same stages." The statement is no doubt partially true, but very far otherwise the suggested inference. For just in so far as it is true, it carries in itself the admission of a common human nature, and that involves, as we have seen, (*ante,* "Human Family," p. 62, etc.) almost demonstratively a common origin. In no unscriptural sense, assuredly, can the principle account for some of the surprising correspondences found in the old customs of the world. Certain of the more special of these undoubtedly necessitate the conclusion of an identical origin. To two of them we would for a moment direct particular attention.

That remarkable *sitting posture of the dead*, so general among the old American races, and traced back through the Pacific islands, not only to the eastern coast of Asia, but even in certain forms to Thibet and Siberia, is, beyond question, a most significant circumstance. It adds convincing proof to the many other evidences of common descent in all tribes of the red man, and plainly presents one mark of the track along which his ancestors made their way to the American shore. Not only so, but it would seem to render certain the fact of early association of some kind between all the people among whom it in any measure prevailed. "Who can doubt the existence of an affinity," asks Prescott, with great force, "or, at least, intercourse, between races that had this strange habit of burying their dead?"

The other fact we adduce, is the even more remarkable series of *correspondences connected with time divisions.* The week of seven days, affirmed to have prevailed over so large a part of the ancient world, is one of the elements in this series. It existed, says Laplace, (Systéme du Monde,) "in India among the Brahmins, and was in use among the Arabs, the Jews, the Assyrians, the Chinese, and in all the East." If, as would seem, the celebrated savan makes this statement on reliable evidence, it must be conceded that it indicates the existence—in a very early period, long prior to history—of some great common influence among that vast range of people, determining custom in regard to the practical perplexities of reckoning time. Nor is this consequence affected by difference of opinion respecting the origin of so remarkable a cycle of days. If philosophers, disinclined to the sacred system of the Scriptures, and regardless of the mighty array of evidences of every kind attesting them, will reject their simple and rational account of this primitive week, (see Genesis, i. and ii. 1–3,)—an account collaterally confirmed, in the most remarkable manner, as we have seen, by the disclosures of geology—let them cherish the idea of its derivation from early subtle astronomical knowledge. It will not affect the testified fact of the singular ancient custom, though it may exemplify the credulity of unbelief; for nothing is more obvious than that opinion can seldom rest on a slenderer basis. That the inconspicuous planets, Mars and Saturn, and the seldom seen bright little Mercury, so commonly lost in the sun's light, should have been so nicely noticed as to have been associated with the sun and moon, the beautiful Venus and the brilliant Jupiter, in an intricate astronomical system, and that such system should have been applied to the purpose of designating days in this peculiar cycle—previously to the separation of Egyptians, Hindoos, Chinese, etc., or that such system could have been, by one of these people, diffused over the rest at the age supposed—must be regarded as altogether improbable. Nor is the source of this idea worthier of credit. It is referred (see Système du Monde) to the Roman historian, Dion Cassius, who wrote as late as the latter part of the second century of our era, and who, therefore, if otherwise of highest character, as notoriously he is not, and if not discredited on this very point by the earlier testimony of Josephus, as he is, (see Contra Apion, book ii. 6–8,) was too far from the origin of this custom to be at all trustworthy respecting it. He certainly could not have known, and must have mainly speculated, concerning such a matter pertaining to from twenty to fifty centuries before his time; and, in all probability, applied backward the convenient designations for the days assigned at an age long subsequent to the origin of the week. Strange that evidence like this can be preferred to that of the Bible!

The mere circumstance that these commonly and occasionally visible heavenly bodies together make *seven* in number, adds really nothing to the probability of such astronomical introduction of the weekly cycle, because it is demonstrable that the number seven sustains relations to the constitution of nature and the history of human thought incomparably more impressive, in connection with the part it performs in the Scriptures, than any such single instance of correspondence suggested in opposition to sacred statement. The singular prominence given this numeral in Holy Writ is familiar to every reader. It marks the completing of creation, the recurrence of sacred seasons, the fullness of spiritual blessings, and the terribleness of divine inflictions. From the first of Genesis to the last of Revelation, we have "the seventh day," "the seventh year," "the seven spirits of God," "the seven vials," etc. etc. In nature and history it is scarcely less prominent. The notes of the musical scale, the seven colors of the solar spectrum, the seven neck-vertebræ of mammalian creatures, the seven decades of human life, etc., are instances in the structure of the world. And the old sentiments of mankind we find handed down in proverbial phrases of universal usage, "the seven wise men," "the seven wonders," and "the seven senses." These sentiments are, however, otherwise testified. No number is so peculiarly used by the ancient bards. Virgil's "bis septem Nymphæ," "septem collectis navibus," "septem ingentia corpora," etc., are familiar; while, from the Greek poets, Eusebius and Clement of Alexandria quote passages showing the prevalent impression of a certain sacredness in this number, especially as applied to the last day of the week. The Pythagoreans styled it a number worthy of veneration, σεβασμοῦ ἄξιος, as referred to by Cicero, when he says, (Tusculan Questions, i. x. 20,) that Xenocrites, and before him Pythagoras, "numerum dixet esse, cujus vis, in natura maxima esset."

In all this there is, certainly, something very remarkable. It would seem to be a manifold testimony—human and divine, in history and in nature—to some extraordinary significance originally assigned this number. And what that meaning but the office of rendering perpetually memorable the great varieties and the important duties connected with the Sabbath of the Patriarch and the Jew, and the Lord's day of the Christian?

Still, if to it all, and vastly more sustaining the incomparable disclosures of the Bible, opposite and most improbable hypotheses be preferred, the fact remains, that ancient week of seven days, affirmed to have existed from Egypt through Asia to the extremity of China; and it undoubtedly indicates some potent common influence of old, through that immense compass.

This, however, is not the only, perhaps not the most striking fact of the kind. In some of these regions the week seems to have been conveniently and yet singularly abbreviated. According to Sir Stamford Raffles, the old Hindoos had a peculiar week of five days, that is, every fifth day with them was a market day. Among the Chinese, according to Dr. Morrison, there existed the same custom of a fifth-day market. And with the old Mexicans, singularly enough, there was a like week of five days. Every fifth day was also peculiarly their market day. (See Antonio de Solis's Conquest of Mexico, quoted by Norman on Yucatan, p 185.) Moreover, in their chronological records or calendar, the Chinese employ two sets of characters or hieroglyphics, designated *stems* and *roots;* and the old Mexican calendar was also distinguished by a double hieroglyphical system. Dr. Schoolcraft, who gives these facts, (vol. i. p. 345,) very justly urges them in support of our conclusion; and in connection with them presses the further question, founded upon others scarcely less significant, "How is it that the Mexicans had a cycle of 60 years, or a double cycle of 120 years, exactly corresponding with that of the Chinese?"

But interesting and important as is the great verity of a common parentage for all races, both as related to revelation and as bearing on the destinies of the world, and certain as it is that "the recognition of this bond of humanity becomes," in the language of both the great Humboldts, "one of the noblest leading principles in the history of mankind," we cannot here elaborate it further, as evidenced by the old monuments. The distinct suggestion, the strongly testified conclusion, we leave to rest on the basis of facts already adduced.

The next inference we deduce from the monumental story is the existence of a far higher than rude condition of intelligence, and adaptation to art, among primitive men. The earlier races in general were certainly very far from being the savage creatures supposed in anti-scriptural theories. This, if the old monuments prove anything, they would seem to place beyond dispute. Nor is it a fact of trifling import. It tallies most remarkably with revealed teaching. It speaks of the original dignity and high endowments of human kind, though it declares something, too, of their downward tendency and wide-spread degradation. If early man were thus, as his oldest obvious works affirm, and as the

Bible tells, a creature not only of high gifts, but of no mean knowledge, bestowed at his birth, the contemplation of him there places us in the immediate presence of his Almighty Father, giving to the earth a son stamped with at least his own intellectual image. But as we gaze upon the scene of that gift, and look up to the great Source of that impress, the intellectual becomes, in our view, blended with the moral; and the conviction fastens on the mind, that not a sagacity enabling him to fashion matter, and subjugate brutes, and battle with physical antagonists, was man's prime distinction, but a large capacity for the true, the beautiful, and the good—an earnest, deathless longing after the Infinite, the Eternal, and the Holy. And when this conviction is received, the final purpose of such a nature, the great destiny of creatures whose pre-eminence is their spiritual essence, beckons thought inward to another sphere. The solemn, endless future rises up to view, with its unmeasured retributions; and religion, spite of all the philosophies, and all the unbeliefs of the world, is seen to be of necessity the all-pervading influence among men.

But this deduction from the remains of ancient races stands immediately connected with another, no less furnished by the monuments: the fact of a strange moral perversion in every early community—the existence of a strictly universal bias toward the false and the bad, in those very relations where the true and the right were of inestimable import. What tremendous significancy there is in the great grooves for blood (human undoubtedly) cut in the old altar-stones of Central America! What abominations are revealed by the monstrous idols of India! What degradation in the sacred bulls and embalmed reptiles found under the shadows of Karnak and the pyramids! It is a phenomenon we see, indeed, every day—the intellect working with energy often surprising, and achieving much that is serviceable, sometimes what is even great and enduring, while the moral being gravitates toward corruption, and grovels in the dust. But nowhere is the spectacle more sadly conspicuous than in the old home of the Pharaohs. Besides her wonders in architecture, her early literature, and her renown for that wisdom which brought the fathers of Grecian thought to her halls for instruction, her skill in metallurgic and other like operations has stamped Egypt's home name "*Chemi*" upon the subtlest of physical sciences, chemistry; and yet the people bowed down to images of stone, yea, worse, to very brutes, and even insects!

As we contemplate this, the mind turns instinctively to that higher instruction which explains the phenomenon, while it furnishes the needed remedy. That better teaching tells of this lapse from the holy in the olden time, and of its progressive mischiefs; but it points out, too, its actual character and its provided cure Place the tent of heavenly-minded old Abraham by the proudest palace ever reared of Egyptian granite, and which is really the greater? Which sends out the influences that have shaped, and are yet to shape, the destinies of the world? Which is identified with the precious truths and holy agencies that train our children, support us in sorrow, arm us for duty and death, and make home so sweet a word? How poor, to minds instructed like the patriarch's, to spirits lifted up to communion with Him who fills heaven and earth, must have appeared, yea, how unutterably sad, those masses of stone so laboriously piled by idolatry in the land of Ham! How significant is the almost total silence respecting them in the inspired narrative!

The debt, then, we owe our Bibles for the readjustments they effect in the lost relations of truth and of the human faculties, comes up as another obvious lesson from the old tombs of the world. Here is the agency that has not only severed the chains which bound intelligence to a loathsome mass of moral corruption, but has imparted the spirit of heaven and the vigor of hope to the great benefactors of the species these hundreds of years. This was the power which tranquilized Europe, when the barbarian hurricane had ingulfed the empire of the Cæsars; and this imparted to modern civilization its distinctive character and its progressive energy. Influences hence emanating opened the eyes of Kepler, trained the genius of Bacon, and placed the torch of discovery in the hands of Newton. Truth, as taught in these sacred pages, and the spirit they inculcate, have given to Britain her chief glory; and the same truth, the same spirit, have founded in the old home of the red man a mighter than British empire. May our people so cling to those vital truths, so cherish that wise and heaven-favored spirit, as to convert into enduring fact what was at best but probable conjecture a hundred years ago, when Bishop Berkeley wrote, with a singular intuition that more than atones for defective harmony:—

> "Westward the star of empire takes its way,
> The first four acts already past,
> The fifth shall close the drama with the day:
> Time's noblest offspring is the last."

But this suggests a final thought, arising also from the old monuments: the end that comes to human things. It may be that Divine Providence sees best to order change for nations as for individuals, even irrespective of their vice or virtue. It may be that in its best condition, yet to be expected, the great moral atmosphere of the world, like its physical, demands the ventilating energy of storm and tempest, though in the rush many a valuable structure fall. But however this be, one thing is certain: the lost races tell it, as history tells it, as the Bible declares, nations, like individuals, suffer for their sins. Vice buried Babylon and Thebes. Wickedness shivered the sceptre of the Cæsars. Nor can any people long survive the ravages of moral gangrene. Be it ours, then, as we love our country, as we feel for mankind, by example, and by every good influence we can exert, to battle wisely against every form of wrong, to cherish whatsoever is right, and to secure, if so it may be, what ten righteous men would have secured for Sodom.

Even if so, however, let us not, writer and readers, forget an end that cannot be averted. Everything tells of a change coming, greater far than the rise and fall of nations, more solemn than the mouldering of generations. The old tombs contain many a bony finger that points to that coming consummation. The old temples meant it when in their prime; their shattered columns are of it prophetic symbols. Of such an issue, deep, mysterious forebodings of the human spirit give warning. To it the past convulsions of the globe awaken attention; and its whole certainty, with all its mighty import, the Bible authoritatively proclaims. Yes, this entire planet shall one day be the funeral pile of all that is consumable in whatsoever has had part with humanity,—or it shall be the purified, renovated scene of a different existence, the enduring memorial of all generations of men. Let us see to it that, if so, it be not for us, in a terrible sense, the monument of a lost race.

NOTE TO PAGE 309.

The facts stated in the following note were furnished in this form at the request of the author, and are here introduced as corroborating the conclusions we have derived from many kindred indications.

Distinguished as an officer of rare merit, and entitled to the gratitude of civilized nations for the benefits, scientific and practical, to be derived from his invention of the "deep-sea sounding apparatus," Lieutenant Brooke is still more remarkable as a man of original thought and active interest in the great questions of the age. Having been lately in charge of an exploring expedition which involved his sojourn for some time in Japan, and subsequently in command of their own war-steamer which brought to this country the Japanese Embassy, so as to become familiar with some leading characters among them, Mr. Brooke is perhaps as well qualified to speak concerning this people as any man living.

May 14th, 1860.

Rev. Dr. Pendleton.

Dear Sir:—Upon the arrival of the Japanese war-steamer Candinmarruh at San Francisco, the Admiral Kini-moo-rah-set-to-no-Cami and his officers were invited to visit the plantation of Captain Frisbie, son-in-law of General Vallejo. After the excursion, the Admiral and his suite partook of a collation at Captain Frisbie's residence. At table, I remarked incidentally to Captain Frisbie, that the Japanese word for *milk* was "*Tche-che.*" He replied, "that is singular; 'tis the same in Spanish." His brother, Dr. Frisbie, said, "No; *Tche-che* is the Indian word adopted by the Spanish settlers of California."

While I was thinking of this coincidence, an Indian boy, "Martinez," who had been taken into the family of Captain Frisbie when a child, entered the room. Captain Mangiro tapped me on the shoulder, and, pointing to Martinez, inquired, "Where you get him?" I replied, he is an Indian boy, a Californian. Mangiro, shaking his head incredulously, exclaimed, "No, no! Nippon! Nippon!" At the same instant, Captain Katslintarro inquired of Captain Frisbie where the boy came from, and when the Captain replied, California, he also shook his head, and said, "Nippon! Nippon!" We had not before noticed the strong resemblance Martinez bore to the Japanese; but, our attention being called to it by Mangiro, Katslintarro, and the other Japanese, some eight or nine, who were present, and who all concurred in the opinion expressed by Mangiro and Katslintarro, we perceived a strong resemblance.

Mangiro then said, "I will speak to that boy; he is a Japanese." But Captain Frisbie informed him that Martinez could not speak the language of his tribe, as he had been taken from them when a mere child. "But," said he, "it is probable that one of General Vallejo's daughters, now in the house, remembers some words, and I will introduce Mangiro to her."

Nothing more was said at the time, although the Japanese kept their eyes upon Martinez, who was somewhat annoyed by the scrutiny to which he was subjected. Soon after, Mangiro came to me, saying, "Captain, what I say is true; these Indians come from Japan, I think, long time ago. I have spoken to the lady, and I find many words the same. I find more than six words the same. I think this people come long time ago *in junk* from Japan; you know junks very often have typhoons, and are blown away from Japan. I told you of Japan sailors I met in Sandwich Islands, and I know plenty junks go that way. Therefore I think this Indian come first from Japan."

I had not at the time leisure to investigate this interesting subject. It is probable that if a vocabulary of the Martinez tribe could be compared with a Japanese vocabulary, an important relation would be established. The subject is worthy of investigation. I shall write to Captain Frisbie, with reference to it. I have in my possession an English and Japanese dictionary, and it only remains to procure a vocabulary of the Martinez tribe to enable us to determine whether the Japanese were right in their conjectures.

Mangiro, who is a very intelligent man, was wrecked upon an island in the Pacific, was rescued by Captain Whitfield of Fairhaven, and spent several years in the United States, where he acquired the English language.

Taking into consideration the fact that westerly winds and currents to the eastward prevail between Japan and California, Mangiro's supposition, apart from the apparent relation of the languages, is quite rational. We know that Japanese junks have drifted from the coasts of Japan to the mouth of the Columbia, and nearly midway several have been, by our whalemen, found dismasted, drifting at the mercy of the winds and waves.

Yours, truly,

JOHN M. BROOKE,
Lieut. U. S. Navy.

www.ingramcontent.com/pod-product-compliance
Lightning Source LLC
Chambersburg PA
CBHW031433230426
43668CB00007B/519